MW01484727

# Army Spouses

## MILITARY FAMILIES DURING THE GLOBAL WAR ON TERROR

Morten G. Ender

University of Virginia Press

CHARLOTTESVILLE AND LONDON

University of Virginia Press
© 2023 by the Rector and Visitors of the University of Virginia
All rights reserved
Printed in the United States of America on acid-free paper

*First published 2023*

1  3  5  7  9  8  6  4  2

Library of Congress Cataloging-in-Publication Data

Names: Ender, Morten G., author.
Title: Army spouses : military families during the Global War on Terror /
Morten G. Ender.
Description: Charlottesville : University of Virginia Press, 2023. |
Includes bibliographical references and index.
Identifiers: LCCN 2023003606 (print) | LCCN 2023003607 (ebook) |
ISBN 9780813950044 (hardcover) | ISBN 9780813950051 (paperback) |
ISBN 9780813950068 (ebook)
Subjects: LCSH: Army spouses—United States. | Families of military personnel—
United States. | Soldiers—Family relationships—United States. |
Terrorism—Government policy—United States.
Classification: LCC U766 .E53 2023 (print) | LCC U766 (ebook) |
DDC 355.10973—dc23/eng/20230505
LC record available at https://lccn.loc.gov/2023003606
LC ebook record available at https://lccn.loc.gov/2023003607

*Cover art:* Prostock-studio/shutterstock.com

*Four generations of women and onetime army wives inspire me
and have given more than they received in return:*

*My maternal great-grandmother,
Johanna "Möderken" Maria Wilhelmine Kruse née Pennekamp
(b. January 11, 1895—d. November 2, 1984)*

*My maternal grandmother, Johanna "Hanni" Eberharde Ender née Kruse
(b. March 26, 1918—d. September 16, 1997)*

*My mother-in-law, Kornelia "Connie" Katherine Campbell-Hambley née Walter
(b. September 21, 1937)*

*My sister, Ingrid "Miezi" Deanna Taylor née Brown
(b. January 9, 1972)*

# Contents

# Acknowledgments

What a long trip it has been. Two decades working on this project brought me into contact with an array of people who collectively are just plain awesome. Broadly they include Linda and Bill Stewart, Jeffrey Simpson, Kira Lopez, Lance Rahey, Dennis McGurk, Kathy Wright, Amy Adler, Lolita Burrell, Diane Ryan and Al Roscoe, Aundre Piggee, Michele and Roger Jackson, Beth and Peter Chiarelli, Val and Keith Walker, Madelaine Lanza, Melissa Weaver, Abby Griffin, Gus and Emily Giacoman, Dailah and Ken Cole, April Griffith, Jenny O'Rourke, Mollie Miller, Suzy Wood, Meredith Kleykamp and John Basso, Jim Gallup, Pat Buckley, Ann and Scott Efflandt, Brian Reed, and Richard Fafara. The hugest thank you to Mike Hunt and Zoe for hosting us in Germany over many years.

Folks at West Point have been especially accommodating to me over the years including Tom and Kay Kolditz, Stoney Trent, Bernie and Candice Banks, Christine Guerriero, Barney Forsythe, Dan Kaufman, Ryan Kelty, Irving Smith, Bruce Keith, Kate Franklin (and Barbara and Mary), Anita Howington, Jim Ness, Donna Brazil, Jan Piatt, Kerri and Remi Hajjar, Darcy Schnack, Lisa Korenman, Elizabeth Velilla, Katie Hauserman, Krista Hennen, Tony Espinal, Jess Gathers, Joel Cartwright, Jim Straka, Bryan Williams, Jess Dawson, Ericka Rovira, Lissa Young, Beth Wetzler, Margie Carroll, and Mike Matthews.

A visiting professorship at Bundeswehr University Munich, in Germany, facilitated a round of interviews. Thanks to Mark Gagnon for championing that opportunity and to members of the staff and faculty at the Uni including Susanna Nofal, Teresa Koloma Beck, Angelika Schoppel, and Nora Knötig. A shout-out to the graduate students in my Military Families seminar that spring trimester.

A special thanks to the awesome physicians and staff at the Schön Klinik Medical Care Center in Munich and Dr. Doris Fleckenstein for helping keep me in Germany after a skiing accident and caring for us through our convalescences. Much appreciation to Pro-Physis in Neubiberg—the best physical therapists in the world.

Research assistance came and left in various forms and with inspiration from Ev Spain, Elizabeth and Todd Woodruff, Cheryl and Mike Endres, Patrick Michaelis, Jacob Absalon, Toya Davis, Natalie Franc, Steve Ruth from Texas, Jennifer Bailey, Kathy Campbell, Kathleen Plourd, Brad Hudson, MJ Ward, Gordon Weir, and Janelle Murray. A shout-out to my students Evelyn Zhang, Mark Kratochvil, Kelly McKeon, and Leslie Willey in our boots-on-the-ground German Life and Culture course who challenged me and one another.

Sociological insights came from Meg Wilkes Karraker, René Moelker, Elizabeth Ziff, Dave Smith, and Mady Segal. Two anonymous reviewers provided superlative feedback on a draft of the manuscript.

A tremendous acknowledgement to the University of Virginia Press staff and board for supporting the book. My editor, Nadine Zimmerli—my German sister from different parents—believed in the project from my opening story and she simultaneously focused and liberated me with ease and care. Indeed, the editorial assistance team of Fernando Campos and Ellen Satrom are a tour de force. Thank-yous to Mary Kate Maco and Clayton Butler for championing my vision. Finally, a salubrious Semper Gumby shout-out to the words(wo)manship of Toni Mortimer, whose emails are like sunshine on a misty morning.

Corina and Axel are the center of my orbit. In 1980, when I was somewhat lost and displaced, Corina came along and gave me a lift. And here I am. Axel completed us with fresh and new boulevards to venture down.

Finally, a thousand thank-yous to all the key informants and spouses and children that opened their lives up to us in the U.S. and Europe. I hope I represented what you said and that you see yourselves in these pages. But know that the views ultimately expressed here are my own and do not purport to represent those of the United States Military Academy, the Department of the Army, the Department of Defense, or the United States government. Learn more about the Munich Alumni Fund and how to contribute to our overseas military family member university scholarship fund on my craft and charity page at https://mortenender.com. Shine on all you crazy diamonds.

# Abbreviations

| | |
|---|---|
| AAFES | Army and Air Force Exchange Service |
| ACS | Army Community Service |
| AD | Active Duty |
| AER | Army Emergency Relief |
| AKO | Army Knowledge Online |
| APO | Army Post Office |
| AVF | All-Volunteer Force |
| BDU | Battle Dress Uniform |
| BNOC | Basic Non-Commissioned Officer Course |
| BRAT | British Regimental Assigned Traveler |
| CAF | Canadian Armed Forces |
| CDC | Child Development Center |
| CIA | Central Intelligence Agency |
| CMAOD | Casualty and Mortuary Affairs Operations Division |
| CMR | Community Mail Room |
| CONUS | Continental United States |
| CYA | Child Youth Activities |
| CYS | Child and Youth Services |
| DADT | Don't Ask, Don't Tell (Don't Hassle, Don't Pursue) |
| DCU | Desert Combat Uniform |
| DDDs | Dual-Dwelling Duos |
| DD Form 93 | Record of Emergency Data |
| DEROS | Date of Estimated Return from Overseas |
| DM | Direct Message (successor to instant messaging) |
| DMDC | Defense Manpower Data Center |
| DMZ | Demilitarized Zone, Korea |
| DOD | Department of Defense |
| DoDEA | Department of Defense Education Activity |
| DSN | Distributed Switched Network |
| EASYs | Emancipated Army Spouses |

| | |
|---|---|
| EFMP | Exceptional Family Member Program |
| ERD | Early Return of Dependents |
| FMWR | Family and Morale, Welfare, and Recreation |
| FNC | Fox News Channel |
| FOB | Forward Operating Base |
| FRG | Family Readiness Group |
| FRL(s) | Family Readiness Leader(s) |
| FSG | Family Support Group |
| FSO(s) | Full-Spectrum Operation(s) |
| FTX | Field Training Exercise |
| GI | Government Issue and Ground Infantry |
| GN | Global Nomads |
| GWOT | Global War on Terror(ism) |
| ID | Infantry Division or Identification Card |
| IIACSS | Al Mustakella for Research Group |
| IM | Instant Message (precursor to direct messaging) |
| IR | International Relations |
| IRB | Institutional Review Board |
| KIA | Killed in Action |
| LAT | Living Apart Together |
| LGBTQ+ | Lesbian, Gay, Bisexual, Transgender, Queer, plus others |
| M1 | Abrams Armor Tank |
| MHPI | Military Housing Privatization Initiative |
| MI | Military Intelligence |
| MIA | Missing in Action |
| MOS | Military Occupation Specialty |
| MP | Military Police |
| MWR | Morale, Welfare, and Recreation |
| NCO | Non-Commissioned Officer |
| NCOIC | Non-Commissioned Officer-in-Charge |
| NTC | National Training Center |
| OCNUS | Outside the Continental United States |
| OCS | Officer Candidate School |
| OEF | Operation Enduring Freedom |
| OIF | Operation Iraqi Freedom |
| OPSEC | Operational(al) Security |
| OWN | Oprah Winfrey Network |
| PCS | Permanent Change of Station |
| PNOK | Primary Next of Kin |
| POA | Power of Attorney |

| | |
|---|---|
| POC | Point of Contact |
| POW | Prisoner of War |
| PTSD | Post-Traumatic Stress Disorder |
| PX | Post Exchange |
| R&R | Rest & Recuperation |
| RCI | Residential Communities Initiative |
| RD | Rear Detachment |
| RDC | Rear Detachment Command(er) |
| ROTC | Reserve Officers' Training Corps |
| SI | Serious Injury |
| SNOK | Secondary Next of Kin |
| SOFS-A | Status of Forces Survey of Active Duty Members |
| STARS | Spouses Traveling and Relocating Successfully |
| STUDS | Spouses Trailing under Duress Successfully |
| TBI | Traumatic Brain Injury |
| TCK | Third Culture Kids |
| TDY | Temporary Duty |
| TV | Television |
| *TWD* | *The Walking Dead* |
| UK | United Kingdom |
| US(A) | United States (of America) |
| USAREUR(-AF) | United States Army Europe (and Africa) |
| VSI | Very Serious Injury |
| VTC | Video Tele-Conference |
| WIC | Women, Infants, and Children |

# U.S. Army Officer and Enlisted Ranks

| MILITARY GRADE | ABBREVIATION | RANK TITLE |
|---|---|---|
| **Officers** | | |
| O10 | GEN | General |
| O9 | LTG | Lieutenant General |
| O8 | MG | Major General |
| O7 | BG | Brigadier General |
| O6 | COL | Colonel |
| O5 | LTC | Lieutenant Colonel |
| O4 | MAJ | Major |
| O3 | CPT | Captain |
| O2 | 1LT | First Lieutenant |
| O1 | 2LT | Second Lieutenant |
| W5 | CW5 | Chief Warrant Officer 5 |
| W4 | CW4 | Chief Warrant Officer 4 |
| W3 | CW3 | Chief Warrant Officer 3 |
| W2 | CW2 | Chief Warrant Officer 2 |
| W1 | WO1 | Warrant Officer 1 |
| | | |
| **Enlisted** | | |
| E9 | SGM or CSM | Sergeant Major or Command Sergeant Major |
| E8 | MSG | Master Sergeant |
| E7 | SFC | Sergeant First Class |
| E6 | SSG | Staff Sergeant |
| E5 | SGT | Sergeant |
| E4 | SPC or CPL | Specialist or Corporal |
| E3 | PFC | Private First Class |
| E2 | PVT2 | Private |
| E1 | PVT | Private |

Army Spouses

# Introduction

It is hard being a military wife.
—SFC's wife in 2003

My appreciation for separated families grew wider and deeper a few winters ago on a skiing trip in the German Alps. Being a college professor is a privilege and one of many benefits are sabbaticals and opportunities to teach and conduct research while visiting other campuses and sometimes other countries. During a sabbatical year, I had secured a teaching post at the Bundeswehr University Munich, in Germany, for a semester. While there, I taught two courses and conducted interviews with U.S. Army families working and living in a German community. I lived alone in the dorms and took my meals with the students in the on-campus dining hall. My wife is a high school social studies teacher and managed two trips over during her school breaks. We are both army brats and spent years living in Germany during the Cold War—travel is in our bones.[1]

Capitalizing on my early years, I became a military sociologist. Part of the job obliges me to go where soldiers and military families go.[2] I have spent summers with troops in Iraq and Kuwait and with them and their families in western and eastern Europe, and across the U.S. from New York to California to Hawai'i.

On this recent Germany trip, we busted our budget and stayed in a wonderful hotel with all the luxury amenities and meals in a family-style dining room with magnificent buffets. Following a late afternoon check in, we went downstairs to dinner. While we both speak German fluently, our appearance and demeanor must have strongly suggested "Americans." The maître d' took one look at us and without hesitation spoke English and escorted us away from the central dining room to a side, more private dining room. Separate, yet still had the traditional Bavarian charm of pinewood with multiple family-style tables, chairs, and bunks. Men mainly occupied the room enjoying dinner. I thought little of it—actually, I was a tad miffed thinking I was being segregated *because* I am American. My wife, however, a lifelong skier and follower of international skiing events, started acting like a total fangirl—all giddy with wide eyes and could not speak full words or sentences.

To my amusement and my wife's amazement, we had been seated with the U.S. Ski Team—the full men's team with competitors, coaches, staff, and various others as well as a handful of women of all ages and children—even a newborn. We knew there were teams in the village and staying in local hotels close to the mountains. A major downhill international competition was scheduled in a couple of days. We had tickets for the event known as the Kandahar—a legendary annual race since 1970 at the base of Germany's highest peak—the Zugspitze. This race would be one of the final competitions before the U.S. team headed to the 2018 Winter Olympics in South Korea in a few weeks.

We could not believe our luck. We quickly realized that the maître d' mistook us for members of the U.S. Ski Team entourage—clearly not professional skiers (well maybe not)—perhaps they thought we were coaches or parents. We did not bother explaining the error. In fact, all our meals—breakfast and dinner for the next few days—were with the team. We met members of the team, the team physician, staff, and girlfriends. My wife took selfies. Being a sociologist, I asked questions about their lifestyle. I eavesdropped on some of their conversations. We learned that coaches and staff are former athletes in the same sport. The team trains and competes together—following the snow from hemisphere to hemisphere around the globe year-round. More fascinating is that like the soldiers and spouses I study—not discounting those that I would be interviewing in a few weeks in a U.S. Army community I had gained access to in another region of Germany for this book after this brief holiday ski trip—professional skiers and their coaches and staff are partnered with children. Spouses and others significant to them are typically home—probably back in the United States. Some loved ones are on the circuit with them either all or part of the time.

The lifeworld of competitive skiers, and amateur and pro-athletes more broadly, competing internationally and domestically in the United States such as in baseball, football, soccer, basketball, and even skateboarding on the professional circuit—and their families—shares more demands with the military lifestyle than many other vocations. Demands that will be discussed in more detail throughout this book but that comprise a high risk of being injured or killed; moving to new locales around the country or the globe every few years often unaccompanied by loved ones; working and training long-extended hours beyond the normal 9:00 to 5:00; working and training on shifts other than normal day hours; living abroad in countries foreign to them; having hyperconstraints placed on one's behavior that are more rigid or different than everyday people; living and working in and around a masculine-dominated culture and structure that is indicative of many social institutions; and having to retire early, sometimes in their twenties or thirties, and thus necessitating finding an accommodating vocation or never working again. These features have implications for family members of twenty-first-century service members that have been regularly highlighted in the military family literature dating back to the 1980s.[3] But sitting in that Bavarian dining room those mornings and nights, I thought about that singular element imposed on both skiers and soldiers and their respective families and the focus of this book: separations.

### Strohwitwe—The Straw Widow

Couple separation is not new, traceable to hunting societies where the men trek off for extended periods of time to locate, kill, and bring home food. Thus, "Strohwitwe" is a German word that means "straw widow" or "grass widow." In general, it denotes "a woman whose partner is away for an undefined period of time."[4] Strohwitwe are the wives of husbands who have jobs that require them to be away from home for multiple nights for their work. The women who sleep in the normally shared bed without their husbands. ("Strohwitwer" is a straw widower.) The symbolism implies that such wives sleep on straw or grass (Stroh or Gras) while their husbands are away. Widowhood in this sense is ephemeral, not eternal.

Strohewitwe is not unique to Germany. The Danes call them græsenke. The Swedes gräsänka. The Finns are more elaborate in their descriptions.[5] In Finland, "repurri" or "reppureissaaja" means backpacker but applicable to a military service member who has relocated. "Vikkoleski" is a slang term for a "weekly widow"—the husband comes home on weekends.[6] "Mmatkatyöläinen" is a more generic term for someone working away from their hometown. A term for night-time working away workers is "Työleski" (work widow) and a seasonal worker, away perhaps during the summer months, is a "kausityöntekijä." A less common term is "vuorotyöntekijäleski" meaning shift worker widow(er). The Dutch call them "gras weduwe" and judges accounted for their status and excused them for adultery—such as sailors' wives—while their men were at sea.[7]

The Japanese refer to the grass widow work-family situation as Tanshin-funin—the practice of, chiefly husbands, living away from their families either abroad or domestically for work. It is long embedded into Japanese work and family life culture with estimates of one-quarter of Japanese working abroad and doing so unaccompanied.[8] Tanshinfunin is translated in Google Translate as "assigned alone" with the rationale being maintaining educational stability for children and elder care for parents.

There are military linkages with grass widows. In Hebrew, anthropologist Erella Grassiani describes "straw widow" as a "term for a house that has been abandoned by its inhabitants, and that is used by the military for strategic reasons. Presumably, it comes from the term 'grass widow,'" in this case used by Israeli soldiers.[9] In this book, being a military strohwitwe(r) today implies that your intimate other—your spouse—is deployed to war away from home. Generations of U.S. Army spouses were strohwitwe (most at the time of the interviews) in a period of perpetual war where separations and deployments were normal rather than exceptional. Grass widow(er)s[10] in this book are exemplars of a growing global trend of people whose loved one leaves the home for extended periods.

## Working and Living Apart

The master narrative of marriage in modern times is a shared residence, a gendered division of labor, and face-to-face communication. Commuter marriages subvert this arrangement as approximately 3.6 million Americans have lived apart meaning they had an alternative residence, although this does not include formal marital separations or divorces.[11] New couple forms have been identified by family researchers. More recent popular categories are Dual-Dwelling Duos and Living Apart Together—defined as "happily married couples who are committed to each other but who are living in separate quarters."[12]

Americans live in dual-earner households where both partners work in paid employment. For those with more education, they might comprise dual-career couples. Both partners are in a professional or managerial occupation requiring highly specific pressures beyond a daily nine to five regimental time commitment plus increased training, education, and specialized growth.

Many marriages are known as two-person, single-career marriages.[13] In this case, "a spouse participates in the other's career," more often behind the scenes "without pay or direct recognition."[14] These educated mavens are professionals in institutions such as college presidents, religious leaders, ambassadors in foreign embassies, small town physicians, First Ladies (and now a Second Gentleman), and senior military members.

If their career requires moving, the spouse may become a "trailing spouse." The trailing spouse accompanies their spouse to new and temporary locales to live and maybe work. New euphemisms for the trailing spouse have followed. Two pithy models are STUDS and STARS.[15] Children that shadow parents are British Regimental Assigned Travelers of one form or another.[16] Research on trailing expatriate (expat) spouses shows more or less support by the organization for the spouses[17] and some limited life satisfaction.[18] Actually, when the spouse does not trail to a foreign country, this is one arrangement of married "transnational professionals"—in this case, "members of a profession or managers, and their families whose work requires them to live abroad, for extended periods of time, often in a range of countries: their transnational movements are part of a considered livelihood strategy."[19]

Tied staying and tied migration are additional practices that provide insight to work and families. Put forth first in the 1970s,[20] scholars now recognize that people—both men and women—migrate or move residences for work not because of purely individual concerns. They do so for a variety of family reasons and topping the list is their devotion to their marriage and children.[21] Tied migration involves a spouse or partner relocating for occupational concerns and the spouse opts to accompany. Tied staying involves spouses/partners that might want to move with their spouse/partner and opt not to because of family reasons. Tied migration transcends the United States or moving domestically. It can be international too.[22] Research on military spouses and tied migration tells us there are deleterious impacts resulting from lower employment for military wives.[23]

Commuter marriages also touch on military family life and can be either transnational or national—the former is international and the latter domestic. Commuter marriage is the term used for couples living apart for work, money, or family factors.[24] They are more often associated with a dual-career, educated group.[25] In her book titled *Commuter Spouses*, sociologist Danielle J. Lindemann interviews ninety-seven couples and defines them as noncohabitating couples, "relatively well-educated spouses who live, or have lived, separately in service to their dual professional careers."[26] Her couples are exclusively married, live apart for work, and maintain different residences. For her study, both partners are in their careers, are career-minded, and have more choices about residence and movement than most. Estimates are that 3 percent of American marriages meet this definition and are commuter for some time. Commuter marriage benefits are increased finances, more attention to work, and solitude. Disadvantages involve time away, extra costs, social isolation, one spouse assumes the day-to-day child care responsibilities, and there is a change in weekend/holiday dynamics. Little is known about military commuter marriages.

"Geographic Bachelor" (or geo-bach) is a military-adopted term to refer to considering a military tour away. An unofficial term, it is slang to describe the service member's status of choosing rather than being assigned to live away from their immediate family (spouse and/or children) in a different locale.[27] A service member can be a "geographic bachelorette." The choice to geo-bachelorette had been somewhat institutionalized in the military for a period but is no longer supported by formal institutional resources on-post as barracks are prioritized for single soldiers.[28] The numbers will rise as multi-job and dual-job couples increase in the U.S. military, but service members will do so off-posts and perhaps at a personal cost.

Strohwitwe, commuter marriages, transnational marriages, and trailing spouses of either dual-worker or dual-career couples bake into modern, postindustrial America and other societies. Groups that involve an absent spouse or parent for a short- to long-term period encompass undocumented workers in[29] and outside[30] the U.S., prisoners,[31] long-haul truckers and commercial fisher(wo)men,[32] amateur and pro athletes,[33] airline pilots,[34] U.S. government civilian "deployees,"[35] public health workers,[36] sailors,[37] and CIA wives.[38] A host of others exist. Indeed, I[39] offer up three recent groups of strohwitwe— the spouses (and children) of physicians and nurses during the 2020–21 pandemic;[40] thousands of Olympic athletes, coaches, and media workers in Tokyo, Japan, in the summer of 2021[41] and in Beijing, China, in the winter of 2022; and finally, the hundreds of thousands of Ukrainian men between the ages of eighteen and sixty who with rare exception are barred from leaving the country because of the war with Russia, while their spouses and family members remain sheltered in the country or flee for border countries.[42]

Many jobs and occupations obligate husbands, wives, and parents to be a nonresident in their immediate family's home for considerable periods— from days to weeks to months to years. I've already noted a few occupations above. To magnify the significance of army spouses, the U.S. Army has declared each November Military Family Month. In the description and justification for the honor the army directly connects families to soldiers through both quantity (percentage of soldiers from military families and married with children) and quality ("strength" and "maintaining ready and responsive forces").[43] Military families are thus both symbolically and tangibly considered an integral element of the military. Certainly not like the contractual one levied on uniformed members of the military but getting closer. They are a kind of subcultural obligatory militarized group. As a popular Month of the Military Child (April) T-shirt on Amazon.com boldly says, "We Serve Too."

The reality of detached families is far from problem-free. Scholars have concluded separation to be detrimental for children and wives, and for fathers and husbands as well. Moreover, there are secondary social forces and structural constraints at work. Grass widows are less likely to pursue jobs, occupations, or professions because of parenting concerns.[44] For the nonresident father (no studies have looked at nonresident mothers or same-sex couples), sociologist William Marsiglio and his associates note that "living apart from children, whether because of being in jail, on military assignment, or being a nonresident father, can lead fathers to engage in various forms of identity work."[45] Types of absent fathers that have different occupational features but similar absent cycles are long-haul truckers and fisher(wo)men,[46] divorced fathers where in many cases mothers obtain custody,[47] and imprisoned fathers.[48] These men have a liminal identity, meaning as a father, they are neither fully in nor out of family and local community life. Absence is a feature of a host of social and psychological properties. Such men (and women) must labor and manage their emotions to construct their identities and negotiate in and around the borders of parenthood.

## Stress, Greediness, Negotiated Triad, and Militarization

Before a researcher or a team of researchers accesses a military-related population, their military sociological perspective is typically situated in three ideal and distinct fields of knowledge: engineering perspective; enlightened perspective; and critical perspective. Philosopher and sociologist Jürgen Habermas and military social scientists Charles Moskos, Eyal Ben-Ari, and Yagil Levy hold that engineering is applied sociology.[49] Here the military sociologist orients and aims her research directly to the practical concerns of policymakers, commanders, and key change agents to intelligently intervene. These groups can directly access and impact the (dis)functional needs of the problems being addressed. An enlightenment orientation is less technical and indirect in application but more about illuminating, broadening, and increasing cultural understanding of and for a range of constituents—mostly scholars and students. Finally, the critical perspective is least about normal applications and more about emancipation, raising awareness, social (de)construction, and identifying systems of oppression and privilege.

This book projects over twenty years anchored most in social engineering but speaks to the enlightened and critical perspectives as well. The audience for this book crosses over from academics to military communities to other occupations and professions to various general publics in addition to grass widowhood in other nations. The voices of the spouses in the seven chapters are framed in four theoretical traditions that have become familiar in most studies of military families: stress; binary greedy institutions; military-family-state triad; and militarization.

Stress models had been the principal model for studying the impact of the military organization on military family members for some time[50] as psychology came to dominate the study of military families. Ironically, the family stress model was originally developed by a founder of family studies, sociologist Reuben Hill, based on his work with World War II families.[51] That research emerged out of and was later verified using clinical studies and large-scale surveys examining findings that dealt with individual family member well-being. The individual and family stress models continue to be robust today and a wide range of scholars utilize them, and it's reciprocal, resilience and coping.[52] Outcomes associated with the more psychological approach offer remedies such as resilience and grit training and other social support and buffering services to help mediate the stresses of military life including deployments. My colleague and positive psychologist Michael D. Matthews has written extensively on these topics.[53] Aspects of stress theory include individuals, families, emotions, cognitions, feelings, resilience, grit, coping, well-being, and increasingly social situations and contexts.

Military sociologist Mady W. Segal's research during the 1980s provided the foundation that brought the sociological directly into military family research theoretically and practically.[54] She first applied the notion of greedy institutions to the military as a group "mak[ing] total claims on their members and [attempting] to encompass within their circle the whole personality." Segal describes them "seek[ing] exclusive and undivided loyalty and they attempt to reduce the claims of competing roles and status positions on those they wish to encompass within their boundaries. Their demands on the person are omnivorous."[55] The military, marriage, and other institutions can be greedy—all placing demands on the service member.[56]

Segal and her colleagues later stressed how the demands of military service (such as risk of injury or death, long and unpredictable working hours, frequent moves to include residences in foreign countries, living and working in a hegemonic heteronormative and masculine culture, behavioral expectations on service members and their family, and separations from short trips to unaccompanied tours to deployments to war zones) have persisted over time not unlike claims on marriage and the family.[57] The demands vary in frequency, intensity, and severity depending on the times (peace or war) and the types of service members and families. These demands are baked into the intersection of the military and the family and have implications for all the players from spouses to children and adolescents to extended kin to service members to commanders to formal and informal military community supporters and service providers. Indeed, these demands create stress across the life course and generations.[58]

Following 9/11 and the subsequent wars in Iraq and Afghanistan, a new light shone on not only the U.S. but militaries around the world. The light generated new social and behavioral scientific scholarship on not only the military and military members but military families as well. The expansion is reflected in studies of soldiers in numerous books such as *Friended at the Front* and *Deployed*;[59] new academic journals that have emerged including *Military Behavioral Health* and *Critical Military Studies* among others; special issues of nonmilitary-related journals such as *Clinical Child and Family Psychology Review* and *American Journal of Orthopsychiatry*; and increased manuscript submissions to traditional military journals such as *Armed Forces and Society*.

A vibrant scholarly literature emerged in the last ten years for the study of military families. It reframes and scaffolds military spouses away from the realm of a functional attachment of two greedy institutions vying for the uniformed members' attention and commitment. Dutch military sociologist René Moelker and his colleagues put forward a triad notion for a more negotiated family dynamic beyond the institutional binary of work and family.[60] Their perspective calls for moving beyond the greedy institution bimodel.[61] Segal and her students recognize the dynamism in the larger society as well and account for military family diversity such as single parenthood.[62] The negotiated triad theory holds however that, based on cross-national comparisons, where three-party dynamics are examined, tensions are magnified, balance is sought, and the family develops a more complex and active relationship with the military—one that includes the organization and the state. Thus, a lively, negotiated triadic model emerges between the military family, the state, and the society—connecting the micro, mezzo, and macro levels in new and novel ways.[63]

Finally, a new scholarship on military families with a focus on military wives holds that ultimately, military spouses become militarized. By "militarized," I adopt Clark University and prolific professor Cynthia Enloe's definition of "a step-by-step process by which a person or a thing gradually comes to be controlled by the military or comes to depend for its well-being on militaristic ideas."[64] The more people and things become militarized the more militarization becomes valued and normal. It becomes pervasive culturally, structurally, ideologically, morally, personally, and institutionally. Enloe argues that militarization bakes into American society, increasingly held in high esteem as an institution, and so the ideas and ideals are more palatable and legitimated. The stage is set and maintained for militarization. Further, she holds that products, chaplains, nurses, women, psychologists, psychiatrists, social workers, social scientists, feminists, educators, fashion designers, and even anthropologists[65] are susceptible to militarization.

Further, new and seasoned military spouses become dependents and helpmates—financial well-being, privileges, social class standing, uprooting and isolation, and availability all come into play in socializing them to be defined as military wife/spouse. Foremost, wives become free and exploited labor for the military organization—labor that directly serves the organization's interests, from the individual soldiers to the overall mission of the state to wage war. Military families are more broadly becoming militarized, and this notion is not entirely new. Military historian Donna Alvah at St. Lawrence University highlights the "soft power" role of U.S. military wives in Europe immediately following World War II, suggesting, "The most prominent of the 'unofficial ambassador' wives were white officers' wives, many of whose husbands were making a career of military service. Like many Americans of the early Cold War era, they envisioned themselves as participants in the battle against communism . . . their efforts to assist and befriend peoples of other nations meshed with U.S. military and foreign policy objectives."[66]

Military historian D'Ann Campbell has noted that a "new military history" is emerging, one that might reveal more insights to how women supported U.S. wars by managing the home front and servicing soldiers in a variety of ways.[67] For example, sociologists Daniel Burland and Jennifer Hickes Lundquist contend that during World War II, the family became the arbitrator and solution for curing the ills of veterans returning from war, creating a new status of veteran spouse, veteran child, and veteran family.[68]

Again, Cynthia Enloe has consistently documented the militarization of women—mostly those impacted by war and the military presence globally, those that work in and around military bases, and women serving in the military.[69] While consistently identifying military wives in past work, she now calls for more direct, explicit, ground up, day-to-day, and attentive qualitative attention to the details of the range of experiences of military wives where "they will willingly absorb their husbands' aspirations and values or to the extent that they succumb to the often-intense pressures exerted on them to behave";[70] yet, in tandem, wives (spouses) become harder to "control" as they become increasingly empowered through education, military experience, outside work, marital options, and full citizenship.

Enloe draws attention to London School of Economics gender scholar Alexandra Hyde's work as representative of this new focus. Hyde found that military power inserts itself into everyday lives, where British military wives in Germany are "both the subjects and the agents of military power."[71] Others have heeded the call to show the explicit relationship between spouses and the uniformed partners—husbands or the implicit militarization of military wives. Through interviews, sociologists Victoria M. Basham and Sergio Catignani highlight the connection for wives in the British army to then-reservist husbands—indeed, militarizing them may not be necessary as they are fully capable of taking on the additional demands as their husband volunteers for duty.[72] Brazilian social anthropologist Cristina Rodrigues da Silva highlights how Brazilian military wives stationed in the Amazon with their husbands are both instrumentally and emotionally connected to the military.[73] In his ethnographic book titled *Making War at Fort Hood* (now Fort Cavazos), Vanderbilt University anthropologist Kenneth T. MacLeish suggests a link between how the army family functions and emotionality. In this case love, and love beyond that which is reserved for others significant to you, is to include loving of the organization, where the military family embraces civilians, reservists, retirees, and veterans—all that come within the military covenant.[74] Similarly, political scientist Harriet Gray offers a compelling perspective on how even in the face of domestic abuse, militarization compounds the difficulty of reporting abuse because of the construction of the notion of the "idealized" military wife and its corollaries.[75] Political scientist Leigh Spanner similarly finds that Canadian military spouses can thrive in their "feminized practices of labour" supporting the Canadian Armed Forces.[76]

More recently, U.S. Air Force spouses have developed fitness plans—like soldiers preparing for war—to withstand the rigors of military family life.[77] Japanese Studies scholar Emma Dalton applies Enloe's militarization notion with a qualitative and feminist gaze to the Japan Self-Defense Forces linking and identifying women, long practiced in Asia, as helpmates to the state, the military, and soldier husbands.[78]

Lessening militarization, spouses in Sweden, Finland, and Norway whose partners are in the military do not perceive themselves as part of the military organization or even as a unique "military family"[79] the way we conceive of them as separate and special in the United States. Military spouses in these nations can fully distance themselves physically, emotionally, and mentally from the military community. Some American wives avoid engaging in stereotypes of the military wife as well—in the military community but not of it.[80] Others embrace the role of military spouse, with (s)hero dimensions while concomitantly transcending their everyday lives beyond the military as surrogates.[81] Indeed, some military family members even actively resisted and protested wars.[82]

The five perspectives—strohwitwe, stress, greedy institutions, negotiated triad, and militarization—provide the framework for insights into the experiences of military spouses and military families since World War II. Previous research focused on peacetime with some more recent scholarship focusing on wartime applications. This book relies on these social frameworks to consider how army spouses and their immediate and extended families responded to deployment separations during the Global War on Terrorism. In addition, recent work has examined deployment separations—some for a war deployment—through the lens of the cycle of a military deployment. This notion helps conceptualize unique movements during "no shit" deployment separations.

The emotional cycle of deployment is said to have been first proposed by K. Vestal Logan in 1987 with the navy in mind and during a time of relative stability for the U.S. military.[83] The initial work involved three stages—pre-deployment, deployment, and post-deployment—where spouses encountered various emotions including anticipation, detachment, and renegotiation, but also engaged in varied activities during the stages. The cycle can happen for the army during peacetime. But in wartime, all is hyper magnified and extra exacerbated.

Military psychologists and social scientists around the world differ on the number of phases associated with the deployment cycle to include three, four, five, or even seven stages and if the focus is on the kinds of activities and emotions reported by spouses.[84] I focus on three during war because my spouses differed dramatically on the timing, frequency, and depth of their deployment separations. For simplicity and ease, I focus on pre-deployment, deployment, and post-deployment as stages. Further, what separates the current study from past work is that many of the spouses had undergone multiple deployments and thus became adept through the cycles of deployment more than once—during war and peace. This framework builds upon past work in peace and wartime, furthers a deeper and nuanced understanding of the three distinct phases in the cycle of a deployment specifically, and examines them relative to other salient experiences of spouses—support services, children and adolescents, communication media, and mass media—and does so from their perspectives and with their voices.

This book provides a venue for U.S. Army spouses to share deployment separations and related struggles and victories during the Global War on Terrorism—the U.S. led military campaign mostly in Iraq and Afghanistan following the September 11, 2001, attacks.[85] Tens of thousands of military spouses dealt with at least one deployment of their spouse from 2001 to 2021. This book provides interviews from 199 of them. The book is not exclusively about the spouse—it extends outward from them to their uniformed partners, their children, and extended kin to the communities and beyond via communication and mass media—two relatively new and formidable features of couple and family separations in the twenty-first century.

Overall, my thesis holds that GWOT U.S. Army spouses, and their offspring, fortify much of what we have come to know about army families during times of peace and of war; yet they concurrently diverge from the past in new and novel ways across the emotional cycle of the deployment and in their uses of social supports and social and mass media. I mean here that army spouses today like those of the past still get lonely, pay huge dividends in emotional labor leading up to the actual deployment, and contend with rumors all before the actual deployment. The emotional and material labor continues into the deployment cycle along with new demonstrable roles and responsibilities. Like the past, reunions continue to be celebrations, homecomings are cautionary tales, and post-deployment is enduring. Pockets of children and adolescents suffer mightily more or less. In some cases, by age, sex, and other subgroups. Communication during deployments is treasured and sought after through any means necessary. Television shapes attitudes and behaviors in matchless ways.

Distinct from past generations of spouses, many are adept and deploy their personal and organizational wisdom before, during, and after deployment separations. There is a cornucopia of military support services cherished, tolerated, and avoided by spouses. Moreover, they engage a host of others in and outside the immediate military community focused on them, their children, and their deployed spouse. Despite deployments, many view the military as a good place to raise children, conspicuously girls. Communication no longer lags but is in real time, hyperpervasive, and intersects with live and taped TV as an imposition and magnifier of emotional labor. In these ways, GWOT army spouses both reflect and transgress the wartime separations of past generations. They are centerpiece and hub for their uniformed partner, children, extended family and friends, the military community, and the broader nation.

Separations can be a challenge and detrimental to the emotional, psychological, physical, and social well-being of all members of the military family of any generation. Separations will no doubt continue in the future and across the world of work. The perspicacity of military families shared in this book may help inform the roughly 3.5 million people in a range of occupations and professions that mandate family member separation today—a growing trend in American and other societies. Commuter couples, transnational marriages, trailing spouses, and dual-worker couples are increasingly meaningful features in modern, postindustrial American life. Military and civilian families are part of the larger community of those living through work and family separation.

While young couples struggle with adapting to the everyday features of the separation, seasoned families that have remained with the military employ their wisdom to adapt to deployments in a range of ways. These include laboring to meet the demands of military family life, transgressing the triad, and (de)militarizing.

This book is about family separation in the active-duty U.S. Army. It does not include the other service branches such as the Navy, the Air Force, or the Marines and nor does it include reservists, National Guard, or Department of Defense or army civilians or contractors.[86] It peeks behind the made public individual and group welcome home videos on YouTube. In this way, it is a comprehensive study into the private lives of 199 active-duty U.S. Army service member families before, during, and after deployments. It pulls back the proverbial curtain where army spouses share their intimate happenings during phases of the deployment cycle and serve as the centerpiece and hub about their children, extended family and friends, the military community, and of course their deployed soldiers at the intersection of support services, communication media, and television. It gives a voice to spouses of privates to colonels to reveal what they encountered and endured during the GWOT.

## Diversity in U.S. Army Families

Like civilians, military families are diverse. The military recruits primarily from the host society but also from within.[87] For the U.S. Army, three in ten recruits have a parent that served at least one two- to three-year enlistment, creating the makings for a military caste in the U.S.[88] Thus, the military is strongly influenced by and representative of the larger society but does not necessarily reflect the same society. The military comprises a host of different racial and ethnic groups. Distinct groups are represented slightly more and less than their national representations. At this writing, the U.S. military allows for LGBTQ+ troops to serve openly and marry. In contrast, the military has always been a youth-oriented institution. Members are young with fewer proportions as age increases. Thus, when service members marry, they are young couples with young children compared to civilian peers. The military is divided into two social classes—the working-class enlisted soldiers and the middle-class officer ranks. The types of military family forms are diverse too. Among the shapes and sizes are members who are single, single with a child or children, dual-military career couples, female military members with a civilian partner, nuclear and extended families, reconstituted families, families that have adopted children, LGBTQ+ families, and even married civilian women that have served as surrogates for others.[89]

Of importance, the military is a gendered space. The U.S. military has long been a masculine-dominated cultural and structural institution. This means every aspect of the military enterprise from beliefs and attitudes to the male body to the historical and contemporary numerical male-majority soldiers to organizational hierarchy to the sanctioned use of violence is masculine. But the military is not exclusively masculine.[90] Women have a long and distinguished history serving in times of war—as a rule at the margins of the institution as nurses and other combat service support personnel—and often pushed out during times of peace. Military spouses are historically mostly wives. Prior to the All-Volunteer Force, far fewer male soldiers came in or married while on active duty. Women had prohibitions against being married in the segregated Women's Army Corps. Only with the advent of the AVF in 1973 did service members begin to marry en masse. This continued into this century, with civilian and military husbands of uniformed women becoming more prevalent. The increase of women and marriages both increased the proportion of women and the military occupational roles they serve. But the pace is slow. Women are approaching 25 percent of the U.S. military despite representing 51 percent of the U.S. population. Likewise, starting in 2016, all military occupational specialties opened to women including combat arms; yet women are sluggish to fill these nontraditional roles. And women in the military marry. However, unlike men in the military, women are more likely to marry men in the military or marry men with prior military service, forming dual-military couples. Consequently, a husband (and perhaps a wife) of a uniformed wife is more likely to be institutionalized (i.e., militarized) than the civilian wife of a uniformed husband. We know even less about same-sex (military) couples.[91]

The data in the table shows the diversity, marriage, and parenting demographic characteristics of the U.S. active-duty army over five-year intervals for 2003, 2008, 2013, and 2018—the course of this research.[92] Of note, the total number of legally recognized family members in 2003, the beginning of the Iraq War and two years into the war in Afghanistan, is 493,563.[93] The numbers for the army topped at 539,675 in 2008 and shrank to 471,990 in 2018. About one-third are nonwhite. Just over half are married and the number of spouses hovers at one-quarter million. Just under half have legal dependent children twenty-three years of age or younger, and most of these children are five years of age or younger. Larger percentages of active-duty women are married to other service members. There are adult-dependents over twenty-three years of age where the preponderance of these are over fifty-one years

Table 1. Diversity, marriage, and parenting demographic characteristics of the active-duty army over five-year intervals during the present study (2003, 2008, 2013, and 2018)

| Demographics | Active army 2003 | Active army 2008 | Active army 2013 | Active army 2018 |
|---|---|---|---|---|
| Total no. active-duty members | 493,563 | 539,675 | 528,070 | 471,990 |
| Ratio officers to enlisted | 1 to 5.2 | 1 to 5.2 | 1 to 4.3 | 1 to 4.1 |
| % women | 15.2 | 13.6 | 13.6 | 17.6 |
| % nonwhite | 40.7 | 37.3 | 31.5 | 32.4 |
| % located in the United States | 79.9 | 87.1 | 89.1 | 89.7 |
| Marriage | | | | |
| % 25 years old and younger | 46.1 | 44.4 | 39.6 | 44.6 |
| % married | 52.2 | 56.3 | 59.0 | 53.8 |
| % in dual-military marriages by male/female | 6.0 / 40.5[a] | 2.9 / 17.9 | 3.0 / 18.7 | 3.0 / 17.2 |
| No. family members | 727,462 | 814,693 | 837,052 | 654,748 |
| No. spouses | 254,739 | 286,984 | 294,150 | 239,873 |
| Parenting | | | | |
| % with children (23 and younger) | 47.0 | 47.4 | 49.0 | 42.0[b] |
| Mean age of birth of 1st child | 24.4 | 24.6 | 25.4 | 25.4 |
| No. adult dependents (over 23) | 3,654 | 5,017 | 5,293 | 8,621[c] |
| % children 0 to 5 | 40.0 | 40.5 | 40.9 | 41.0 |
| % single parents | 7.7 | 6.6 | 6.2 | 4.9 |

[a]Percentages are of all AD army marriages not all AD army members.
[b]22 years of age and younger is reported in the 2018 survey.
[c]For all AD military for that year.

of age (not in table). The percentage of army single parents is low, noting that the mass of these are single fathers, not mothers (not in table).

The spouses interviewed in this book are diverse. Like the U.S. and the combat arms branch of the military, they are typically white and women. They are overrepresented by officer spouses (the methods section in the appendix provides more detail about the spouses). Women of color are represented, enlisted spouses make up more than half of the interviews, and male spouses have a voice too. I intentionally and systemically identify the latter three groups in terms of race, rank, and sex throughout the book when they represent a topic and theme in the finest.

For military civilian spouses of the GWOT in the U.S., Britain, Estonia, Denmark, Germany, Fiji, and other countries, separation became aberrant normality. Their lives resembled the lives of other institutional contexts where a spouse/parent/family member is absent for extended periods and in some cases multiple periods with the added elements of extreme danger, uncertain return times and continued deployments, limited communication, and psychological and physical changes.

Mass and social media brought increased attention to military families during the GWOT, unlike any previous wars. This has contributed to not only increased reporting in both broadcast and social media, but in the emergence of not-for-profit organizations, film, and music.[94] Indeed, art imitates life. A popular fictional television show dubbed *Army Wives* ran for seven television seasons between 2007 and 2013 (see the conclusion),[95] and a reality television show titled *Married to the Army: Alaska* had a shorter run for one TV season with eight episodes in 2012 on the Oprah Winfrey Network.[96]

With this backdrop, my positionality for the reader is that I am a white, straight, cisgender male whose age varied from early midforties to midfifties throughout the study. I left Bremerhaven, Germany, for New York as a toddler with a military stepfather and a German immigrant mother on the troopship USNS *General Alexander M. Patch* (T-AP-122) with a green card and subsequently became naturalized as a U.S. citizen. I later spent my childhood years living with working-class parents in Southern California. For high school and undergraduate college years we again became a military family and moved to army towns across the U.S. and abroad. I know my way around military communities.

I value service. But my definition of service is broad. I grinded for a few years doing public service in nonprofit organizations in and around San Francisco and Santa Rosa, California, working with the mentally ill homeless, at-risk youth, environmental conservation organizations, and Holocaust survivors. Later, I headed off to graduate school in sociology on the

East Coast of the United States. Today, I work as a professor and live near an army post. However, I am a civilian and civilian trained as a sociologist from an undergraduate degree in California through completing a PhD in Maryland. I have taught at civilian schools in the U.S. and abroad. These insider/outsider statuses and encounters have been fortuitous and valuable.

As I said above, army families reflect and deflect civilian families. Army spouses today share what many other freestanding spouses are undergoing in the postindustrial world—a split due to work and institutional demands—from incarcerated people serving time in prison to athletes competing at the highest international level in their sport. All such spouses are grass widows in form. Families are culturally universal in their love, devotion, and commitment to one another. Army spouses are set apart in the gated community and institutional requirements of the military that have become a normal feature in the post-9/11 world—one that had somewhat melted away before 9/11. But it reemerged with extreme prejudice between 2001 and 2021, temporarily subsiding as the U.S. and other nations have all but left Iraq and Afghanistan. But sabers continue to rattle belligerently the world over.

The U.S. Army family is apart from but a part of the larger U.S. society. They are isolated with personal stresses related to the unique demands of the military lifestyle, expressly separations during times of war that civilian American families do not share when only a small percentage of their compatriots opt into the military. Military families find themselves at the intersection of two greedy institutions vying for not only the service member's loyalty but the spouse, children, and any others significant to the service member. Additionally, they integrate with a more dynamic, negotiated triadic model that exists between not just the family, but with individuals, the community, the military, the state, and the larger society in which they are members. Finally, there are elements of the militarization of army spouses in the post-9/11 era. One that envelops spouses, their children, and in some cases, their extended kin, into a potentially exploited position near to the front lines and when troops return home as a combat service support element that is intimately tied to soldiers, family, the state, and society. Some army spouses and army brats wholeheartedly submit to the position—"Drinking the Kool-Aid" is the euphemism used in the army to connote hyperorganizational conformity. Others feel a push and pull with some facets of military family life. Others resist quietly or loudly. All however should be appreciated and understood for what they have been through.

I conclude here reminded of the 2002 popular Eminem song "Lose Yourself" about his being an absent father because of his traveling musician lifestyle. During the late 1970s and early 1980s, for extra money while in college in Germany, I worked as a local roadie setting up and tearing down stages and working security for rock concert events. I recall talking with bands and their crews about the relentless touring—eavesdropping on their lives back then as I did with skiers forty years later. Reading biographies and watching documentaries today reinforces the fact that even for the famous, wealthy, and world renowned, the touring experience meant missing family time. Indeed, the band Journey, still popular today, has two songs from that period like Eminem's about being separated from loved ones—"Faithfully" (1983) and "Wheel in the Sky" (1978)—and easily available on YouTube. Countless others have such songs. Years later I still think about those skiers in a hotel in Bavaria separated from their families as are the spouses, partners, and children of other athletes, musicians, and other professions and occupations. What they share with military families are separations for extended periods of time. Certainly, musicians and skiers, like soldiers, are having the time of their lives. Both are applying the trade they trained countless hours for. But what of their loved ones left at home?

This book aspires to be a singular and unique venue to the living out of separated families: specifically, army families during the GWOT. What follows is an in-depth look at stages of the deployment cycle during war, encounters with live war media coverage, communications between the war and home front, children and adolescents during the emotional cycle of the deployment, and informal and formal support services made available to army families. Perhaps the spouses I interviewed, and millions like them along with service members and other family members, will find some comfort in these experiences as might all the others across the globe interested in or impacted by family separation.

# 1

# "The Deployment before the Deployment"

## PRE-DEPLOYMENT

The problem with pre-deployment sometimes is hurry up and wait. It was difficult too because his parents were here, and they were kind of waiting for him to leave too.
—Enlisted soldier's wife and mother of two boys

Military family life across history is replete with separations of the service member from their family. Nowhere is the separation as intense as war and related conflicts such as humanitarian crises, nation-building, peace enforcement, or other formidable intervention. All require troops on the ground, across oceans, far from home, for significant periods, and in dangerous contexts. All U.S. Army families encounter duty-related separation at some point during their career with unprecedented numbers in the first twenty years of the twenty-first century.

Separations are a major demand of the military lifestyle. Separations can comprise taking part in overnight field training—bivouacking in the woods at the backend of the post for training exercises—to Temporary Duty away overnight or across weeks or months. Broadly, there are unaccompanied assignments to other bases and places for month- and yearlong-plus deployments to dangerous situations and contexts, among them in or near theaters of war. Given the past twenty years, most people today think of separations as associated with war—service members deploying to a foreign land engaging in a military mission anywhere in the world for extended periods but specifically to Iraq and Afghanistan. So intense is the event, that we tear up watching YouTube reunions of military families at schools, homes, and on sports fields. One reunion, of Sergeant First Class Townsend Williams with his wife and two children, occurred albeit awkwardly in the U.S. Capitol Building during President Donald J. Trump's 2020 State of the Union speech on live television.[1] The emotional toll reflects the long and dangerous separation and our empathy for family life.

Deployments, in particular combat ones to Iraq and Afghanistan, are exceptional. They are lengthy, dangerous, bleak, restricted, and unaccompanied, garnering both international and national attention. Not since the Persian Gulf buildup and subsequent war in 1990–91, and before that Vietnam, have so many soldiers been in such austere and dangerous conditions.

This chapter focuses on army spouses at the first of three major stages of the emotional cycle of military deployment—the pre-deployment stage. The next two chapters focus on subsequent stages of deployment and postdeployment. I focus on three stages for sound reasons. The opportunity to study spouses did not occur until March 2003 and we capitalized. First, in 2003 and 2004 I supervised a small research team that visited two posts to conduct interviews.[2] Most were going through their first deployment to Iraq and a copious number of our interviews at the time occurred in the earliest part of the deployment there. The reality was fresh for them. Second, by 2008 and 2018, I worked alone in Germany to interview spouses whose deployment occurrences ranged from short ones (one to three months) to longer (nine to fifteen months). They also had more and varied deployment encounters. Finally, in the interviews, focusing on only three phases provided a chronological flow and efficiency in the conversations.

A pre-deployment phase begins formally with the first notification of an imminent deployment through to the actual departure of the soldier. The departure may not be to the war zone. Rather, it may be to a war staging area such as Kuwait but notably it is away from the home front and the family. It marks the beginning of the strohwitwe's long engulfments to come— the soldier is not sleeping in their home-front bed next to their spouse. The reality of an impending deployment from notification up through the departure is a significant demarcation period. It distresses every member of the immediate and extended family, exacerbated more for those with children and adolescents. However, the spouses I interviewed, notably those in 2008 and 2018, could recognize the signs of an impending deployment. They were able to identify and pinpoint the time leading up to the official notifications for deployment that would demarcate the pre-deployment—the pre-pre-deployment. A period chock-full of anticipation, rumors, expected unit rotations, and types of units and skills needed in the war likely to be deployable. Later, deployments in some cases became so regular during the 2000s that divisions (comprised of roughly ten to fifteen thousand soldiers)[3] knew their place in the Iraq or Afghanistan campaign plan rotation cycles. Moreover, the pre-deployment, like the actual deployment, can vary in time as well, ranging from a year's preparation to only a couple of days in numerous cases.

Operation Iraqi Freedom officially began with an announcement by President George W. Bush from the White House Oval Office at 10:15 EST on the evening of March 19, 2003.[4] The so-called, and perhaps only temporarily labeled, GWOT had begun prior, on October 7, 2001, when President Bush launched Operation Enduring Freedom to locate and capture or kill Osama bin Laden and dismantle the Taliban regime in Afghanistan following the September 11, 2001, terrorist attacks in New York; Washington, DC; and Pennsylvania.

CNN had embedded reporters with select U.S. Army units as they prepared and then rolled across the desert from Kuwait toward Baghdad, Iraq, in March of 2003. Likewise, CNN began interviewing the wives of those deployed soldiers. At the same time in March of 2003, I was well into the spring semester teaching classes at West Point—business as usual—teaching a course called Sociological Theory through Film, and I had a basket full of independent study projects underway with senior cadets. We long followed war efforts in Afghanistan that began seventeen months earlier and, at the time, were carefully monitoring an invasion of Iraq by the U.S. and other military forces.

A colleague of mine, a male army captain on a three-year teaching assignment at West Point, anxious to get into the fight in some way, watched an interview of an army captain's wife on CNN. We had a large-screen television in our hallway for all to monitor the war unfolding live on CNN. He says, "I know her" and her husband—an army colleague commanding in the war with CNN reporters embedded in his unit. This insider connection provided the impetus for us to contact the Rear Detachment Command unit and the captain's wife. I soon after assembled a research team of two women and us two men and with institutional support and encouragement scheduled a visit to the post in the southeastern United States to interview wives watching their husbands roll into Baghdad.

It was an unprecedented and compelling opportunity to visit with those spouses. One quote has remained with me from an army wife from Ohio living on-post. She had been married for two years before September 11, 2001—to an army tanker (a crewman operating a tank such as the M1 Abrams)—and enthusiastically quipped to me regarding her husband's involvement in that initial invasion of Iraq: "I was watching CNN [an embedded reporter] with [his unit] on and it showed them going into the desert and my husband had to have been having the time of his life. That is what they trained to do and that is what he was doing."

We visited with that unit twice that spring. Later, in the summer of 2004, I found myself in Iraq conducting research. It proved to be a productive research journey in Iraq on three fronts: helping facilitate major studies of Baghdad adults[5] and Iraqi adolescents[6] and surveying and deep hanging-out with American soldiers, subsequently published as the book *American Soldiers in Iraq*.[7] A senior American commander in Iraq, keen on our insights, asked that I inquire into the well-being of the family members back in the States. Later that fall, I assembled another mixed-sex and -race research team of six and we visited a large military post in the southwestern United States. We interviewed wives (and a handful of husbands) living across the post and in the local community.

As the wars in Iraq and Afghanistan continued and even surged in 2007, I thought it necessary and warranted that I continue interviewing army families. Few Americans had any idea both wars would rage on, but it seemed an appropriate time to conduct follow-up interviews. In 2008 I secured research funding to spend the summer in Germany—the logic being access to diverse units in Germany and efficiently covering less geography than traveling around the United States where military posts are spread farther out. During that solo trip, I visited four different military communities throughout the summer and interviewed a spectrum of army spouses and different army units. Finally, in 2018, while on a visiting professor semester in Munich, Germany, I again did a solo visit to a U.S. Army unit in Germany with an interest to study how spouses were faring after almost two decades of war.

Emotions and other facets of the pre-deployment have been consistently studied among military families since World War II—much of it with a stress and greediness focus.[8] Features of the pre-deployment realities reported by scholars included reactions to a notification, uncertainty, unpredictability, fear, preparation issues, long working hours for the military spouse, length of deployment, rumors, leadership issues, the definition of the situation, and media. These elements of the pre-deployment emerged in the interviews with spouses we conducted. Finally, I discovered a new element from our interviews with army spouses: their gleaning of experience from personal struggles, victories, and skills from previous deployments.

A senior NCO's wife and paid Family Readiness Group Assistant in 2008 shared her views in an interview with me.[9] She has some wonderful insights about deployments from three different hats: an army spouse, a volunteer group leader, and a paid FRG Assistant. She shared:

[Our responsibility is] in assisting commanders and trying to ensure that their Family Readiness Groups are ready to support family members in deployment, and even non-deployment. Again, soldiers are training more so even though they are in garrison. They are away a lot more. It just depends on the family. Some people can handle it, some people can't. I think it just depends on your level of experience, level of maturity, and also, I think that it depends on your level of commitment to really what your husband is doing. That is probably where I sit because I have been a military spouse for over eighteen years, and I have always been committed and I have liked it. I have been committed because this is what I chose. Nobody made me marry anybody in the army. When I married him, guess what, I married the army. Because I think that if you are committed to your marriage, to what he is doing, then you are going to do whatever it takes to make sure that you are self-sufficient. If it is all about you, you, you, and you tend to have a more or less lackadaisical attitude, and when that rotation comes up, you are spazzing because you don't know what is going on. My role is threefold, believe it or not. My husband is a deployed soldier, I am also a senior adviser, and then I also sit in this position as site manager for this program. I have been that young spouse and my husband went to Desert Storm [the first Persian Gulf War in 1990–91], I had a newborn baby, I was young, and I was immature. [I went home.] Boom, everybody knows how fast those deployments kick off. Having to mature and realize, man, I need to be within that environment so that I can grow and learn the military as opposed to pulling myself out of it and just acting like okay, this is another phase we are going through in our lives. I can speak from experience because, again, I have been married for eighteen years. But you take a younger spouse who left the nest from mom and dad, came into the nest with the husband, she has two small children and just basic high school education. What does she do?

In the quote she captures endless features of the pre-deployment phase including preparations from a psychological orientation relative to availed formal and informal services. It is a rich illustration of someone militarized as she "married the army." She begins by defining the role of the FRL and provides insights into the deployment before the deployment. Notably, she highlights and fully captures the significant role of linking, both having struggled and then surrendering the self to "committing" to militarization. She also shines a light on those less experienced—most military spouses—and those that leave to the detriment of themselves and the community. She embodies in one person much of what the spouses reveal collectively. I now turn to the spouses generally and themes they highlighted about the pre-deployment phase.

## The Spouses

Spouses interviewed in 2003 and 2004 had husbands in Iraq on their first deployment during the GWOT. The number of troops on the ground in Iraq nearly doubled by 2004 with 130,600[10] but most were still on their first rotation into the war. By 2008 (30,100 in Afghanistan and 157,800 in Iraq), and certainly by 2018, service members and their spouses had multiple deployments under their proverbial belts. Since spouses in Germany in 2008 had gone through at least one deployment, I asked each point-blank, "What phase of the deployment cycle do you find most difficult?" A handful of spouses referred to deployments in addition to Iraq and Afghanistan such as South Korea and Kosovo. As the distribution in table 2 shows, about one-third found the pre-deployment phase to have the second-highest threshold of difficulty (31%). The deployment phase is identified by 44 percent as the top difficulty and just under one-fifth (18%) found the post-deployment to be the most difficult. One spouse laughed and said, "Every phase of the deployment cycle is difficult." Two spouses (4%) said no phase is hard. I will return to this table in subsequent chapters. Here I focus on the portion of the interviews that dealt with the pre-deployment phase, uncovering what goes on in their lives during the period of the deployment.

### *The Official Deployment Notice*

The first feature of military deployment is formal notification for soldiers by their leaders that they will deploy. (S)he can then share the news with family. Historically, this has varied. In past American wars, such as World War II, Korea, and Vietnam, a draft notice in the mail while still a civilian, or oftentimes volunteering, implied that one would deploy to the theater of war after completing basic military training. During Vietnam, deployments were typically individual replacements—soldiers went to war alone but joined already engaged units around the theater of war. Just prior to, during, and long after Vietnam, the U.S. military maintained a large standing force—mostly oriented toward preparing for communist aggression coming from Soviet Bloc countries in Eastern Europe during the Cold War. In the wake of the advent of the all-volunteer force in 1973 and the withdrawal from Vietnam in 1975, deployments changed with serving members mobilizing with entire intact units, preparing, deploying, and returning together. The U.S. also began deploying to not only war zones but other types of missions such as peacekeeping, but again, more often as cohesive, intact units, rather than as individuals replacing other individuals in units who

Table 2. Percentage of army spouses identifying the most difficult stage of the deployment cycle to Iraq, Afghanistan, Kosovo, or Korea

| Deployment cycle stages | Percentage responses as most difficult* |
|---|---|
| Pre-deployment | 31% |
| Deployment | 44% |
| Post-deployment | 18% |
| All deployment stages | 2% |
| Other responses | 4% |

*Percentages do not equal 100% due to rounding error.

completed their tour. Units deployed, served, and returned together, with few exceptions based on outstanding circumstances such as injuries, personal or family hardships, the Date of Estimated Return from Overseas, or officer rotations.

Yet, while broader unit rotations are predictable today, with individual cases, notices of deployment are localized and situationally dependent. A stateside private's wife in 2003 shared, "He was actually non-deployable because he had broken his kneecap. I found out two days, three days before, that they were supposed to go. So probably the 17th or 18th of January. That next Monday, or whatever that was, they had left. Because he broke his kneecap in November and he had a brace on and everything, the doctors said he was non-deployable. They said, 'Okay.' And then the next day he went to work, and they said you're going."

The notices of a pending deployment came to the interviewed spouses months, weeks, and sometimes even within days of deploying that their spouse would head to Iraq or Afghanistan. A captain's (company commander) wife in 2003 anticipated the notice, saying, "[We knew] they were going, but it was the actual date that came down to just a couple of weeks' notice. You knew that it was coming. For preparation time period, as long as you did something, until you just got the date." A battalion commander, lieutenant colonel's wife commented in 2004, "We knew pretty far in advance, but just didn't know the exact date or time frame." During times of war, military leaders and savvy service and family members can gauge military unit rotations. While not an exact prediction, the long wars of Afghanistan and Iraq and dwell times (the amount of time between deployments for units and individuals) allowed for a better reckoning of when people might find themselves deployed again.

Finally, in 2018 in Germany, a brigade commander's wife and stay-at-home mother of three agreed to meet and interview. I will call her Monica.[11] We met over coffee and cake in an Aldi's grocery store café—popular throughout Germany. We sat across from each other at a quiet table for two. Monica provided insights related to her peers. She would be my first interview that summer and like other senior spouses at other posts provided me with entry as a gatekeeper to other spouses in the unit. Her struggle and insights about the pre-deployment represented the perspectives of a host of others that I would later interview. She found the pre-deployment difficult. She found post-deployment to be easy because they had continuity. Providing the title to the chapter, she said the reason for the pre-deployment difficulty is because it is the "deployment before the deployment"—comprised principally of long working hours and the overall gear up. Monica says she loathes conflict and "likes to make everyone happy." The period created stress on her. But she notes that at least for her, everything seemed to work out.

### Uncertainty, Unpredictability, Fear, and Rumors Coupled with Long Working Hours

In past wars, scholars found patterns of uncertainty and unpredictability to exist for military spouses during the actual deployment. The spouses here talked far less about uncertainty, unpredictability, fear, and rumors than expected given past research. The four topics appeared more where we might not expect them—in the pre-deployment phase. A stateside captain's wife in 2003, whose husband participated in the initial invasion into Baghdad, provides the leitmotif of the topics in the weeks leading up to the deployment:

> There were just rumors going around that maybe they were going to leave, maybe they weren't. They weren't sure. My husband had been telling me that if there was a war, we are leaving, no matter what. I am like, "Okay," but it was around September [2002]. I was scared. I didn't know what was going through my head. Especially because I was by myself over here [Southeast USA] and I didn't really know anybody. We had only gotten here in August. So, it was like ready, set, let's go. I am like, "Okay, what am I going to do?" I was thinking about going back home with my family in California, but we didn't think that it would be this long, so I was like, "Let's just stay." I really didn't know that I was pregnant at the time. But. I just decided to stay.

Another captain's wife, this time in 2008, reflected on the events and the broader military demands of uncertainty and unpredictability. In this case, the time before the deployment represents a feature of the lifestyle that requires a couple sacrificing and surrendering themselves to the organizational demands. She said, "Pre-deployment [is the most difficult] because there is that time, there is no control, he's leaving, and you know it and you're just having all of these things you're going to do without him. I think in the military you never have total control and that's kind of in the civilian world too, but here it's this entity that says where you go and when. So, you surrendered."

These views are not unique to officers. A corporal's wife I interviewed on an army post in Germany in 2008 reflected on her fears about the impending deployment.

> I think pre-deployment honestly was the hardest part. I think the buildup to him leaving was the worst. I was actually talking to another spouse about that last night. That, that was the absolute worst. The kind of not knowing, you know, doubting yourself and fearing for what was to come and you know obviously there's some fear and things like that. Just the whole, I'm going to have to be everything to everyone. And feeling how I didn't know if I can handle it and didn't know, I mean, this is his first deployment and he's never been away for more than two months, I guess before [the pre-deployment is the hardest part]. So, I mean, this is, you know, a major thing for us, you know.

At the end of the quote, she too surrendered to the milieu of military life during the 2000s. Spouses of both officers and enlisted service members had similar socioemotional sentiments during the pre-deployment.

Once units, soldiers, and families become aware of their deployment status and begin to cope with the reality and feelings of the impending deployment, long working hours are imposed on soldiers and spill into the family. An array of necessities become vital, and a series of activities begin to unfold all before they are "wheels-up" headed to the posting abroad. Monica, the brigade commander's wife in Germany, had twenty deployments behind her by 2018. Again, this phase is difficult because it is the "deployment before the deployment" confirming German anthropologist Maren Tomforde's research.[12] She stresses there are exceptionally long working hours and an overall gear up and high intensity of activities for both the soldiers and the immediate families where no detail is not worth addressing.

A Latinx/Hispanic sergeant major's wife in Germany in 2018, whose husband is also a helicopter crew chief, said, "I never saw him" in the weeks leading up to the deployments because of the preparation requirements. Going back ten years to 2008, a white master sergeant's wife shared her mixed feelings during the pre-deployment phase:

Before deployment [is the most difficult]. My husband took command
[of a unit] on the 13th of July. We had just come back from Germany.
He was home a week, two weeks actually. He went in the field for
a week [a regional deployment for training exercises], was home
for three days, went to the field for another week, and was home
for another couple of days. That continued until they went to NTC
in the Southern California desert in November. NTC, as you know,
is monthslong. He wasn't home. It was like, "Okay, what about my
time?" We knew before we got here that he was heading to Iraq. My
husband was trying to get back [to Germany] in April 2003 so that he
could deploy with them. I understand. I was in the army for ten years
and I understood why he wanted to do it and I didn't have a problem.

Long working hours for the soldier leading up to the deployment are a
common feature of the pre-deployment—from senior leaders to rank-and-file
soldiers.[13] Like family preparation, leaders and their troops are occupied preparing their units and themselves militarily for varied contingencies of the
deployment and impending war. Stress results because the two institutions
are competing for the time of the service member during this phase. Family
members want their soldier at home—more so because of the impending
deployment.[14] Less time for anyone creates stress and disappointment. Innumerable spouses sulk in dissatisfaction during this period because of the lack
of time their soldiers can spend with their families.[15] Others turn to and focus on their own family preparations. Indeed, researchers identify practical
planning as a buffer for hyperemotive feelings during the pre-deployment.[16]

### Family Preparations

I have already noted that both soldiers and families begin their professional
and personal preparations for the impending deployment once they learn of
the official deployment. Preparations during the pre-deployment feature both
practical provisions and emotional and psychological preparations. Among
the spouses, when I asked probing questions about the pre-deployment phase,
preparation received the broadest discussion. Practical preparations involve a
wide range of activities among them obtaining powers of attorney, updating
life insurance policies, organizing financial affairs, notifying credit card companies, updating passwords, and other personal, financial, and legal matters.
    Overall, while preparations discussions occur often during pre-
deployments, a teeming group of spouses projected an ease with arranging

matters and while admitting it is stressful, felt confident they processed everything correctly—both with and without formal assistance by the army.

Uncertainty hindered preparation for spouses. It makes them skeptical. In the quote below, the on-again, off-again feature of the deployment made them cynical and impacted their preparations. A brigade[17] commander's wife in 2004 shared:

> No [the spouses were not well prepared for the deployment]. It is not because of the time elements that they were given, it is more of a mindset. Because [the division] was earmarked to go the prior year, I am sure you heard this before, the date changed a few times. They are going. They weren't going. They were going. I wasn't here for that, but people have told me that it was a horrible up and down rollercoaster for them. When the word did finally come down, in fact even the order that [the division] was going and dates began to become apparent, still, I was talking to wives, and they were not believing it. Wives had been here. We arrived in July 2003. Last year at this time when we would go to our coffees [spouse social gatherings], our monthly coffees, we would talk and many would simply say to me, "I don't believe it. I won't believe it until he is on the plane." ["So, they weren't doing anything to prepare themselves, they were just not dealing with the uncertainty?"] Exactly. I think that even when we started putting classes in place for the deployment and getting them [other spouses] ready, there were even then doubts or disbelief.

Two enlisted wives from the same brigade in a fun-loving and jovial dual interview confirmed the senior wife's standpoint:

*Wife 1:*  We did not have adequate time prior to deployment—they were going, they weren't, they're going *now*. We did not have enough time to work out child care issues.

*Wife 2:*  I had to quit my job. I stepped down as a manager to curb my hours and responsibilities. Neither of us had *any* family time prior to deployment.

*Wife 1:*  Our husbands worked long hours every day with no block leave [military vacation time] or days off. We would have liked at least thirty days' notice that they were going so we could get things in order. She had a POA before he left, but I did not prior to deployment.

*Wife 2:*   We did not have any communications with or from FRG or
chain of command regarding any deployment issues, concerns,
info. (emphasis in the interview)

By 2008, not everything proved as challenging as the early years of 2003
and 2004. Subsequent spouses with wisdom highlighted the ease of preparation—attributed directly to their past. A colonel's wife in 2008 simply said:
"I relied a lot on past experiences and just my own experience sending him
away two to three months [at a time]. No one from the post needs to help
me." A male civilian in Germany, former sergeant, and married to a woman
sergeant with two teenagers that summer highlighted: "For us none of it [no
phases of the deployment are difficult] because we have been through this
before. For my family, specifically, the pre-deployment was a no-brainer. I
got everything here. All right, we will see you when you come home for
R&R. We had it handled. We knew. I knew what to expect for her and she
knew what to expect for me." A staff sergeant's wife in Germany I interviewed graduated from an American Department of Defense high school in
Germany—a former and fellow military brat—and her husband was on his
fourth deployment in 2008. She shared that preparing for deployments is
the norm of military life, not the exception. Practical preparations for them
as a couple are like an old hat. She said:

> This deployment was different than others because like I said, for us,
> it's the fourth [deployment]. We kind of prep a whole lot. We were just
> starting to get normal, and he left again. So, we didn't get back into
> deployment mode until probably three to four days before he left.
> Instead of before, we'd go in deployment mode two to three months
> before he left. Because we already had everything settled. We didn't
> have to worry about anything. I know where all the accounts are.
> The cars are running, and everything is done. It's just easier to leave
> it alone because we always know he's going to leave again.

Overall, the spouses from across the three regions—the Southwest and
the Southeast U.S. and regions in Germany—conveyed only moderately different struggles depending on units and even within units. Differences reflect best by time in the unit, rank, and type and degree of exposure where
all three intersect—the longer the time in the unit, the higher the rank, and
the more experienced and skilled people fared better. For example, one battalion commander's wife in Germany and mother of three teenagers who
had been with the unit for a long while and who worked with spouses said,

"We knew pretty far in advance [about the deployment], we just didn't know the exact date or time frame. It was almost too much time because it heightened the anxiety among spouses. I am personally glad to have had the extra time to start up. I would like to see classes on motivation. It was hard to motivate spouses initially."

Note that she also said, "when I took command," meaning she took over the FRG for the battalion. She perceived her role like that of her husband. They are a command team for the U.S. Army—he officially, she quasi-official but militarized.

In addition to practical preparation, emotional and psychological preparation came through from numerous spouses. A CSM's wife in Germany—the highest enlisted rank and in her early forties—shared her hurt indirectly. "I am going to sound really mean, cold, and heartless because you just have to be that way sometimes. The minute he gets on that bus, I say, 'goodbye.' That is it. I am done. My heart just got cut out and I am not even going to try to put it back together again until after he gets back, and we get back in the groove of things. You are just a voice to me over the phone and I have to keep it that way."

In an infrequent but valuable opportunity, I interviewed an army sergeant—a staff sergeant's wife—from a dual-military couple, with two children, and who had trained for the deployment but did not herself deploy. She pulled back the curtain to reveal the soldier perspective on family. Here she opened:

> I think there should be less pre-deployment planning, prepping [as far as the soldiers are concerned]. A lot of it really doesn't get utilized downrange [military slang for the deployed area where the fighting occurs—downrange meaning down the firing range where the bullets land]. Simply put, we spent a lot of time [pre-deployment] doing field exercises, FTXes, things to where we were away from our family, and it had absolutely no point. Complete morale, not a booster, the other one—crusher. The soldiers are out there thinking we're never going to do this. Why are we doing this? This is time I could be with my family. My family is grieving over the fact I'm going to be gone for frickin' twelve months. Now I'm not with them—even if it is for a three-day exercise—it's the principle.

Throngs of spouses seemed to want to say something to us about emotions, but they proved too guarded in the interviews. Following rapport- and trust-building, they relaxed some and their feelings about pre-deployment came through, nonetheless. Often comments came in conjunction phrases opposing an objective perspective with a subjective one. For example, an enlisted soldier's wife in 2004 said: "DCUs [a Desert Combat Uniform being worn] was not a problem, it [the pre-deployment] was just a different kind of worry." Here she's referring to the symbolic adoption of and change into the new combat tan camouflage uniforms for the desert deployment—from the traditional green Battle Dress Uniform. But something more real than the uniforms would be unfolding. An LTC's wife said, "The pre-deployment is [the most difficult because of] everything. Emotions are high because you're ready to take over the wheel so to speak. Everybody is cranky." By "take over the wheel," she later told me when I asked for clarity, she referred to all the family responsibilities that were coming. "Cranky" here is a soft euphemism for extreme familial stress. A different mother of two boys, a major's wife, noted the stress of the anticipated deployment that characterizes the pre-deployment, "Even when he was gone to South Korea [for one year], that was the easiest once you got into the groove. I mean, the pre-deployment's never easy, because there is always that stress because you know it's coming. Really, if they could come home one day and say they are leaving and leave the next day it would be great." An enlisted soldier's wife with six daughters reflected on visceral reactions to the stress associated with pre-deployment. She verbally reflected on both her and her husband's anxiety confessing, "My husband and I were both on nerves. We both have upset stomachs most days anticipating him leaving."

Spouses mentioned carrying sentiments differently. Their familiarity allowed them to look beyond their own emotions. They empathized with the emotional planning shouldered by their army partners. Here I have two exemplars from army wives that represent this viewpoint. The first is a battalion commander and LTC's wife in Germany. Maggie hails from New Jersey and is slightly older than other spouses, having married her husband after she had some success in the private sector herself. They have three young daughters. Maggie invited me into her home for the interview. We had a built-in trust because of our colocation at West Point where I teach, and her husband had served on the faculty for two years. Like Monica ten years later, Maggie became a gatekeeper for me to other interviews. She said: "I just think again I have been preparing for it for a year and a half, I kind of field myself against it for the moment. The biggest worry that I have is Marvin has a KIA soldier. The effect that would have on Marvin because it will crush him. I worry about him in that way."

I had the privilege to interview a perspicacious specialist's wife in Germany who grew up in Hilo, Hawai'i. Her grandfather served in the U.S. Navy and survived the bombing of Pearl Harbor. She grew up around the army and the navy in Hawai'i where her father had served in the army. She stayed in the family business marrying her navy husband who came from a career navy family. He later reenlisted in the army with eight years of service. She, like Maggie, showed immense maturity, selflessness, and a steeling of her husband and their six-month-old child. She said, "But you prepare your husband for the deployment too. He was so sad because we had a newborn, and he was just born. He was always sad as he knew he was going to miss having his infant times. I told him just be strong and he'd be fine."

Preparation is a major feature of pre-deployment.[18] The spouses here reinforce that like others interviewed, preparation takes two forms: practical and emotional. In the quote above, this young spouse must prepare emotionally for two people: herself and her husband. The significance of knowledge with the earliest phase of the deployment stands out as army spouses champion their credentials as kind of institutionally savvy trekkers.

### Leadership and the Definition of the Situation

The U.S. Army is not the Google company. Rather, it is a hyper hierarchical organization compared to new, flatter, decentralized, and more informal organization forms of many newer for- and nonprofit start-ups. Publicly, there is a civic echo in the military organization and the echo begins with the senior leadership. While a slew of military scholars highlight that leadership assistance and engagement are major issues from past deployments, few spouses commented on the role of uniformed military management in the pre-deployment phase. Virtually no one remarked on the FRG leadership across all four interview periods. A handful of spouses pointed out how army leadership related to the timing of the actual deployment from the unit level to the army level. The majority highlighted a lack of satisfaction with leaders' articulation of the exact dates and times. Some feigned satisfaction, nevertheless. For example, a stateside battalion commander's wife in 2004 with two tweens and a teenager was concerned about the families at their post. She said, "The army needs to stop telling the families to remain if they do not want to. With electronic communications the way they are, it doesn't matter anymore. If they need to be near their family, real family, they need to go home." Others felt satisfied. A specialist's wife from Texas living in Germany in 2008 said, "Yeah, I think we were pretty well informed [by the leadership]. I think that especially they were straightforward with us when they were leaving, where they are going. I have heard of places where they don't. You don't know exactly what you are getting into. I have been really well informed. We were ready for it. They are pretty good at communicating."

New army leaders reading this will be disappointed that so little reflects on them and their leadership during the pre-deployment phase of the emotional cycle of the military deployment. It reflects a long-standing, hands-off tradition of allowing everyone involved to get both their professional and personal affairs in order, including their own, for the impending deployment during pre-deployment. Take comfort. You will have plenty of time to lead during the deployment.

Leaders can however be crucial in defining situations for followers.[19] Organizational members also have agency and can decide how to interpret the reality of a situation. Military sociologists have long taken from the sociological notion of the definition of the situation. This refers to how people in general construct reality. In an army family deployment context, the family socially constructs the reality of the deployment in terms of what it means for them. The genesis of this notion dates to families during World War II.[20] Spouses told us about how they perceived and made meaning of the pre-deployment. In 2004, a tanker's wife whose husband had deployed to Bosnia in 2001 and Iraq in 2003 said, "I don't think that stress is going to help anything. I talked to my mother-in-law yesterday and she is a big whiner, crier person, and I basically told her that if you are going to act like this, then just don't call me. That is not the way I am. She doesn't really like me. She thinks that I am not worried about him, and I don't care, and that is not the case at all. Getting upset is not going to help."

Again, the greatest number of comments like these can be subsumed under the heading of "experience" where the social construction of reality becomes a military habit. The spouses evaluated their ability to cope and manage the pre-deployment phase and the impending deployment based on past military or other related events. They projected confidence given past personal encounters no matter how relative the events. Even a young wife with two toddlers and three years married but whose husband has five years of service. She told one of my interviewers in 2003 how her limited familiarity with separation has constructed her current definition of the situation where separation is the norm rather than the exception, saying, "No [it did not affect our Christmas]. He leaves a lot. I mean, I guess I didn't think there was going to be a war. I would have just thought they would go there, and nothing ever really would happen, honestly. I did okay. I was a bit worried, but I did fine. We are used to it. We leave. Last year he didn't leave, but usually, he leaves about every year or so."

Once more, sociologists refer to the definition of the situation as how actors individually and collectively construct expectations of them and others in any given situation. In this way, the spouses like the one quoted above created a healthy social order for themselves. Family members and soldiers have some agency in terms of how they define the situation of a deployment. Later chapters will define the military lifestyle further. In this case, the pre-deployment and deployment that came, based on past separations, are something they are skilled in and qualified for.

## Conclusion

This chapter introduces the reader to army spouses and their first phase of a military deployment—the pre-deployment phase. For them, looking back, it is a difficult phase and for about a third the toughest of the three. This chapter is one of three highlighting the emotional stages of the military deployment cycle. Subsequent stages such as the deployment and post-deployment (sometimes called redeployment, reunion, or reintegration phase) are discussed in the next two chapters.

Over fifteen years, the spouses we spoke with continued to identify the pre-deployment as an emotionally challenging phase of the deployment for them. Keep in mind, the duration of the pre-deployment phase ranges from a few days to a year or more. Longer ones highlight how the deployment phases lengthened with the emotional impacts beginning before the deployment, not only for troops but families as well. For some, merely weeks and months, but for others even a year out. After the first notification of an officially impending deployment, spouses bared emotional labor worked around uncertainty, unpredictability, fear, preparation issues, long working hours for the spouse, questions about the length of deployment, rumors, leadership issues, and the definition of the situation. These are standard elements gleaned from previous studies of military spouses during past wars and related deployments.

Experience is a new element introduced here from the standpoint of army spouses and deployments. Life experience coupled with practicality from previous deployments buffer the most against emotional labor, fear, anxiety, uncertainty, lacking leadership, and extended absences while still present. It also helps to construct the situation into something manageable. While some leader spouses have rank, experience, and education, even junior-level spouses with separation or other personal upkeep can become hardened during the pre-deployment.

From a conceptual perspective, the pre-deployment is a greedy period of military family life imposing itself on members of the family. Those that surrender to the demands appear to become militarized as they circle the family home-front wagons by preparing to leave jobs, consolidate personal and administrative affairs, put on their emotionally protective battle-rattle armor, cheer on soldiers and one another, and engage the military community either personally or professionally as leaders and followers.

The next chapter delves into the deployment phase of the deployment cycle—the most difficult phase of the deployment according to many spouses with at least one deployment behind them. However, we learn again that experience with the military buffers the separation in dramatic ways for this new cohort of veteran army spouses.

# 2

# "The Temporary Widow"

## DEPLOYMENT

The beginning was hard. But honestly, it was really hard before he left, but it was just like, all of this education and all of this drilling and all of this waiting. I remember like the day he left, and the next day I woke up and I was almost relieved because it was finally like, we started.

—Army sergeant's wife and mother of a two-year-old

A deployment "refers to discrete events in which Soldiers [sic] are sent with their unit (or as individuals joining another unit) to a particular location to accomplish a specific military mission."[1] Since 9/11 through 2021 the frequency of separations for service members increased. Most soldiers left for Iraq and Afghanistan with others in Kuwait, the Philippines, Honduras, Syria, Iran, and the African continent, among other locales, supporting the GWOT. My research team wrote in 2007 of an ironic and arresting sociological fact: that while the U.S. Navy endures the most of virtually all their military movements as deployments aboard ships and submarines even before and after 9/11, members of the U.S. Army began surpassing the Navy in terms of "average number of nights away from the permanent duty station."[2]

There is no surprise that deployments are high risk of injury or death and are the most difficult feature of military family life. Soldiers and families recognize that deployments are part of military life. Indeed, a deployment is an opportunity for a soldier to prove her mettle in a real-world environment rather than a training one.

This chapter focuses on the fully away phase of the deployment cycle by U.S. Army spouses and their families. Deployments lasted from weeks to fifteen months. All wives at the time of the interviews in 2003 and 2004 had a deployed spouse to Iraq. In 2008, spouses at the time of the interview in Germany had a spouse in Afghanistan, Iraq, at home with deployment experience, or on other training deployment. By 2018, the wives of American soldiers interviewed in Germany had husbands at home in the garrison or on a six-week deployment to eastern Europe at the time of interview with previous GWOT-related deployments. The experiences of all spouses ranged from one to multiple deployments. Most had undergone Iraq or Afghanistan deployments. Others had both or multiples of one, the other, or both.

Among the spouses I interviewed, a multifold had occasions with deployments dating back to Operations Desert Shield and Storm in Saudi Arabia and Kuwait (1991–92) and Bosnia and Herzegovina (1995–2004). Wives referenced unaccompanied tours of husbands to South Korea and Kosovo. Going back further, still other wives alluded to and shared, without a query, that they gained experience because their fathers (and in a few cases mothers) had been deployed on navy ships or submarines or as army soldiers or Marines to Vietnam.[3]

Returning to table 1 from the pre-deployment chapter, we see that collectively within a deployment—combining early, mid, and late deployment phases—spouses identified this portion of the separation as the most difficult when directly asked. We should expect this. The soldier is away. But the reader should keep in mind, the number represents just under half of the spouses that I interviewed—44 percent. The remainder identify the other two phases as most difficult.

The themes shared here represent typical topics expected during deployments including the five major themes of loneliness; new roles and responsibilities; deployment length and frequency; the Rest & Recuperation period; and the Family Readiness Group. More minor themes emerged including fear; finances; transitions; Early Return of Dependents; Germany; bureaucracy; casualty affairs; Rear Detachment Command; inexperience; wearing rank; pregnancy; activity; and experience. While these latter subthemes became universal across and for deployed U.S. Army families, the details of the experiences are new and exceptional to the GWOT.

## The Spouses

### Forms of Loneliness

Feeling lonely is a complicated and unpleasant emotional response to being isolated physically and/or emotionally from others. Loneliness is a major feature of military family life. Army families tally steady and persistent relocations from friends and extended family. Separations within the family foster feelings of loneliness for military family members. Feeling alone is the first emotion army spouses shared facing once the deployment got under way.

Notably not the major theme of the deployment for spouses, spouses did reveal being lonely when asked about their primary issue during the deployment. Spouses in Germany in 2008 and 2018 shared feeling this emotion more than those back in the U.S. (keeping in mind the spouses from 2003 had only been separated for a fleeting period and did not anticipate long or multiple deployments). Loneliness for the spouses manifested in four forms: (a) general loneliness; (b) senior wives feeling lonely; (c) reflecting on junior spouses being lonely; and (d) not being lonely.

As a general variety of loneliness, a pregnant sergeant's wife represents her peers, commenting: "There haven't really been hard times, it is just that I get lonely. I get mad at him." Another sergeant's wife, thirty-five years old, reflecting on the middle of deployment and being with people, said, "Um, after about three months, the shock is worn off and you know it just feels real lonely, um, it's very isolating. I live in a stairwell with non-deployable people that have no idea. And it is nice to see, every now and then, they'll ask, you know, they'll ask questions about it. 'Well, what is it like?' And that's cool they recognize there is a difference. They don't all just say, 'Well, that is his job.'" A captain's wife represented the views of the more senior wives. She moved to Washington, DC, during the deployment and opened:

> No. I was alone. I was in DC, and I worked hard at it. I had a system. I'd get up in the morning, I'd put an earpiece in on my cell phone and I'd walk to work which is about twenty-five to thirty minutes. It was in Morgan Circle. I worked right downtown in the district [of Columbia], and I called my Battle Buddy,[4] my other captain's wife friend who had the baby and she and I would vent for thirty minutes every morning Monday through Friday. And that still didn't cover it. That just hit the surface. That kept me sane. And we did that for each other, and we visited each other and that was it. But she wasn't across the street, she lived in Kentucky. And so, you have to have somebody safe that understands.

Reflecting on her observations of loneliness among junior spouses, the wife of a senior officer commented on what she perceived to be the major issue during the deployment: "I think being lonesome. A lot of them haven't dealt with being alone before."

Returning to the role of experience and maturity theme, loneliness can become routine. An army wife said, "I'm used to being alone. We've been apart, ten years' marriage and we've been, you have your marital bliss. We get so much time apart, I don't need, so some of my friends are, so much time apart. So. I know how to deal with it. He went to South Korea. That was a whole year."

A captain's wife from Ohio with two children and a third on the way represented a surplus of spouses on buffering loneliness: "Not so much being alone, because when the soldiers deploy, both spouses pull ranks and you form your own little family groups and you know, have friends and that part. I don't think the loneliness is so hard."

Loneliness is a salient feature of military family life. Constant and persistent relocations and separations can create feelings of loneliness for military family members.[5] Loneliness due to separations dates back throughout wars including Operation Desert Shield/Storm in Saudi Arabia and Kuwait (1991–92)[6] and Operation Joint Endeavor in Bosnia and Herzegovina (1995–2004)[7] and Operation Restore Hope in Somalia (1992).[8] Early findings on surveys of spouses with partners in Iraq and Afghanistan reported high incidences of loneliness.[9] Features of loneliness include a lack of companionship, intimacy, sharing, missing their partner, lack of community, and missing significant family rites of passages such as birthdays and graduations.[10] Moreover, these emotions can be pervasive and significant.[11]

Loneliness crosses cultures too. German partners reported loneliness early in deployments.[12] Some three-quarters of British army wives recounted feeling lonely during the deployment.[13] One-third of Canadian spouses held "strong feelings of loneliness."[14] Australian spouses felt loneliness and isolation during deployments.[15] Overall, almost half of American military active-duty spouses at home identified loneliness as an extensive problem during the most recent deployment—second to "safety of deployer."[16] Another research study conveyed that 90 percent of spouses identify loneliness as a source of stress.[17]

## New Roles and Responsibilities

Army spouses of deployed soldiers to Iraq and Afghanistan continued the long tradition of an earlier generation of military spouses. As they contend with being lonely, they then begin taking on and coming to terms with developing new roles and responsibilities in their relationships and families. While feelings of loneliness seemed to persist, many buffered and mediated the emotions with new roles and responsibilities. By far the top theme for spouses during the deployment had them emphasizing new roles and challenges placed upon them. The scholarly research on military families tells us that while spouses have difficulties during deployments managing every-day matters associated with the home front, most, over time, thrive and a bountiful number say they find themselves acquiring new skills, resilience, and competencies. A typical response comes from a sergeant's wife with three children: "I am concerned about how to fix and take care of the car. I just learned how to change the oil." More than half the spouses described new roles and dealing with challenges.

Legions of spouses brought up to me the new role and challenges of being "single" and single parenting—a new feature in military family scholarship. They specifically addressed feeling single and the grass widow sentiment. A wife married for two years to a junior enlisted soldier said, "A lot of times on a day-to-day basis I feel very single. It feels more like we're just dating, and he happens to be gone for a while. I'm back in my routine in my house, doing the things I always did. I do pretty much what I want when I want."

For others, they characterize grass widowhood as more a liminal stage[18] between being married and single. An LTC's wife from Texas with a twelve-year-old daughter shared, "You are in a weird—you're not, you're single but married, married but single. So. You are kind of in a no man's land. Because your married friends—it is tough to do things with. I finished my master's degree while he was gone—that was a lot. I also worked with single adults, college students that were so much younger. That was nice because they were so much younger, and I felt like I fit with them better than a married couple. So. You are both. It was a very odd place to be."

Still for others their status represented a temporary state and had a pre-cedence. A wife with a master's degree in psychology in Germany and an NCO husband noted her status in third person, "More like the temporary widow basically. She's there and she must be missing her friends and I must be sad all the time. There is a German word for it, but I don't know if there is in English. 'Strohwitwe.' It means that you are single for a short period of time while your husband is away."

Spouses referred to single parenting rather than a single marital status. A CSM's wife with three children and prior military service herself noted flatly, "'Cause I am. I call myself a single married mommy."[19] ["You don't really have a spouse?"] "No, you don't, and you need to get it in your mind. He is not there. He or she is not there. Don't think that they are because you are setting yourself up" [for failure].

Some spouses cautioned about the single-parent reference. The wife of a West Point graduate and captain with three children challenged the single-parent analogy, angrily suggesting to me that one's situation might be more challenging. When I asked about single parenthood, she said:

No [I do not feel like a single parent] because I've been a single parent. Because I had my daughter before I got married and that's hard, to truly be a single parent. I *hate* when women say they feel like a single parent in the army because it's not true. A single parent is what the women across the street deal with there [referring to the Army Community Service office]. They have two kids, they have no husband, and they take care of everything. That's a single parent. Not working, getting a paycheck, husband in Iraq is not a single parent. No, I never feel like a single parent. (emphasis in the interview)

Others highlighted the unique challenges of living abroad during the deployment. Living abroad for military families can be the best and the worst of times.[20] They slam into culture shock and are farthest from social supports. Demands of separation and risk of injury or death are more magnified in an alien culture. Some wives shared feeling overwhelmed by roles and responsibilities while living overseas. Still others shared they overcame new roles and responsibilities with resilience.

Other spouses mentioned the role and responsibilities of parenting during the deployment. An illustrative example is a mother of a two-year-old and wife of an SSG deployed merely a week into a twelve-month deployment: "Um, balancing everything. Being a good mom because we decided to go the no spanking route. It is so challenging because I was spanked, and you have it in you. I don't think we have any resources here at all. When we were at Fort Benavidez, we had parenting classes the whole way. For her first year, I was on it. It was great. I was motivated. Over here [Germany], you know, it is so much more challenging because you are on your own. I deal with her. I put her in her room."

Challenges and readjustments involved everyday living situations such as altered sleep patterns, dealing with increased discretionary time, and household matters. One last group of spouses stressed the ability to roll with new roles and responsibilities.

In sum, once into the breach of loneliness, military spouses (and children and adolescents) then take on different and additional roles and responsibilities when their partner separates from the home front for a military deployment. Such behavior is not new. U.S. women experienced role changes before, during, and after World War II as dramatic, transformative, and liberating for women.[21] By the 1990s, military spouses missed the assistance of their partners in household labor and chores but found they could manage tasks both inside and outside the home.[22] But war militarizes, moving them deeper into roles. Tasks are especially burdensome such as "arranging for childcare, working at their paid jobs, managing house and car maintenance, and having to quit a job or schooling."[23] Like their sisters from earlier decades, military spouses conveyed a sense of autonomy, independence, and self-reliance associated with their partner being deployed. So much so, they have had difficulties relinquishing some of the roles and responsibilities when their partner returned home.[24] The negotiation of new roles and responsibilities continued when army spouses deployed to Iraq and Afghanistan.[25] Some scholars refer to the situation as "role boundary ambiguity"—at least for reservist spouses—where both spouse and service member are unclear about the degree of psychological and practical presence in family life.[26]

Spouse roles transcend culture too. Two-thirds of Canadian spouses of active-duty deployed soldiers reported difficulties in managing their day-to-day activities such as parenting, household chores, and care maintenance.[27] Norwegian spouses constructed the military deployment to Afghanistan as a nonevent—a private affair, unique to their family—a normal feature of their family-work life.[28]

### Deployment Length and Frequency

The length of past, present, and future individual deployments arose as a dominant theme in the interviews. Historically, military spouses have had strong views about length and frequency of deployments. For spouses whose military partners deployed for the first time in the initial phase of Operation Iraqi Freedom, they had no inkling of the foreseeable number of deployments. They already began speculating about a return date. A spouse from the 2003 invasion in Iraq represents the sentiment of others: "Um, the only thing that really bothers me is just the time. Like the timeline as far as just a date. I know they don't really know. But just like say, 'Okay, well they're gonna be back by August 1st.' If we just had something to look forward to. Some kinda date. That would help a lot of people."

A year later, in 2004, wives had different expectations concerning their lives. A battalion commander's wife, mother of three children, FRL, and fully read into the military role, outlined the coming months highlighting the price wives pay personally for exercising their autonomy but also the relativeness of return dates, "Our battalion, our brigade mission is changing. We are now going to be, I don't know what the situation is, but basically, we're the reserve unit for the Iraq War, where the Iraqi army needs them. I don't think that my wives realize that yet. It was told, I don't think that they know what that means. Potentially it means the army is subordinate. Scary.

The redeployment timeline, unfortunately our unit put out the word that there was a possibility that they were redeploying."

Wives mentioned the duration of deployments. They ranged from shorter to longer. Two examples represent the concerns. One wife called for short deployments. A specialist's wife from Texas said, "Shorter deployments. I am sure you hear that over and over. I think it is a little harder for wives in Europe because you tend to not have things you are used to." The wife of a warrant officer with five deployments in eleven years shared, "I think sixteen months is too long for a family. Our family has not experienced that particular deployment, but I see a lot of families and it takes its toll and they really don't want to stay in the military after experiencing that. Even our neighbor, whose husband is a captain. They have been in for eleven years. When he gets back, they don't want to stay. They don't want to have to face it again."

There seemed to be a certain level of submission to number and length of deployments as the inevitable reality of family life for spouses. An understanding that the business of the army is separations and deployments, and you simply recognize that and in military jargon, "move out with purpose." A civilian male husband of a sergeant, Mike, with two adolescents represents this sentiment:

> Yeah, I mean when we got into it, we knew that she would be deployed. We knew. I knew, because I was in before she was, what it was going to be like. That's helped me anyways and a lot of stubbornness. Marriage is not an easy thing. I do not think anyone has ever had the perfect marriage where there is no arguments or anything. So definitely knowing what I was getting into prepared me a little bit. I'll give you an example of her deployment schedule. At the beginning of 2002 she went [away] to BNOC, which at the time it was an eight-month class. Six or eight. I think it was eight months. No, it was a six-month class. We flew to the States to watch her graduate. We spent a month in the States, and we came back. We were here for two weeks. She went to Kuwait. She came back for two weeks over Christmas and then went back to Kuwait. And then in March rolled [deployed to Iraq]. And then she was over there for a year. So out of that two years we saw her maybe about three months scattered.

Historically, the length and frequency of a military deployment is significant to military spouses where six months or less appear most manageable.[29] Early in OIF and OEF, difficulties began to manifest and magnify as deployments approached twelve months or longer.[30] Research shows that longer deployments negatively impact health, especially for female spouses;[31] increase the likelihood of divorce;[32] reduce male civilian spouse marital satisfaction;[33] and alter coping strategies.[34] Shorter deployments showed fewer psychological problems.[35] Others have found few to insignificant problems as frequency of days deployed increases, at least related to marital dissolvement.[36] Similarly, past research has shown that the frequency of deployments impacts military families in a negative way[37] but may also increase coping strategies as experience increases.[38] A study of Canadian spouses—where the deployments had been shorter than the American norm—typically three to six months—found deployments to be less prominent in mental health.[39] Research shows that frequent deployments impact interpersonal relationships among UK military personnel.[40] Thus, studies vary by the objective criteria of length and frequency of deployments within the U.S. but the finding is culturally universal.[41]

## Rest & Recuperation

The R&R period for U.S. soldiers is typically a fourteen-day respite from all deployment-related military duties and responsibilities. Soldiers are encouraged and, in some cases, ordered to leave the theater of war to a rear area such as another country, including flying home. Affectionately called R&R, it provided some cracking contentions for various spouses, and they wanted to speak about it. R&R proved to be a foremost feature in the deployment cycle outside of communiqués for spouses (discussed in a later chapter) and became front and center in their consciousness during interviews. But beyond the recency effect, the sheer number of spouses highlighting undergoing R&R impressed us.

Like other topics, R&R is not a topic for the 2003 wives we interviewed. They concentrated exclusively on their husbands coming home on the heels of the initial invasion and "success" of Iraq. They are not anticipating year-long deployments or respite periods at the time of the war. However, in just over a year in Iraq, R&R became an institutionalized feature and policy associated with the emotions of the deployment cycle for 2004 spouses. Next to new roles and challenges, it emerged as a leading theme during the deployment phase. The R&R had both proponents and detractors among spouses.

Most spouses responded favorably to having had or anticipating the next R&R. One emblematic response came from the wife of a sergeant major with two boys when asked, "Could the R&R be better?"

Absolutely not. It was seamless. He called me on Friday morning and said, "I would be there tomorrow at 1:20" and the next day at 1:20 he was there. Now, if that had anything to do with his rank, I don't know, but I was shocked that it went exactly like he said it was going to. The fact that he was even here, I credit the chain of command 100 percent because he wouldn't have been if they hadn't walked in and said you will [take an R&R]. So, I love them, love them, love them. They will forever more have a special place in my heart.

A handful had negative experiences. Mike, married to the sergeant, referred to his wife's two-week R&R a month before the return as "a joke, a tease." Most of the negatives had to do with emotions—emotions of children, the spouse, and even the soldier. A captain's wife with four children all under five captured all the sentiments best:

The two-week R&R. Not difficult in the sense, obviously you want to see them and spend time with them, but that he took his R&R at six months because he wanted to see the baby. Well, the baby was so small. That month following that R&R was like you are starting over. You're like, "You got to see him." But you had to explain it to the kids again. I mean, they knew, they had talked about it. He's going to have to go back. He's only here for a couple of weeks. But the month following, it's really like, "Oh my word. We're starting all over again." It kind of puts you in a slump. It's like you got to see him for a little bit and now we have to go back. So, for me, if the army were to allow you to not, I think my husband is the same way, he admitted while he was still in Iraq that the few weeks that going back was really tough. It makes you question. "Is this really what we want to do for the rest of our career?"

A sergeant's wife with two small children candidly shared their family withstanding a passed R&R while living in the States and a pending one while living in Germany. "Mostly because he's nuts [affectionately referencing her husband and spending time with extended family]. So, he wants to see his family, of course that's what happens when you go to a war zone. You all of sudden want to see everybody. When we did R&R the first time in the States it was horrible. So, I don't think I want to do that again. But he does, so I'm going to suck it up. It's really difficult."

Spouses also seemed ambivalent in the interviews about the R&R. No emotive reaction, simply accepting what the army provides. The young wife of a second lieutenant in Germany said, "We're gonna go back to Texas where his parents live and we're probably gonna spend a week with his parents and pretty much any relatives that want to see us can come to us . . . and then we'll probably spend a week, and I don't know, go to a bed and breakfast or something, something like that."

Spouses shared what they did during the R&R as well. Almost all responded selflessly regarding who the R&R should benefit including their military spouse, children, or extended family members. When they did refer to themselves, they suggested they were being selfish—another example of spouses internalizing the military values of humility and selflessness. Another 2LT's wife from Chicago confessed: "It was nice. It was good to share with the family. I would have preferred to be selfish and had him to myself, but it didn't work out that way."

Activities ranged from coming home and integrating back into the family, visiting family around the country, or traveling to exotic locales. Garmisch-Partenkirchen in the southern state of Bavaria in Germany got the most likes—the same ski area my wife and I visited and where we met the U.S. Ski Team. Several women mentioned getting married during the two-week R&R. A captain's wife boasted: "Yeah, that was when I was six or seven months pregnant, and we had our wedding during that time. Oh, yes, yes! That was awesome. We had friends and family at the wedding, and we had a really short honeymoon in DC."

Families also spent the R&R with extended kin. Notably, few to no spouses responded favorably to spending the R&R times with extended kin. An NCO wife in Germany who met her husband on Match.com mentioned meeting both her husband and their extended kin in Boston for the first R&R. They then proceeded to drive with them—full extended family in a caravan—back to their home in South Carolina and remained there for the duration of the R&R. "He is close to his mother," she says grudgingly. "This will not be happening again. Not now in Germany." She'll "put her foot down now." The family can visit, "on her terms," but not during an R&R.

In sum, the R&R is another feature of the deployment phase of the cycle. Historically, this is a new feature of deployment as soldiers return to their families for this period.[42] Studies examining R&R found the practices to be mixed[43]—with a sundry preferring no R&R in favor of shorter deployments.[44] Similar to what I heard. Others reported disruption within the deployment phase.[45] The R&R program was discontinued in the U.S. Army in 2008 for deployments less than twelve months,[46] although the UK continued to grant it for six-month deployments,[47] as did the Dutch.[48] Positives of the R&R include family being together and negatives include poor timing and readjusting a second time.[49] Saying goodbye a second time is hyper painful compared to the first.[50] Something we heard regularly as well.

### The Family Readiness Group

The Family Readiness Group, historically known as the Family Support Group, is a formalized organization for army spouses and dependent children but increasingly girl and boy friends and family members such as parents and other extended kin. The FRG engages in a range of activities to connect the families to the soldiers and serves as an organized body both during non-deployed times but certainly during times of deployment.

Surprisingly, spouses commented little on the association with the FRG during deployments despite spouses having an almost formal tie to the FRG. Enough responses emerged during the interviews to warrant it a formal theme, but less perhaps than army leaders and researchers might expect. Enhanced aspects of informal and formal support groups feature in chapter 4. Up front though, most spouses, by far, continued to prefer informal supports to formal supports such as the FRG. Informal supports are immediate, personal, and organic compared to the delayed, impersonal, and bureaucratic aspects of formal supports such as the FRG. One popular division commander, a two-star major general of a post where we interviewed spouses, took FRGs beyond their purview and engaged in humanizing the formal. While in Iraq, I could not forgo an invitation to participate in one of his numerous and regular Video Tele-Conferences with the FRG back home. It seemed intimate, genuine, fun, and thoughtful. Stateside, spouses I interviewed months later praised those same VTCs.

Historically, the organizational cultural norm is the expectation that the commander's spouse (i.e., wife) function as the FRL. Today, fewer wives are obliging. Some wives simply bail on the role. Yet, the expectation that the commander's wife leads an FRG has little changed over the years. Military anthropologist Margaret C. Harrell interviewed army spouses across the rank spectrum and found that half of army wives, in the years leading up to 9/11, felt compelled to participate in military life or their husband's career would be tainted.[51] A captain's wife in Germany in 2018 said her husband expects her to lead the FRG. He insists that "I need to run the FRG" when he takes command in October. She doesn't want to but "probably will have to." She says she "isn't the army" and "doesn't appreciate being voluntold. It isn't genuine." With no children of her own, she feels the FRG is "more oriented toward family people." Despite living in Germany and working full-time, she plans to go home to Montana if her husband has a long deployment again. The first one was "the worst nine months of my life." These findings point to continued gender ineq-uities and uncompensated labor where no husbands shared such expectations.

Others pointed out that while commander spouses are forgoing FRG leadership, FRG responsibilities are expanding to embrace people not for-mally connected to the army such as extended kin and fiancés. American families are increasingly diverse and military families reflect this diversity in composition and in attitude. While the U.S. Army officially recognizes new forms of family formations and others significant to the soldier such as single parents, dual military, and elder care, some people are clearly not acknowledged. The informality manifests during the deployment where the rear detachment and FRG assume some responsibility. How does this expan-sion of others significant to the soldier work? A spouse leading an FRG—a battalion commander's wife in 2008 and mother of three children—shared:

> [The first couple of months of the deployment were] very busy for me as an FRG leader. Very, very bumpy. There was a lot of insecurity for the wives. I only have wives. It was very hectic. We have this, I don't understand it, because I didn't set it up, it is a group mailing that is on the Internet where we post messages, pictures, and we have 250 members to include parents, aunties, friends. So. At first, we con-centrated getting that online and getting all the wives emails so they could be part of the list. And as an example, in January, there were three thousand messages. One thing that I wish we had done prior to the deployment in that six-month window was touch base with the out-of-town people better.

In sum, FRGs are mostly face-to-face associations but have become in-creasingly virtual as spouses are highly mobile and geographically diversi-fied. During the GWOT, FRGs accommodated an expanded nuclear military family to support extended kin beyond the married soldier to include the single soldier and her family. Historically, army spouses told researchers that they have significant awareness of the FRG where 85 percent identify it as beneficial.[52] FRGs continued to play a vital role in the GWOT, by being present, but were seemingly less utilized by all army spouses[53]—especially by at-home, male spouses during the deployment.[54]

### Other Deployment Cycle Topics

A range of other deployment topics—less significant than the ones above but notable—came out in the interviews. Some spouses are old hats worn during previous wars. Others are new to the GWOT. These topics include fear; finances; diverse types of family transitions; Early Return of Dependents and going home; and living in Germany. The spouses also discussed military bureaucracy and the casualty process. Other themes include the Rear Detachment Command; inexperience; wearing rank; pregnancy; activities; and having experience.

Fear and uncertainty manifested in a host of ways and are magnified during a military deployment. Fear emerged as a moderate theme among the spouses. Spouses again were often other oriented and atypically did they discuss their own fears without some probing questions by me. A mother of three teenagers mentioned fear for other wives: "Making fifteen months go by without needing to be medicated. You get excited. 'Oh, it has been two months. We have thirteen to go.' A few months has gone by quick, but that doesn't mean thirteen more is going to. I think that for me, in this leadership role, the fear of going to fifty-nine memorial services, [a] brigade lost fifty-nine soldiers. They came back last November, and they lost fifty-nine soldiers. Going into this thinking, 'Okay, there is a possibility of going to fifty-nine memorials.' Daunting. Scary."

Research shows that fear of infidelity,[55] serious injury (psychological and physical),[56] and death are common during deployments.[57] German military spouses report that fear intensifies during the deployment, and they have adopted coping techniques to overcome them.[58] Dutch and Canadian spouses are similarly distressed during the deployment phase.[59] Concern for the safety of the soldier remained a top concern during the GWOT.[60] Notably, GWOT spouses seemed to overcome their fears with communication (discussed in chapter 6) and experience. The wife of a first lieutenant deployed to Iraq and a previous two-year unaccompanied tour in South Korea said when I asked about being fearful for his safety, "He was on the DMZ [in Korea], so yes. A lot of times I did. Now that he's not there, I realize that they do this every year, they have the 'North Korea's going to storm South Korea if they don't supply them with energy,' and um—I didn't realize that when he first moved there, and didn't know anything about South Korea, so. ["Did it help after?"] Mm-hmm. It wasn't nearly as bad." Fear subsided even more after she visited him.

Army families report concern about financial well-being during deployments.[61] Studies show that family financial burdens heighten during deployments—less for senior spouses as their families amass money. Longitudinal research has shown that financial concerns stabilize from pre-deployment to the actual deployment.[62] Financial burdens, especially for junior soldier families, have historically resulted from deployment-related financial expenses such as communication costs, supplies being mailed to the soldier, and child care.[63] In the GWOT, these burdens continued but subsided somewhat as many of these costs became dramatically subsidized. Some spouses shared their own financial burdens with us, and senior spouses gave voice to junior spouses who experienced financial burdens during the early deployments and during the early phase of the deployment.

Spouses also shared that the Finance Office at some posts are obstructionist, at least initially into the deployment. The army Finance Office is the equivalent of combining a bank with a payroll office. Soldiers overdrew a considerable amount of funds during their initial deployment creating conundrums for spouses at home.

Contrarily, a novel number of spouses related having considerable income and an ability to manage their money well. And indeed, their financial status followed the privileges that come with rank and status—where 15 percent of the army are officers, and another nominal percentage are senior NCOs. Their financial fitness is notable but not universal. A stay-at-home wife of a captain studying to complete a college degree and be mother to a toddler revealed: "We were okay because he was a lower-ranking officer at the time. So, I qualified for financial aid. So that really wasn't a budget issue. But again, once it came to decisions, that was a big thing."

Transitioning as a military family during a deployment is less about transitions during the deployment process[64] but involves full-family geographic mobility both within the continental United States and outside the continental United States to such places as Germany, Italy, or South Korea, among other locales. Relocating within the organization, roughly every three years, is a normative feature of the military. And there is a massive bureaucracy in place that assists soldiers and their immediate family members with these relocations. Spouses I interviewed discussed transitioning. Transitions include both moving to Germany and deploying simultaneously, dual-military couples trying to maintain a marriage, and parenting and deploying separately and adjusting to parenting.

Early Return of Dependents and spouses going home during periods of deployment are two examples of transitions.[65] ERDing is a formal process that allows a family to formally Permanent Change of Station back to the United States while their soldier is deployed—usually earlier than normal given the deployment. This means the military would treat the move as an official relocation and cover all the expenses. Actual numbers on ERDing or simply returning home during the deployment are difficult to come by. In addition, some simply return home for the period of a deployment at their personal expense—these numbers are similarly difficult to gauge. Some early research found that moving back home for extended periods alleviated immediate set-backs only to create a separate set of new problems.[66] A company-level FRL provided a perspective from one vantage point: "Out of forty spouses [in the company], you have fifteen that have chosen to go back to their hometowns. Umpteen of them with children, young children not in school but there are a few with school-age children. Of the twenty-five remaining, fifteen partici-pate in the FRG. We can call this the 38/25/38 percent FRG rule."

Living in Germany, South Korea, England, or Italy, where most U.S. military families reside, as a unique location relative to being stateside is a normal feature of military life. In his classic book-length ethnographic study of the U.S. Army in Germany during the Cold War, anthropologist John P. Hawkins concluded that "soldiers and spouses living in Germany believed both the soldier's life and army family's life to be more difficult in Germany than in America."[67] Living abroad during a deployment is novel, isolating, and stretches people psychologically and socially, and emerged as a promi-nent theme. Foreign residence and stressors are not exclusive to the U.S. military.[68]

Negotiating the bureaucracy of the military organization is a reality for military spouses and some research has pointed to problems,[69] especially for junior enlisted women who feel invisible and incompetent within the very structure set up to assist them.[70] A notable number of spouses I interviewed mentioned difficulties, riddles, and glitches associated with the bureaucracy of the army during the deployment. For example, a spouse highlighted how the paid FRG Assistant position needs more military precision, definition, and responsibilities outlined between the FRG Assistant and the RDC. As it is "very unclear right now and some things are falling between the cracks because one thought the other was handling it."

The U.S. Army Casualty and Mortuary Affairs Operations Division (for-merly the Casualty Affairs and Memorial Operations Center) is a system that touches every army spouse and soldier over and beyond during times of war. Historically, the casualty process becomes hypersalient during deployments as every family and the soldier must prepare for the possibility of a deploy-ment to the theater of war—where military activities such as combat are oc-curring—and by default, they could be wounded or killed. Each U.S. service branch has a special system in place to process casualties.[71] "Casualties" is a broader term including fatalities and includes three distinguishable groups: Seriously Injured; Very Seriously Injured; and fatalities (the Red Cross is the home-front equivalent if a family member of a soldier dies or is ill). The term "casualty" is often misleading, used as a euphemism for fatality in popular culture. The initial period after notification that their loved one has been injured or killed has been described by scholars and featured in popular films.[72]

In the interviews with us, spouses discussed formal and informal aspects of casualty affairs during the deployment. The casualty process is an administrative feature of the military—hyper magnified during deployments.[73] A brigade commander's wife highlighted how the system works when there are casualties, and the news media announces it:

> When it comes to injuries or casualties [she means fatalities]. We all . . . Okay. We had a casualty last month, recently. I got a call at 2:00 am. I would get the call right away because it was one of our battalions. All the other brigade spouses probably got calls at 7:00 or 8:00 in the morning—a negative notification—so that if any one of their FRG people called and said, "I saw on Fox News blah, blah, blah" they would say, "don't worry about it, there was a death in the division, it is not us." I think that has worked very well from my perspective. For the most part, I think that getting those negative notifications is wonderful and it has helped me whenever someone calls or I see somebody and they say, "My God, did you see CNN, whatever." I am able to say, yes, the division suffered four losses, no it wasn't [our unit].

The Rear Detachment Command is the military chain of command working out of the unit's garrison headquarters to manage military and family affairs. This is usually an officer between the rank of captain to colonel. The Rear Detachment is a group of non-deployed service members (although they may have been or will deploy) occupying the garrison, home base of the deployed unit. The RDC manages equipment and personnel not deployed. They have increasingly extended to assisting and supporting families.[74]

The RDC emerged as a notable theme among the other themes—not a stand-alone theme, but prominent among the deployment topics. From my observations during visits to posts, the RDC worked diligently but was overwhelmed to meet the needs of families. Most RDCs react to continuous requests for information. Inquiries directly resulted from live coverage of the war in the broadcast, legacy media. As media attention waned, so did the operational tempo of the RDC. The sergeant major's wife in 2004 again empathized with RDC, sharing a story:

> Um, rear detachment is placed in an almost impossible situation. Let me start off by saying they have 100 percent of my sympathy, because

God knows, I wouldn't want to deal with a bunch of women, it isn't just women, it is men. We had a soldier who broke his arm. Nothing major, but the spouse had gone to some weekend trip with a family member. When she did that, it took us a day to call around and find where she was. We were begging people. We found her and she was able to come and meet him and get him to the hospital. It would have been a little bit more seamless if she had told someone, her Battle Buddy. Absolutely impossible task. I don't ever see a solution unless they put chips in people.

As the above quote suggests, young, inexperienced army families is another theme highlighted mostly by senior spouses. This did not emerge from young families themselves—indeed, they scarcely thought of themselves as young—rather it came from wives of senior army leaders explaining overall delinquencies associated with a lack of maturity.

Rank of spouses emerged as a pronounced theme for a handful of spouses during the deployment. Again, anthropologist Margaret Harrell suggested, on the one hand, that the role of wearing your husband's rank is archaic and that only a "gentle" generation of stratification remains among officer spouses.[75] Although, in her other accessible, readable, and popular piece on the perspective of junior enlisted wives, the rank among spouses is perceived to be real and consequential.[76] Rank between spouses, in this case, has to do with perceived differences between officers and enlisted. In addition to interviewing senior officer spouses, I spent time hanging out with them, when not interviewing. They hosted me, and my research team in some cases, in their homes, at coffees, for lunch or dinner, and over drinks at the on-post community club. Officer spouses deployed their privilege in many informal conversations and felt compelled to inform me about the research project. They held strong opinions of enlisted spouses and spoke candidly about them. For example, a common theme across many officer spouses—especially the older and senior wives—was that enlisted women lacked social and self-control particularly when it came to socializing children, mannerisms, and public behavior—oblivious to social class differences.

Similarly, enlisted spouses shared in their interviews with us how they felt demeaned by officers and their spouses. One wife of an enlisted spouse reflected on their saga when her husband deployed out of Hawai'i: "Wives wore the rank of their husbands. They use their husband's rank." She recognized that the officer's wife is the "one in charge." "But," she says, "You aren't carrying the rank of your husband." She understands the desire not to fraternize, but the officers' wives "talk down to her and others." She declares,

"Respect is earned," not given because of rank. Officers' wives believe "they get respect because of the rank but rank is earned." She pointed out that her education exceeds theirs in innumerable cases. Some noted that the rank cleft could be bridged. A sergeant's wife offered, "My stepfather was an officer [we lived at West Point]. So, I grew up in his household and sometimes there is a conflict between officers and enlisted men. [The FRL] was an officer's wife and I was unsure how things would be when the husbands were gone. Like my mother, as an officer's wife, she did more of the officer's stuff. She didn't deal at all with the enlisted wives. I wasn't sure if Cary [FRL] would be like that, and she wasn't. She was involved in everything with the company, which is nice."

A plentiful group of spouses found themselves pregnant during the deployment. Pregnant spouses of deployed partners deliver earlier than their non-deployed peer wives,[77] have larger infants,[78] and differ in their pregnancy experiences and support by rank.[79] There are slight differences as well between deployed and non-deployed wives of deployed partners[80] although the impact of deployment on pregnancies appears mixed.[81] Communication media can link delivering mothers with deployed partners in unprecedented ways and the popular press highlighted a number of such births.[82] Another notable event unique to the grass widow during the GWOT, although I encountered none in my travels, is experiences of military women surrogates.[83]

Last, the experience theme emerges again for spouses during the deployment. "Give me a task to do each day, to fill the time when he's away." With this quote from the army Wife's Prayer, so begins Abby E. Murray's revealing chapter about coping and staying busy with military life.[84] Activity is not cliché here. Spouses spoke of how their experience with deployments correlated with their family background and the maturity as a feature of the deployment. They had become comfortable, developed a routine and rhythm, and kept themselves engaged during the deployment. By 2008 numberless are already old hats with two, three, six deployments.

In summary, the overall deployment is the most difficult phase for spouses with the segments of the deployment—pre-deployment, deployment, and post-deployment—being relatively difficult. The deployment envelops the spouses into a primary status of grass widow. The spouses experienced much of what we know of them during the pre-9/11 era. The myriad of themes is traditional, uncovered by military sociologists and psychologists studying previous deployments. Indeed, there are research findings now found across other nations and armies around the world deployed on similar missions in Iraq and Afghanistan. These themes include loneliness, new roles and responsibilities, deployment length, R&R, and the FRG. The themes center on topics associated with stress and demands imposed from a host of others in-cluding family, the community, the mass media, and the military. There is a direct and indirect need for spouses to embrace new roles and responsibili-ties during the deployment, to overcome their emotional labor of loneliness, fear, and financial insecurity. Additionally, how the spouses experienced the themes relative to Iraq and Afghanistan paints an ongoing view of them as they move across the deployment cycle and across the decades.

In addition to the tried and true, old and new experiences for 9/11-era grass widows emerged but to a lesser degree. Notably, the expanded feature of others significant to soldiers—single or married—is new and important in the post-9/11 era. Further, the perceived contested cleft between ranks is not particularly new but beginning to be revealed through boots-on-the-ground research rather than traditional survey research. What is fascinating is that spouses with experience appear to have a more swimmingly positive deployment compared with younger, inexperienced families that are barely treading water. Transitions continue and many are leaving the home when the soldier leaves. Pregnancies during a deployment can leave families vul-nerable throughout the pregnancy, birth, and postpartum. The RDC and the FRG appear to play an ever increasingly key role in the process.

# 3

# "The Big Group Hug"

## POST-DEPLOYMENT AND REINTEGRATION

You can make a soldier do anything; you can't make the spouse do
diddly-squat.

—MSG's and prior enlisted wife

We have killed all our own spiders, we've opened all our jars, we've
taken out our trash. It's almost like to say, "We didn't need you for
fifteen months, we don't need you now." I hate to say it that way.

—SFC's wife, military brat, prior enlisted, and mother

Coming home is beautiful—a hyper meaningful event for strohwitwe. More
so for service members and their families—as soldiers return after months
rife with difficulty and life-threatening missions. Sometimes called the *redeployment, post-deployment,* or *reintegration,* this period extends from the
reunion day through months after coming home. The *post-deployment* phase
is the broadest term associated with soldiers returning from war. It is the
last phase of the emotional cycle of a military deployment. Capturing a
shorter period after deployment, *reintegration* is a modestly restrictive term.
It encompasses the time after the soldiers return home. It comprises not
only the immediate time but the process to assimilate, mix, acculturate, or
simply rejoin families, communities, and society. *Redeployment* means as-
signing troops to another locale. Redeploying could involve returning to a
rear area or a multifarious front-line position in a different locale. For illustration, troops redeployed from Iraq to New Orleans, Louisiana, to provide
direct humanitarian assistance in the immediate aftermath and devastation
caused by Hurricane Katrina.[1] Redeployment is yet an additional term used
interchangeably with reintegration and post-deployment.

Homecoming and reunion are two common and essential terms associated with post-deployment in the U.S. Army. *Homecoming* is associated with
a time narrower than reintegration—usually, a day or three when individual
soldiers or their unit return home. Homecomings are the narrowest period

but receive the maximum public attention. They are the return and immediate arrival. Pomp and circumstance accompany the singular event or moment in a day. In YouTube videos with millions of views, service members arrive on tarmacs and at gymnasiums, schools, and sports events into the waiting arms of wives, fathers, parents, siblings, and children.

*Reunion* is slightly broader and encompasses the homecoming and beyond. It envelops the entire spectacle and pageantry of the homecoming and the days and weeks following as the soldier rejoins their immediate family and the broader military community at their home station. It embeds in features of reintegration and then official leave (vacation time) during the earliest parts of the post-deployment.

A third term capturing post-deployment exists after the homecoming and amidst the reunion and is known as the *honeymoon* period.[2] Defined by clinicians and other professionals, the honeymoon phase is a period of glee, love, and well-being that subsides ultimately when challenges and problems associated with reintegration could begin to manifest.

The terms are used interchangeably here at times specifically to refer to the periods after the deployment. And spouses use them interchangeably referring to soldiers simply coming home. These events are unique and specific but commingle in several ways, including anticipatory expectations, structured and unstructured aspects of the event, realities of the redeployment, and impositions imposed by the commanders, unit, and organization on the family. This chapter highlights these notions for the reader. The spouses in the interviews underscored themes confirming the post-deployment period that are well known. As well, they served up new insights on soldiers coming home to families after the war. After a bit of background on post-deployments, the spouses will share their accomplishments. Their prominent concerns at the post-deployment stage are stress and uncertainty; homecoming couple and family activities; psychological problems and PTSD; social changes; reintegration activities and classes; reintegration support services; and a handful of other salient reactions.

## Post-Deployment: Homecomings to Reintegration

Reunions in the wake of deployments are a common element of U.S. military deployments today.[3] During World Wars I and II and the Korean War, soldiers simply showed up at the doorstep of their families without any fanfare. Soldiers had no indication when they would return, and any return notification via traditional mail carriers or once popular telegrams would likely only arrive after the soldiers. Telephonic contact was available but sparse. Both would have only provided inaccurate information as tens of thousands of troops were bombarding transports trying to get home.

The 1946 Oscar-winning Best Picture, *The Best Years of Our Lives,* is a rich model. A personal favorite film of mine, I encourage senior military spouses to watch with other spouses.[4] In the opening scene of the movie, three service member characters star—an army Air Corps pilot, an infantry sergeant, and a sailor, and all are trying to return to their respective unsuspecting families in the same hometown after World War II.

By Vietnam, American soldiers usually knew their DEROS. In Vietnam, soldiers were part of an individual replacement system serving 365 days in the warzone—the theater of military operations.[5] Soldiers had "short-timer" calendars that marked down their dates until they returned to "the World" (United States). One week away from DEROS, a GI might say they are "short" with six days and a wake up until they take "a freedom bird"—a commercial flight to the West Coast of the United States usually for out-processing from the military and then home.[6] Their families are fully aware of their DEROS, although they could take a few days to weeks to travel from Vietnam to small towns and big cities throughout the United States.

After Vietnam, soldiers commonly deployed and redeployed as part of a larger collective of units with time for preparation and time for homecomings. U.S. soldiers have returned from a legion of deployments since 1980.[7]

Again, army spouses from 2003 and 2004 had uniformed spouses deployed at the interview—a myriad on their first deployment to Iraq. Although some have previous military deployment acumen depending on their time in service, few are aware of the decades of deployments to come. By 2008, a vast number had gone through multiple deployments, homecomings, reunions, redeployments, and reintegration. By 2018, uniformed spouses on shorter deployments appear to flow in and out of their homes with relative ease and less collective fanfare.

## The Spouses

### *Stress and Uncertainty*

Reunions after both peace and wartime deployments are stressful for soldiers and their families.[8] Whole groups of spouses I interviewed highlighted the uncertainty and unease they felt about the pending homecoming and the stress that accompanies the period. Some wives said they just feel "anxious." Others discussed how extemporaneous rumors emerged in not knowing exact redeployment dates, which exacerbated the stress of homecoming.

A pregnant wife of a junior enlisted soldier—a heavy wheel mechanic—captured the stress familiarity finely. She told me in 2004:

> Yeah. Because if we had a date, I would feel better. Like okay, it is okay. You know he is not going to be home until this date, you know, it is okay. Not the exact date, but approximately. We just don't have a date or approximately, or anything. Whenever the mission is done, they will let us know. I am like okay. Yeah, we do listen to the news, and there are soldiers dying over there and a lot of soldiers are coming back on [Fort Benavidez] or [South Carolina], just other places and not here. We are like, me and my friend are kind of getting, not worried, but anxious because we are like, we haven't heard anything. Her husband called yesterday, and he said they are fine and everything, but they seem like they are stressing out too because they don't know what is going on. They don't know when they are going to be home. They are hearing the rumors just like we are. We just want to know what is going on. Are they going to stay or are they not? We just want to know so we know what to do. I mean, it is just really hard. That is what is hitting me right now, that we don't know when they are coming back. We can't make any plans. If we do, they are going to be ruined because they can call us tomorrow and say they are not going to be home until September or October. It is hard.

Another pregnant wife of a sergeant in Germany in 2008 shared what others mentioned, "It comes in waves. For me the hardest part [of the deployment] is right before the end. It just seems like it's never going to end. The middle you settle into the flow of things. We're getting really close to them coming back, so it's starting to get hard again. What am I going to do? I can hardly handle the reintegration."

In a double interview, two mid-level NCO wives went back and forth on the redeployment:

*Wife 1:*  Yeah [said sarcastically]. They are coming home anywhere between February, March, or April.

*Wife 2:*  I am like, Come home?! You can't really get excited about a certain date. They are like March 6 is the magic day. You can't really circle it on the calendar because you can't count on the army's days. It could be earlier; it could be later.

*Wife 1:*  Even though I am not as, I know, don't try to [do anything].

*Wife 2:*  Either way, there is still poopy diapers and kids to be fed.

*Wife 1:* I am looking forward, but I won't make myself crazy.

*Wife 2:* Maybe [I will make plans] before they come.

*Wife 1:* I am not making any plans. When my husband came home on R&R, I had plans to make a big dinner, make a big deal of him coming home. All he wanted was a Blockbuster movie and a pizza. I am not even going to try this time. I am going to wait and see what he wants to do. I don't want to push him. It is stressful enough.

A senior-level person, well respected among the spouses and serving as a paid FRG Assistant and with prior enlisted service, put the stress of dates and redeployment in perspective in the greediness of the military offering:

I see OPSEC as being important. I know spouses want information and they want it, you know, especially this is going to come up more so when they start getting closer to coming home. "When is my soldier flying?" We actually did it in a very timely manner that gave people a little time to plan; however, were we considering the soldier's safety . . . when they got ready to redeploy, I started to look at where parents lived in relationship to their soldiers, especially my single soldiers. If they were within the five-state region of Texas [where he had been stationed as a Non-Commissioned Officer-in-Charge], I would try to call them immediately upon getting official information. There is a possibility that they may make it there for their son's or daughter's homecoming.

As I shared in the previous deployment chapter, FRLs remarked on the number of wives who returned home to their families of origin during the deployment or ERD'd to another post. In nominal cases, lieutenant wives would even head off to graduate school for a year. Mostly, when asked for a number, the 50 percent rule came up. In this case, half of the unit is married. Half of those married expected to leave for extended periods—going to family or other destinations. The time away can be weeks or months. Displacement occurs often in the summer months when children are out of school.

Nevertheless, others might pack up altogether and leave during the entire deployment. One captain's wife in 2018 mentioned flying home to Minnesota to be with her parents and siblings once a month from across the country for the entire deployment—an expensive affair—and she worked full-time. Notes to such mobility emerged elsewhere in interviews and I pick up on them in other sections of the book such as the experiences of children and adolescents. Spouses leaving created added stresses for the FRG and RDC as the homecoming approached. Teeming numbers of wives, children, and extended kin returned to the unit as the new phase approached. Self-displacements such as these may buffer against stressors during the deployment phase. However, the transitions back re-create stress and uncertainty.

Reunions after deployments are a characteristic element of U.S. military deployments today.[9] However, plans change. Research shows that changed dates can cause administrative and emotional upheaval.[10] All the plans made by the military post, the surrounding community, and family and friends create strains, and any postponement or moving the return date earlier discombobulates everyone involved. Research shows that reunions after peace and wartime deployments are stressful for soldiers and their family members.[11] Typical examples of stresses vary. They take in unmet expectations, return delays, soldier culture shock, lack of adequate decompression and reflection time, adequate family time before resuming military duties, reintegrating home and family routines, and finally, minor and significant mental health problems.[12]

### Post-Deployment Activities

Post-deployment activities are another central theme for the wives I interviewed. Some describe what they expected of other wives as FRLs or what the individual wives wanted to do or had done. Of all the topics discussed in our interviews, spouses became most animated and excited to talk about their upcoming homecoming and post-deployment anticipated plans. Their experiences ranged. Activities include encouraging others to participate in reunion or reintegration training, preparing banners and posters for the homecoming, planning who would and would not attend, visiting families, baptizing children, getting pedicures, and visiting Sea World. A wife from 2003 with two small children, a co-FRL for a company and married to a sergeant, shared that she prepared by:

> I have of course the house. Everything is going to be clean. My husband is a very clean person, so my house is usually cleaner when he is home. But when he is gone, you know, the kids. He cleans when he comes home. You know, we will do the banners and I will have everything he loves. It will be all about him. It is always usually about him when he comes back from deployment. He is so tired and so just worn out and he just wants to be home. We'll do a lot of stuff

with the family and then one on one time. My parents are going to take the kids for a while. I am just really, really looking forward to when he is coming back.

The sharing of post-deployment activities is a new dimension to deployments. Spouses and family members regularly plan and execute activities done with the tenderest concern to reestablish a semblance of normalcy for the entire family. However, the army, its paternalism, militarizes the post-deployment in a host of ways.

Initially, the system typically imposes a set of criteria once the soldiers landed at their home post. A mainstay among them is a three-day pass, followed by fifteen half-days of reintegration activities and training, trailed by thirty days' leave [vacation time]. An FRG Assistant emphasized: "The reason that they do the fifteen half days for reintegration is so that commanders have eyes on soldiers for two weeks." In this case, monitoring them for individual-level irregularities.

### PTSD and Other Psychological Problems

For countless army families, the fear and reality of psychological problems incurred during wartime, Post-Traumatic Stress Disorder, major depression, and Traumatic Brain Injury, are common. Substantial numbers of wives mentioned concerns about psychological issues and specifically PTSD for their homecoming spouses. This theme is significant with typical responses however scattered across a spectrum of concerns related to psychological problems. The spectrum embraces children, perceptions of wives and soldiers by senior FRLs, spouses, and soldiers.

One army spouse, herself with military service in the Air Force and an army husband not deployed at the time of the interview, reflecting on her psychological well-being and with him deploying alone without the benefits of a unit, said:

No, we weren't given any pre-deployment or any reintegration. I cried in the airport, then cried in the parking lot for an hour. Then went home and cried at my house for three hours. Then, on coming back I just picked him up at the airport. I think that's one of these places where the army, all the military, there is a huge focus on the unit deployed with the units, there are a lot of these programs, but individuals, we have a lot of onesies and twosies [one or two isolated cases] and their families are not taken care of in the same way.

Other responses had to do with specific perceptions and anticipations of how soldiers might be upon their return. A first lieutenant's wife provides a typical response—a multiracial couple, Asian and Latinx/Hispanic, that married straight out of college:

> I would say it is um, I think it is a two-way tie between the initial deployment and the coming back [as the most difficult part of the deployment]. Not the reintegration part but the coming back. Just because there is more, more of—the first few days, he's gone, I'm really worried about him, and then at the end. It is like—he is coming back. I wonder [how he has changed]. Like, over the phone, he sounds the same. But is there, is there something he hasn't told me? Is he going to react to something different whereas before he wouldn't have? It was after he deployed that I started reading a lot about post-traumatic stress disorder and I remember seeing it on TV on the news and such.

Serious mental disorders and TBI vary by the amount of combat exposure, especially following early deployments to Iraq and Afghanistan, and are estimated to impact approximately one-third of service members.[13] There is evidence that soldiers returning from Iraq or Afghanistan with clinical symptoms impact their families negatively and in turn adversely impact soldier recovery.[14] The fear of spouses and adolescents is justified, authentic, and warranted. War continues to insert itself into the family domain just before and long after the soldier returns. And the experience "militarized" families.

### Social Changes

More general than PTSD, soldiers, spouses, and children change normally during the soldier's time away from the family. A significant feature of returning soldiers is the concern for sociological rather than psychological change. In the interviews, the spouses shared types of change among military families, including the need for adjustment time, mood and personality changes, reestablishing communication within the marital and familial relationship, disciplining children, and reestablishing familial and marital roles and household routines. Change is not necessarily a negative occurrence or outcome. A variety of spouses emphasized positive features associated with reintegration. Wives highlighted how they and their husbands changed for the better—that these were developmental opportunities.

At first, there were discussions about needing adjustment time following a deployment. A white wife of a staff sergeant, both from Phoenix, Arizona, married with two toddlers, shared how her husband needs time away from guys he had spent day and night with for fifteen months, saying, "Just the normal concerns of readjusting to life and then the time. The little bit of extra time he spent with friends that he was with for so long. But I think that it is all normal. I don't think that it is abnormal. My husband, when he gets back, he wants to be home and he is like I spent the last fifteen months with those guys, and it is okay that I don't see them right now."

Regarding mood and personality disorders, a pregnant wife in Germany of a junior enlisted soldier spouse said, "You see the commercials and stuff, and you read about how [trails off] . . . He's really in a relatively safe place and he doesn't seem overly like, I use the word 'shell shock' because that's the word my grandfather used, he was military during World War II. He doesn't seem overly shell-shocked to me, but he's changed a lot. In a year, who is not going to change? I've already sensed a lot of the change."

A handful of spouses mentioned communication in the relationship or disciplining children. Regarding children and discipline, a military brat herself with prior military service, married to an enlisted soldier, and mother of a three-year-old mentioned:

> 'Cause, as my husband would put it [as I would say], "He screws up my chi." We have everything. Like when he came home on R&R. We fought the first week, cats and dogs, because he couldn't understand why something was here, why something was there, and he wanted to be really nice to our daughter when I had spent all this time instilling certain things in her. Then he comes back and he's like, "Oh, it's okay if she does that." No, it's not okay! I just find it hard adjusting. We have killed all our own spiders, we've opened all our jars, we've taken out our trash. It's almost like to say, "We didn't need you for fifteen months, we don't need you now." I hate to say it that way.

As Michael Matthews stresses, people can grow, expand, and develop during crisis.[15] Again, spouses emphasized the positive side of change coming out of deployment—how the soldier changed for the positive. A worthy instance comes from a senior army officer's wife whose husband had recently returned home from a deployment:

> He has grown on the plus side. He has grown to appreciate me much more. A lot of the things that he has taken for granted. He has learned to appreciate me a lot more. ["So, he gets what is going on at home?"] I did say today that I am going to leave him alone. There

was a little frustration level this morning. I would leave him alone as a single parent for a month to realize what was going on. He would say, "Please don't do that to me." But I do think that he gets a little bit better at understanding everything that I have to do. If I wrote down everything that I did, he would be astounded. All he is doing, not all he is doing, he is just going to work in a war zone, gosh darn it, he has nobody really else to think about, where I have different responsibilities, but a lot more of them.

Wives also perceive change for the better. An African American wife of an army major on his third deployment with three adolescent sons and an adult child not living at home shared:

For me the hardest is the pre-deployment and reintegration. We change . . . You know if something is going to happen, or something is going to go wrong, it's going to go wrong as soon as he leaves. So. You are bracing yourself for that. Then everything during the deployment is pretty easy because you get in a routine, you start to do things you didn't do when he was here, like go to school or lose weight, just certain things that you do. Then the integration part you are connecting. Even though my husband and I connect well, we don't have any problems, it's just that is he going to accept the change in me or am I going to accept the change. How much has he changed? Or how much have I changed? Those are questions you have in the back of your mind. ["Has he changed?"] No, surprisingly, no. Not much at all. I have. ["How have you changed?"] I've lost weight. My appearance has changed. I've started working. I haven't worked for fifteen years. So, I've got a new job. ["Are you losing weight because you're not eating or you are working out?"] I'm working out and being healthy and spending a bit more time on me. My family was the most important thing, making sure they were taken care of. Although I'm still doing that, my role with my husband being gone allows me a little bit more freedom.

Soldiers, spouses, and children change during deployment separations. Spouses and children develop, and soldiers conceive of them as when (s)he left. This axiom is realistic as soldiers experience intense and traumatic events during deployments, in addition to the separation itself. For many, all this extends the healthy post-deployment family reintegration.[16] Relationships, roles, and family dynamics require time for renegotiation.[17] Earlier research found that healthy reunion integration required couples to renegotiate their roles, expectations, and levels of independence.[18] During deployment, frequent communication (as I discuss in chapter 6) assists with marital satisfaction post-deployment, and preparation pre-deployment is associated with higher satisfaction with parenting post-deployment.[19] Prior to Iraq and Afghanistan deployments often required weeks of adjustment post-deployment, and conflicts arose around pre- and post-deployment roles and relationships.

Past post-deployment difficulties for army spouses found in the research literature from most to least reported include a soldier's atypical mood or personality; disciplining children; reestablishing roles; communication within the relationship; daily household routines; making household decisions; meeting children's expectations; and 20 percent identify marital intimacy issues.[20] Couples are more likely to have magnified dilemmas during reintegration if they had unresolved problems before the deployment. Add to this those spouses—predominately wives—that had gained some independence, and families that circled the wagons when a soldier left and provided limited to no space for him or her to return to.[21]

### Reintegration and Other Post-Deployment Classes

Counseling and similar reintegration classes came up in interviews for a legion of wives, especially FRLs. Overall, such courses have the perception of doing positive things for families. Two quotes from wives provide insight into the range of responses. I asked a massage therapist interviewee if she planned on reintegration classes. She responded, "Yes. That's one of the ways, men and women often speak very differently in the same town. The army has the chaplains for counseling and things like that. They have been helpful; we have used a lot of that, just because you just don't think you understand each other. Having someone say—'This is what she's trying to say' or 'This is what he's trying to say,' that helps. So, I think those classes are going to be great. I've heard that they have a lot of them. I think they are going to be great."

I asked a German-born, junior enlisted soldier's wife what precisely she wanted me to tell the major general (division commander) during my outbriefing that she needed for a successful reunion with her husband. She responded with a broader need for counseling in advance of reunion:

I guess individual counseling. That would be really, really nice. The same way that we don't know what is going on with the other women, they don't know much about us. I know that the problems that I have had and that Korinna [a friend] has had since the guys have been gone. I can only imagine what these women are going through that they have more children, full-time jobs and everything. I think that it would help everyone out to have some individual counseling. Even if it is just fifteen minutes to sit down and do like a checkup. It would be like, "How's life?"

In handfuls of social science studies, various spouses have reported positive features associated with deployments and reintegration. These have included greater marital closeness, increased independence, participating in decision-making, and soldiers participating in household chores and child care compared to before the deployment.[22] Programs designed to assist families can be impactful.[23]

### Support Services and Other Reintegration Concerns

Programs and strategies in and around the army have been around long before deployments in Iraq and Afghanistan. Wives provided sundry general topics associated with redeployments, reunions, homecomings, and reintegration relative to their relationship with support services other than counseling and minor reintegration concerns. I make more of this in the chapter on supports (chapter 4), but I will provide a little space here. An African American, retired army, and FRG Assistant shared views of this topic. He focused on spouses that had left the community, something I discussed in the deployment chapter (chapter 3), saying:

My personal feeling is that everyone should stay because this is their best source of support. The Reserves and National Guard go through it every day. It is because they have people spread out all over the place. "Hey, if you know you have people out of the area, provide them with a resource of some sort." Whether it would be going down to [the local volunteer center] and picking up the book, *Reunion and Families* [a popular booklet at the time], or if they have children, maybe extend that by a couple more pamphlets. Put all that stuff in an envelope and send that off to them. Of course, here locally, we have the actual reunion training. The bad part of it is that you can't force spouses to do anything. I would say that is the bad part, but I guess it is also good in all actuality.

Before Iraq and Afghanistan, formal and informal programs and strategies existed to assist soldiers and their families adjust to post-deployment, and a congregation of these continue to exist.[24] Participation rates and perceptions about the level of helpfulness were mixed.[25] Cross-nationally, families shared some of the same encounters as the U.S. cases, including Belgium, Canada, Germany, Portugal, Turkey,[26] and United Kingdom military families.[27]

Additionally, less significant themes from the spouses hold insights to broader, hyper profound problems during the years after the early part of the wars. For example, wives simply did not bargain for their partners to be gone so often and for so long. One wife, an army brat married for a brief time to a sergeant and pregnant, provided an ironic perspective where she is comfortable with him preparing for war but not necessarily going to war. She said, "Come home, it would be nice if he could come home. I would just like him to be home every night. That is all I want. Have him home every night. I can deal with him going in the field. I can deal with NTC, I can deal with him working long hours . . . I can deal with it."

In other words, some demands of military life are acceptable, but long separations to war and the risk of injury or death are less so.

Another unique concern that indeed mounted in the first few years was the potential to return for additional deployments. Spouses began sensing the potential for multiple deployments in 2004. An MSG's wife from a military family told me, "When are you all going to take him again? How short is that list that he is on for going back, for being recalled? Rotations and they have ninety days after he comes back, after the stop-loss,[28] after ninety days, they can recall him. I know there is a list, like Reserves. People they are pulling now, a lot of those are Reserves."

One more issue emerged regarding physically wounded soldiers and the process of their homecoming. This occurs at the individual-family level either at home or at a U.S. hospital as Sigrid and Jamie below experienced. Technology to extract casualties from the battlefield more expeditiously along with medical advances have dramatically decreased the number of fatalities in a combat zone and with it, increased ephemeral or lifelong injuries for wounded soldiers.[29] One wife of an army engineer and a brigade-level paid FRG Assistant highlighted a conversation with a wounded soldier:

> I was asking him the whole process of how they bring home a wounded soldier and I said, "Did your family receive any kind of training?" and that was kind of a hotspot with him because, no, they don't get any type of training. When they come home and they redeploy, there is a big reunion training, stress and all that stuff and everybody, we call it, "The Big Group Hug." And he said, "I was

wounded, the onesies and twosies are not happening." I know that they are addressing that, and I know they are aware of that. I can see us helping that out.

An interview I did with Sigrid in Germany dramatized the significance beyond being wounded. She and her husband, Jamie, were a white couple that grew up in a small town in upstate New York with no military family members. Jamie was commissioned through the OCS. At the time of the interview, they had been married eight years. I interviewed Sigrid seven months into their first tour together abroad. They had four young children at the time of the interview. Jamie was home during this interview but away on a temporary assignment elsewhere in Germany. Jamie and Sigrid would have been a typical interview had Jamie not been seriously wounded in Iraq. Two years before, during a sixteen-month deployment, his vehicle was hit by a suicide car bomb. He sustained significant internal and external injuries, spending almost one year convalescing in military medical hospitals in and around Washington, DC, during the time of major scandal at the Walter Reed Army Medical Center.[30] My first question to Sigrid was, "How is he doing?" She said, "Good. He's fine now. He looks a little different because he had structural damage on the outside too, but he career-re-figured, and we didn't take the army retirement. So, we didn't medically retire. They let people stay in if you push fairly hard for it. It's easier now than it was in the beginning."

Sigrid goes on to describe the yearslong convalescing process from a spouse's perspective and parenting in the military. Jamie is one of just over fifty-five thousand wounded U.S. service members in Iraq and Afghanistan as of 2020.[31] The wounded warriors could fill almost every seat in the Los Angeles Dodgers' baseball stadium in California.

Last, there is the broader issue of the quandary of (in)dependence. Most military family members came out of civilian society. Americans value highly both individualism and independence. So, on the one hand, the military reinforces the independence value. Indeed, the hyperpopularity of grit and resilience training in the army reinforces this individually oriented value. It places extraneous responsibility on and may somewhat undermine individuals as it concomitantly expects soldiers and family members to be selfless, consuming and depending on the resources it has established and funded. One spouse articulates this quandary. I asked her for ideas on getting spouses to reintegration classes. The prior enlisted wife married to an army MSG said, "Not at all. That is the one part. You can make a soldier do any-thing; you can't make the spouse do diddly-squat. You can highly encourage, beg, plead, sweeten the pot, but you cannot make them do anything they don't want to do. If they don't perceive the need, and most of them are in the superman, superwomen complex—somebody else, not me, that is not happening in my life. So. I am not going to do it." An American military jam of sorts—a Catch-22.

## Conclusion

Everyone wants to go home. Perhaps no one more than a soldier at war. Most come home to family and friends. The post-deployment is full of experiences from homecomings and reunions to honeymoon periods to reintegration. Spouses in 2003 had yet to have homecomings from Iraq and Afghanistan, but they were coming, and they have concerns. Some in 2004 had, while others anxiously anticipated a homecoming in the coming months. By 2008, a legion of spouses of service members had gone through one, two, or three deployments and had become knowledgeable but continued to manifest problems. By 2018 spouses rode the peaks and valleys of short deployments to eastern Europe while familiar with and practiced in much lengthier deployments years earlier in Iraq and Afghanistan. They had little to say about post-deployment with three- to six-week deployments. They had become the dutiful strohwitwe of the now almost post-Iraq and post-Afghanistan U.S. Army (a small contingent remains in Iraq at this writing).

Again, stress and coping come with the post-deployment period—both leading up to and during post-deployment. Soldiers arrive as a collective group in typical scenarios. However, there are strict organization demands placed on their time for weeks after the homecoming. The demands spill into the family. Spouses are hypersensitive to behavior, and engagements with children can be awkward and varied. Children are released from school and other activities to accommodate the homecoming and reunion and the honeymoon period. The nature of the post-deployment is one of intense emotional labor on the part of spouses, children, and others significant to the soldier as they await their reintegration into the family. It all but completely envelops them and their family in military culture and structure.

Both spouses and services members participate in classes and briefings about the post-deployment phase individually and later together. Such classes and training further militarize the at-home spouse to the personal and professional needs of their service member. Countless opt out of the draconian-appearing sessions and accompanying activities. They engage in emotional labor to integrate the service member into their familial roles, the community, and the larger American nation-state on their own accord. They are tools. They put arms around the service member and help absorb them back, only to prepare and restart the emotional cycle of deployment all over again as the next political defense-related strategic affair looms on the horizon or they leave the military altogether—for other jobs and occupations requiring separation. Nevertheless, the war never leaves the soldier or the family. They are a cohort enduringly post-deployed and exceptionally seasoned, skilled, and trained at it: veterans. Ready if called to accommodate new separations in the military or at other jobs, in other times and places.

# 4

# "I Have No Idea about Services"

## (IN)FORMAL SOCIAL SUPPORTS

The CDC [Child Development Center] is amazing. They just don't
keep them alive.
—SSG's wife in Germany in 2018 with two daughters under five

Family members have been steadfast supporters and providers for armies
since the dawn of the republic. They camp followed or sequestered on forts
during the eighteenth and nineteenth centuries and accompanied loved ones
to military posts around the world in the twentieth century. In the post-9/11
age, they still follow, sequestered on and off military-designated gated communities, and become (de)militarized as essential elements of military life.
With the changes in geography and increased institutionalization over the
years has come an increase in the number, quality, and types of social support programs and services that buttress, assist, and aid the service member
and her family in coping with life in and around the military. The dizzying
array of programs and services are an integral part of the day-to-day activities and the unique challenges of specific military life demands, including
deployments. This chapter first introduces social support in the U.S. Army
and then describes formal and informal social service champions and los-
ers identified and used by them from highest to lowest worthiness when
prompted during interviews.

## Formal and Informal Social Supports and the U.S. Army

Social supports have long served to help individuals and groups with a range of
needs, among them emotional, psychological, social, and material resources.
Social support encompasses more than emotional and relational backing and
encouragement from people. Social support can be help, assistance, and provisions. Social support can be direct or indirect, formal or informal, instrumental or expressive and can be time, money, or resources. Sources of social
support include family, friends, colleagues, bosses, subordinates, neighbors,

and acquaintances in one's preferred institutions such as religious, clubs and associations, workplaces, recreational activities, and schools. Social support can also be real or perceived.[1] Social support is a common feature of studies of military families and the U.S. Army has long relied upon social supports to assist families and soldiers.[2]

Army spouses have universally favored their own spouse, family member, friend, or coworker as informal go-to sources of social support. Only after these intimate others might they move to bureaucratic, formal others and sources such as specialists in their church, medical, and military communities.[3] That appears to continue in the post-9/11 era. Both past and present, the military affords families with supports to assist with such significant demands of military life, comprising relocating, injuries, death, living in foreign countries, and separations such as deployments and other assistances. The U.S. Army upholds effective support services receiving praise by families.

Many of the same sources of support in the army exist in civilian communities, particularly in professions that require relocations and separations, such as internationally oriented businesses and the U.S. State Department. U.S. civilians have formal sources of support fulfilling every human need from dog walkers to dancing lessons to a personal trainer to a surgeon, but they come at a substantial financial cost. Individually they are available, but collectively they are prohibitively expensive. In the military, services are free or availed at a modicum cost compared to civilian society—something that expanded dramatically during President Reagan's administration.[4]

For informal social supports, the primary source for married military spouses is their husband or wife. Extended family members can be relied upon, but geographic distance is a significant challenge, more so for overseas families. Friends have proven to be an outstanding source of social support. Friends can be old or new in military communities and come from living in the military extended network through work, recreation, children's activities, or, most likely, their soldiers' military unit. Neighbors are another source of social safeguarding for military family members. Military leaders are cognizant of family needs, more so because they benefitted from such supports coming up through the ranks themselves, and they too have families that utilize the supports. Besides, they believe and know that supported troop families make for combat-ready troops.

The military has a long history of providing sources of formal support services for military families. Certainly, the military prides itself on "we take care of our own" as immediate and extended family members are becoming "our own" too. Military municipalities are company townish where the business of the military touches every aspect of the post and surrounding community. Formal social supports have changed in name over time, but programs and support services for specific needs have been consistent and growing.[5] Other nations provide similar sources of aid.[6] Readers can easily Google support services and the army and a fire hydrant of formal and informal support services will blast forth.

U.S. Army family-specific programs in the United States and Germany have about seventy formal services. These have included the Family Readiness Group, various sources of child care and youth services, K–12 schools (DoDEA), New Parent Support Program, marriage enrichment, spouse employment, relocation assistance, veterinary service, bowling alleys, and golf courses, and casualty and memorial assistance, among a host of other programs and services.

In addition to informal and formal supports provided within and by the army, each civilian municipality surrounding a military post has various suppliers of services accessible to members of the military. These involve not-for-profit organizations, support groups, a retired military population, faith communities, recreation sources, battered-women shelters, and for-profit and local government employers. Federal and state programs are available to military families at the macro level such as educational assistance. Finally, a range of services are tappable online for military family members.

In the U.S. Army, social support links directly with army family well-being.[7] Social support service usually involves providing or receiving real help from others. According to sociologist Bradford Booth and associates: "*Informal social support* for army families typically derives from relationships between the soldier and spouse, extended family members, friends, other unit members, and their families and neighbors. *Formal social support* for army families derives from participation in and use of the unit, installation, and civilian community-based resources designed to promote well-being and offer necessary intervention services."[8]

Five arenas—formal military and civilian support, informal support, online sources, and federal and state support—provide a rich fountain of sources available to army families. Will they get used, if created, and how are they received? The ensuing section turns to the spouses and the formal and informal resources that have upwelled since the GWOT began and identifies a new group that forgoes any supports—emancipated army spouses.

I asked spouses about formal and informal social support and services in their military network area. I encouraged them to identify any social supports and services they felt worked well for them and which ones did not work well—indeed, which ones might need improvement, or others that are simply broken. Formal services were consistently identified first—both working well and not so well. It took probing questions to get at informal services. In both cases, instances came unsolicited or came to light with probing.

## The Spouses

### *Emancipated Army Spouses (EASYs)*

Before addressing support services available to army families, I want to highlight a remarkable group of army spouses that emerged over the years: emancipated army spouses. EASYs are a sizable group of people that proudly projected a classic rugged individualism about not utilizing any of the formal services provided by the army. I suspect countless more exist, but they never came into our research orbit, such as when my team or I visited a community. They might or might not know of us but opt out of engaging with us because they are disconnected, unfettered, and liberated in and out of the community.

EASYs are in the community but not of it. Completely disengaged or maybe aloof, they avoid the formal activities of the communities either by choice or of necessity. Still, others among the EASYs utilized a handful of services, such as the inexpensive military commissary (i.e., grocery store), but have no opinion one way or another about them. For example, some shared they could as quickly use off-post grocery stores, securing provisions from local stores and farmer's markets in Germany. Many EASYs lived off-post and reveled in their exceptionalism and autonomy, independent of army services. Historically, these women could be wives of junior enlisted soldiers kept or keeping purposefully away from the post or the unit or civilian husbands of military women with(out) previous military service and experience or not wanting to project any weaknesses by utilizing supports but also not welcomed as a minority.[9]

Today, there is a new emancipated army spouse in town. One that is individually unique, emancipated, on the margins or in plain sight, collectively more prevalent than she might think. Their emancipation transcends elements of stress, institutional greediness, and militarization. These are precisely the systems in the military structure, culture, and community that they perceive could drench and overtake their liberties.

In interviews, EASYs emphasized not relying on military services to any degree—being *of the military* but not in it. A representative of this group of spouses comes from an SFC's wife with an eight- and nine-year-old living in Germany:

I have no idea about services. In ten years, I've never fallen back on any part of the military. My sister called me from the States one day reading to me out of the paper about this woman and her kids and her husband was in Iraq and how sad it was. I was in tears thinking it's got to be terrible for her. My sister's like, "Helen, I'm reading it to you because it's a woman with two little girls and her husband is deployed—it's the same situation as you." I didn't see it that way. It was funny. My husband was deployed, and I did have two little girls. It was just me, but as far as the support services—the coat section of the PX? [is the best formal support—she says with sarcasm]. Honestly, there is nothing. The FRG has done nothing for me. The FRG is in Düsseldorf, and they sent me this cute little email, like from time to time, that I have no idea what it does. Because I'm not about to drive in the car, with the gas, for anything. The FRGs had never done anything for me anyway in all the years, all the Kuwait trips, none of it. They had a potluck dinner one time. I recall they were very picky eaters. Otherwise, I don't need them.

Spouses in 2018 stressed their desire to remain on the margins. A twenty-something captain's wife in Germany underlined that "she loves her husband." However, she is "gonna lose it." She "hates moving around." She doesn't know if she can handle additional deployments. For now, "I'm riding it out." Her husband had been doing several short deployments, mostly to eastern Europe for weeks at a time. She goes on, "I have nothing against" [their small community in Germany], "but we were forced to live on-post" [required to live in U.S.-subsidized World War II renovated apartments]. She and others in this community resented their forced living arrangements preferring to live immersed in a German hamlet away from American accouterments. She said, "This place is terrible [referencing an apartment across the street from her job]. It is a step back for us. Living like a new 2LT couple." During the interview, she repeatedly apologized for complaining—stressing her marginalization. She felt trapped institutionally in Germany. She noted she flew home to her parents during her husband's Afghanistan deployment as much as possible even though she worked full-time.

In contrast, another EASY, living in and outside the community, said she liked her renovated on-post housing, mainly because they received an extra bedroom despite being officially unauthorized to have it because of their family size. It became her home office. She had little time or inclination for the military community formally or informally. She teleworked from three to eleven p.m. 5 days a week from Germany to her office on the U.S. East Coast from nine to five. She had no time or inclination for local involvement. Her technology killed space, and she manages time differences too. She is physically in the military community but not of it.

How individual family members and the family as a unit interpret the deployment mission plays a critical role in how they respond to it—in other words, their social construction of event predicts outcomes.[10] The question becomes, how might we encourage such adaptation found among EASYs? Such independence of formal support services exists among militaries of other countries such as Norway.[11] How can the U.S. foster less dependence?

### Formal Social Supports for Army Spouses

For numbers of military families, however, they come to expect formal social support services as a standard part of their military benefits packages, and consequently, they become a normative feature of military life. Moreover, the formal programs meet both the global needs of most army families and the unique needs of small and specific groups of army families.

Spouses responded with an equal number of formal working well and not working so well. However, while spouses quickly and easily identified delinquent services, a critical mass of spouses identified services that work so exceptionally well for them that "they could not do without." Services ranged from the general to the specific, with uncommonly detailed samples of each.

The overwhelming majority of spouses identified many formal support services that worked well for them. They referenced the Family Readiness Group, Army Community Service, Child and Youth Services, and Morale, Welfare, and Recreation in particular. These tried and authentic programs are historically popular among army families dating back decades.

The central feature and strength of the FRG lie in providing both formal and informal support for spouses. Among the formal sources of social support available to spouses, the FRG is the most often mentioned by the spouses interviewed here. The FRG stands alone atop all other formal services combined as the centerpiece to bridging both overcoming and facilitating stress, greediness, and militarization among military spouses and their families. Many spouses had direct and indirect, recent, and old experiences with FRGs notably given that their spouses served on deployments at the interview time. Some spouses volunteered with the FRG as leaders. Others participated regularly, others irregularly, and still others avoided it. As one spouse adamantly noted, avoiding it with "every fiber in my being." However, spouses have a love-hate relationship with their FRG. Other spouses noted joining FRGs of other units to either avoid theirs or the others offered them something better. A twenty-four-year-old and married wife of a specialist—a tanker on his second major deployment—provides representation of a conflicted relationship:

> Nobody is going to find out what I said? ["Right."] Ours doesn't have a lot of communication. There is the Alpha Company FRG leader and then each platoon has a point of contact. My POC is wonderful about getting stuff to me, but the thing is, there was something on Friday, some kind of city hall thing which I couldn't go to anyway, but I didn't find out about it until Thursday because that is when my POC found out about it. I don't know when the FRG leader found out about it. But, like there was a rally Saturday to support the troops. Every other troop from the battalion was there with a T-shirt on that had like A Company on the back of it. Our troop didn't have one. It is like, you know, there is no unity or anything. Like I said before, these people aren't my main support group. They aren't really my friends. If we had some unity, they might be. It has never been there to find out if that would be something. I have gone to every meeting, except for one because I was out of town. I want to be a part of it. I am willing to volunteer, but there is really not anything there.

A typical disparaging comment on the FRG involved the following from a Latinx/Hispanic wife of a WO with a five-year-old in Germany: "The FRG [needs fixing]. I think everyone says it's important, but nobody really acts like it's important. It depends on the commander, of course, and depends on where you are. Yes, they push it, but there are so many rules. You can't do this, and you can't do that. You can't spend money on that; you can't spend money on this. It's just complicated so much that it takes away from what it really is, and it just really becomes so complicated. It takes away from being fun."

However, most spouses praised the FRG both in Germany and stateside. Their statements are succinct about their FRG encounters when they praise. A pregnant sergeant's wife said, "The FRG has been fine. They have been great. Charlene [FRL] has been awesome about the whole deployment. She is very supportive of all the wives."

In the same vein, praise rained down for Army Community Service in general from the spouses in Germany. Again, historically, ACS has been a staple support service in the army community. An LTC's wife of twenty-six years with two adult children shared, "I would say ACS [is working well], the community support. It's there wherever you go regardless of where you are, there is usually an AER—the financial readiness to help people when they have to fly home for Red Cross emergency or soldiers get into trouble. The services that ACS provides, like the Exceptional Family Member Program for people with special needs children, all of the support services that ACS does I think that's a definite plus no matter where you go. Even the more poorly resourced one has something to teach you." A retired military wife of an active-duty commander, two years married and no children, praised ACS and offered some insight, "I would say ACS is working very well; however, it has stigmatism associated with the different services it provides. They use it in a negative manner or punitive manner. So, if you bounce fifty-five checks, I'm sending you to the budgeting class or I'm sending you to the money management class."

Numerous stateside spouses praised the ACS in interviews, mainly the senior women. A brigade commander's wife said, "We have the best ACS agencies that I have probably seen in my army career here at Fort Corbin." Spouses of junior officers and enlisted mentioned it sporadically and if so, only in passing. A captain's wife in 2003 noted, "If I need it, I know the services are there. Like ACS, I know it is there if I need it, but I really haven't felt the real need to use it."

Established in 1968, Youth Activities Programs remain central to army families today. Umpteen find it related to soldier readiness, soldier career intent, and soldier morale. In the interviews, Child and Youth Services received a good deal of positive endorsement. A captain's wife with three children in Germany captured the sentiment: "I think the services like CYS, like with different sports, I think that's working pretty well. They provide quite a few different varieties for kids to choose from."

Other spouses praised the CYS but offered sage advice. Mike in Germany shares his view: "I think they should make it cheaper. Because 90 percent of the coaches are volunteers. I would like to see the volunteers get something out of it to make them want to volunteer more. I think they should be allowed to have an hour and a half off before their practice starts. They should make it cheaper. Because I don't agree that my son should have to pay sixty-five dollars for a season of soccer when nobody is getting paid."

Another formal support service is military child care—known as the CDC—renowned in the U.S. for quality and low cost based on a sliding pay scale equitable to rank and income. With over half of soldiers married and approximately 45 percent with children and the majority under five years of age, child care is vital to family stability and army readiness. There are other sources of child care in military communities too.

Likewise are the military children and youth schools, known as the Department of Defense Education Activity, which received praise for quality. Virtually all military posts have elementary and middle schools—both stateside and abroad. American high schools exist overseas with only one or two DoDEA high schools on-posts in the United States—such as Fort Knox High School on Fort Knox in Kentucky. Some military children abroad attend international institutions or boarding schools depending on the country and location of the stationed parent. Military-family teenagers attend high school (and a few middle schools) with civilians outside the stateside base. For example, I graduated from Leavenworth High School with umpteen fellow military-affiliates from Fort Leavenworth, Kansas— Go Pioneers! Also of note, DoDEA schools educate children of U.S. civilian citizens living and working on military posts abroad, and the families utilize other support services.

I provide a fresh and deeper focus on military children and teenagers in the next chapter (chapter 5) but address some support issues here. A handful of spouses provided condemning comments about child care access and the school system in Germany in general. A captain's wife with two children—a four-year-old and a twenty-month-old in Germany—begroaning aspects of militarization said, "I think they [the CDC] are pretty understaffed right now and so a lot of times it's hard to get your kids in, and you need it. There are a lot of army functions, if you will, and just things you are required to do, and they are not always put out in a timely manner, then you have to find something to do with your kids. I think that's kind of difficult." Another captain's wife with prior military service and with three children—eight and five years old and six months old—in Germany said:

> I think I'm not impressed with the school system here at all. It made me think I wanted to home school and that's never ever been something I want to do. My kids are way too social for that. They'd just go crazy having me all the time. I think the kids are going to be very far behind when they get back to the States, and I'm concerned about how we are going to deal with that. Maybe not so much for my kids. I think my kids are bright enough they can pick up on it, but some kids need extra help, and I don't feel like they are getting the help they need. My biggest complaint here right now is the school system. I think it's atrocious.

Responses about child care and schools are mixed. Spouses noted that the schools created programs to recognize the deployment of parents. A battalion commander's wife with three children highlighted, "I love our schools here. My little kids go to elementary school on-post. My teenager goes to high school off-post. I think they do a fabulous job at supporting the military. For example, in high school, in the attendance office. There are excuses for being tardy and not excuses for being tardy. The military is a reason not to be tardy. My heart gets warm."

A wife in a double interview quipped, "I can't put him in day care because he is a preemie [born premature], so he has weak immunity so I can't expose him . . . I don't really trust them. I guess that is the way that I was brought up."

Working spouses had difficulties securing child care. Here one grumbled about time—not having enough to work out child care issues before the deployment. A different one says she had to quit her job—stepping down as a manager to curb her hours and responsibilities. Most, however, praised the CDC. An officer, company commander's wife with one child and the company FRL, extolled:

> They do. They have hourly care, which I use a lot. They have every Friday night they are offering child care. The first Saturday of every month, you get free child care. I have harped on it, harped on it, and harped on it, to take advantage of it. They [mothers in her FRG] are not taking advantage of it. They have it. It is not free, but it is only $2.50 an hour per child, which is not that much to shell out, really, if you need a break. I have really tried to encourage my ladies to use the CDC. Some of them take advantage of it, some of them haven't. It is out there. A lot of them expect a lot of things for free. Can't get everything for free, but come on, $2.50 an hour. I am just like, you know, you can't have everything for free. If you really need a break. It is there. I usually put mine in CDC two days a week from like 9:00 until 2:30. [Note that this amounts to roughly $220.00 per month for two children—a hefty sum for a junior enlisted family.]

Another captain's wife with one two-year-old in Germany applauded the CDC: "Oh, the services the Child Development Centers offer, the playgroups. They do field trips, you know, all over and everything like that. It is nice to know that I have a place to take Nicholas where he can play outside. So, yeah [the CDC is working well]."

Finally, spouses identified the Family and Morale, Welfare, and Recreation programs and services. Like ACS and FRG, FMWR has longevity in the army community. Soldiers, civilians, and their families frequent FMWR. In the interviews, FMWR received positive accolades from a critical mass of army spouses interviewed in Germany but less so stateside. Two spouses provide representative comments of the overall group. A specialist's wife and military brat from Hawai'i with two children under four said, "The MWR lets us know what kind of recreation and special occasion is happening like bands, games, and everything. We really get a host of things." An SFC's wife from Texas with three children under twelve in Germany, leaning in on being an EASY, extolled:

> I don't know. I really don't. Like I said, I really did withdraw. I am just now starting to come back in. I have never been a big army wife and I am just now starting to understand rank and that sort of thing and who is who and what is what. I think that I came to the point where I realize that he is making a career out of this, and I might need to learn some of this. So as far as programs are concerned, MWR does sports for the kids. To me, that is one of the most important things, combined with male mentorship and keeping the kids occupied. Anything that keeps the wife or child occupied during deployment, whatever program it is that is what needs to be done. Because you have wives like me, when I first came here, I was terrified to drive and wouldn't know anyone. For almost a year, I didn't go anywhere.

Other topics commended by spouses to a notably lesser degree are high gas prices in Germany [four to five dollars per gallon], the PX, the post libraries, and the movie theater. Specific services coming under MWR included, among others, child care, respite care, EFMP, Army Family Team Building, the Edelweiss Hotel in Garmisch-Partenkirchen, Germany, and the Nurturing Parent Program. Among the commendable comments directly from the spouses is an SSG's wife with two kids under four years of age, noting, "In Germany, they have really good programs. For example, the Edelweiss. They do ridiculously cheap prices."

In addition to a slew of formal program praises, spouses identified a plethora of formal services that needed improvement, were not working well, or were simply broken. No primary services outstood. Nevertheless, collectively there are formal service problems. Hindrances with medical care, the FRG, child care, and the school system came close to overrepresentativeness. In terms of medical issues, a typical criticism came from a military brat wife of an enlisted soldier with four children sharing, "I think our medical system [is broken]. If I were to complain about anything, it's probably the timeliness of appointments, the dental program, and things like that. I understand the troops come first, absolutely as you have to have them mission ready, but if you're really that short and you can't get any appointment for a month, then I think you need to bring in a few more people."

A specialist's wife, new to the military, said she felt the OB/GYN staff at the local military hospital were "rude to her."

The Rear Detachment Commander receives scarcely a mention in 2004, 2008, or 2018. However, the spouses of members of the unit I studied in 2003 had much to say about the RDC. Sometime called the "Rear D," in this specific case, a captain led the rear detached soldier unit. And in this case, he turned out to be the least deployable captain in the battalion. He drew the unfavorable straw as the highest-ranking officer not eligible to deploy to Iraq and remained with the stateside unit to command other non-deployables—the chief number are for medical reasons.

The RDC serves as the conduit between the deployed soldiers of the unit and their spouses and family members worldwide.[12] Adding, our RDC case managed the barrage of media inquiries and requests, among them print and broadcast media that besieged the military post during the war. The reporters lived in the community for months and occupied a coffee shop just off the post. The RDC appeared to work hard and championed the needs of families but often seemed overwhelmed and fell short. He existed in crisis-action mode, constantly responding to a firehose of requests for family information, specific forms of support, and providing context from the ever-changing combat environment. At one point, a member of our research team severely chastised him for hanging his freshly pressed Class A uniform in the back window of his car (the military members wore Desert Camouflage Uniforms exclusively at the post). He parked all day in the visible and highly prominent designated commander spot at the unit. The captain was oblivious to formal military uniforms on army posts during a war being a telltale sign of an impending and infamous "knock at the door" fatality notification.

He understood context and performed some needed functions. For context, his work existed at the intersection of the unit, the family members, and live press coverage of soldiers of this unit that had significant press coverage. For countless wives, they do not know what their soldier does as part of the war effort. Most wives praised his efforts on providing context—"He is doing a great job." A 2LT's wife hailed his efforts in one particular area, "[The] FRG had a meeting this past week. It was good. He [RDC] did a really good job explaining what exactly my husband does. My husband is patrolling. Then he talked about the destructibility of armor. He talked about what happens when a tank is hit. He was saying that if all else fails, they can still live. He speculated about positive scenarios. He did really good examples of how to watch the news."

Others questioned his ability, suggesting, "Oooooh. For me personally, I mean, he's okay." [For another wife], "It could have been handled differently"—again responding terribly diplomatically.

Other formal services having hiccups had onesie and twosome responses but included Women, Infants, and Children; the Army Post Office; and toddler activities that individually amount to little but collectively implicate formal support services as problematic. Disappointed in the WIC program, an SSG's wife—Filipino American with two children in Germany, carped, "The WIC [is broken]. Like they didn't count the household like for my stepdaughter. My husband has a legal dependent. She has an ID card, but she doesn't live in the household. She's German. She's actually half German and American. She gets the benefits of a German citizen here but not American receiving these benefits."

Finally, an SSG's wife with two children under three years of age lamented about toddler activities, "Well, they have lots of programs out there. Only one thing, there is not enough activities for toddler age children. That is probably my only concern . . . obviously it is because I have a toddler-age child. Most of the classes start at age four. ["What do you want?"] Anything. Anything. Our kids started doing gymnastics at eighteen months, and they had a great teacher. It was fantastic. Anything, sports, swimming. Swimming, gymnastics, or dance—activities to get out of the house."

Disapproving of the post office, another SSG's wife from a military family and no children said, "Like I said, I work. If I didn't work, I don't think I'd have as many problems. Like the post office is not open on the weekends anymore to mail packages. It's only open from ten to four. If I come at lunch, that's my whole lunch. You have to stand in line. So that is not good. The CMR to pick up packages is open till six p.m., so if I run straight after work. They are closed on the weekends as well."

Along post office lines are shipments and deliveries to APO addresses in Germany. While no spouses complained directly, some spouses shared that online, stateside companies will not ship to APO addresses abroad. Of a handful of standouts, the richest insight came from an SGM's wife, African American with prior service and three boys in Germany: "No, it is not really even the cost. When I call an 800 number and ask them why they will not ship to an APO, they say it is because of this form that we fill out. They just don't want to deal with it."

Spouses identified a range of other formal programs from finance to legal services to commissary services, among others. Individually, the programs differ and account for few mentions. Nevertheless, collectively they point to the diversity, range, and number of services army family members patronize—services that meet specific needs but make military family members dependent on the military—and due to expectations of impeccable service, inevitably fall short.

Again, encounters proved mixed for services. A case in point, innumerable spouses had challenges with their finances and criticized financial services. An FRL—captain's wife—confirmed what she had heard about finance: "Moans and groans about finance." These grumbles come from junior enlisted women married to soldiers making far less than officers, and the senior spouses perceive they and their spouses are financially inept (notably, an E4 specialist in the army makes approximately 27 percent of what an LTC makes in basic salary).[13] Perceptions of significant challenges with finances came through—a senior officer's wife said, "I have been the link between finance and the spouses. We have had problems with finance and not wanting to help the wives at all. They basically told us we don't want to see wives." A private's wife with two children confirmed the outlook: "My biggest problem right now is finance. If we could just get finance right. I am sick and tired of everybody telling me, 'Oh, you can't do anything about it. You have to wait until your husband comes back.' That is why he left me here so that I can take care of everything."

So again, experiences mix, even on the terribly mundane but often perceived to be sacred resources the army provides. For example, a sergeant's wife living on-post related: "The commissary, PX? The commissary is like two minutes from my house. It is right there. I love it. It is easy for me. They bring the groceries to your car. Which is a big deal when you are pregnant." Yet, a sergeant's wife living off-post told our interview team, "No, I use the grocery store off-post. ["Isn't the commissary cheaper?"] Yeah, it is cheaper. I don't like post. Something happened to me a long time ago with a couple of soldiers. I was sexually assaulted by some soldiers. That is why I don't like going on-post by myself."

The highest negative responses are associated with backlash connected with Early Return of Dependents. Unfortunately, I did not interview any spouses who'd ERD'd to learn about their experiences. The sample represents those spouses commenting on others ERDing from a communal perspective. Research shows that high stress brings on wanting to move, but the best predictors are youth, recently married, and limited experience with the military—and this with already stateside spouses.[14] In a handful of cases, spouses who'd ERD'd need resources and information from the spouses that remain at the post. A spouse critiqued: "Yeah, ERD. It makes me think there's a lot of spouses who think they can handle it or say they can handle it and then just realize they want, need that support once they leave."

Essentially, ERD encouraged a legion of spouses to return to the United States from abroad.

Pregnant wives could return to the States or communities where understandably familiar familial support existed. In the case of ERD, it challenges the notion of the once shared event of all active-duty spouses commiserating in one locale and sense of community as the unit deploys collectively. In its place is a patchwork of families and others significant to soldiers across the U.S. and abroad and remaining on or near the military post and who may or may not depend on one another for support during their unit's deployment—but all connected virtually in some way through email, cellular telephones, and expanding into social media. Their experiences may more mirror those of deployed army reservists.

Spouses who return stateside, while they might undoubtedly have immediate family and friends to rely on, lacked a formal and broader informal face-to-face community support network that is the military municipality of sorts both stateside and overseas. A secondary outcome, according to spouses, associated with ERDing included few adults to take key public positions and few children in programs resulting in programs not running. ERDing does have benefits for some, as does remaining. A 2LT's wife with no children contrasted her situation to that of a commander's wife:

> I think it totally depends on the person. Like for me. I would definitely not want to leave. I, ya know, I'm so glad I have my friends here, and the community really is supportive, but like, for example, my husband's commander's wife, she just had a baby, you know. She's going to school, distance learning, and her parents and his parents live like twenty minutes away from each other. So. For her to go back to the States and have that support while she's finishing school and while she has a newborn, it's perfect for her. But moving back in with my parents wouldn't have been the right thing for me.

Summing up, the military has a long history of formalized support services, priding itself on "we take care of our own."[15] Immediate and increasingly extended family members are becoming "our own," too. Military municipalities are company townish, where the business of the military touches practically every aspect of the post and surrounding community.[16] Formal social supports have changed in name over time, but programs and support services have been reasonably consistent and growing.[17] Other nations provide similar sources of support.[18] Army family-specific programs in the United States have ranged and changed.[19] Additionally, each military has a civilian neighborhood and state and federal agencies available to military families—at least stateside. As much of social life moves online (both formal and informal), so do support services. Informal social supports are primary in the lives of military families, and I turn to this topic next.

## Informal Social Supports

In addition to formal social supports, informal social support networks in the army mirror the civilian sector. These typically consist of one's spouse, immediate and extended family members, neighbors, friends and coworkers, and others who may be available face-to-face or at a distance through communication technologies such as email and telephones. Nevertheless, family, friends, and supporters become fewer and further between army posts worldwide and during deployments, ironically when support is needed for most grass widows, children, and adolescents.

Army spouses mentioned informal support services in and around their German and American communities and army posts. Spouses shared far less on informal support services in general, but when encouraged by us to elaborate, the responses were commonly positive.

Formal and informal support ties directly to the relative degrees of stress, greediness, and militarization. A notable, insightful, and candid comment regarding the informal support system that represents the ongoing irony faced by military spouses comes from a childless captain's wife in Germany— another leaning into becoming an EASY:

> Yes. The problem with the formal structural things is the commander is always there. I've never been to an FRG meeting where the commander isn't sitting there. I've never been to a meeting when a Family Readiness Group Assistant [paid military staffer] isn't sitting in the command building. And if you just stop and think about that from a psychological perspective, that is support that is intrinsically tied directly to the entire system that at that moment is causing you stress, grief, whatever. And they can help, but there is no guarantee written or otherwise that that help doesn't come with something, either something that will impact your husband's career, something that will come back to haunt you. These are small communities, and that to me, the support system has to be based on trust. I believe in the army. I believe in what my husband does, but I do not trust the system. I have never trusted the system. The system failed me when I wanted a job. The system failed me in so many ways . . . And so, to say

to me, here is your support network, come use it, trust us, my instinct is to say, "Why?" You can stop-loss my husband without telling us. You can extend him for fifteen months without telling us or telling me after the fact. You can keep him, if he was enlisted, past his contract date, which is the thing that we agreed on. Why in God's name should I trust you? That's my honest to goodness reaction. And so, in that sense, I think my response has been to find women and men in the system, either active duty or spouses who I do trust who will give me honest answers and who will stand by them. And those answers are never on a piece of paper or in a courtroom.

An archetypal quote representing the empathetic feature of the commonality of military life with a twist, chiefly in Germany, was offered by a senior army chaplain's wife with two children, who told me, "Oh, the informal, I think, has always worked. Families help each other even if you don't know someone and you have a problem, they are very quick to lend a hand, I think. ["Why?"] Because, they all have been there. They all know what it's like to have been some place and not anybody to help them. So, most of the time, they are very responsive to each other, I think."

Spouses indeed noted being lonely during the deployment. The import of loneliness is salient here. The soldier spouse is the foremost person an army spouse turns to with a personal or family trouble, trailed by a family member and a friend with host of others coming in far behind.[20] Responses are often associated with their intimate spouse rather than their platonic friendship and acquaintance network. Below is an illustrative exemplar from a pregnant wife of a junior enlisted vehicle mechanic in 2003 who opened, "My schedule is really hectic. I do have a lot of family problems, and that would add more stress on top of everything else. That is what I mean when I really stress out. I can't control it anymore. So now it's like, my husband is the one that is always helping me to not stress out and all that stuff. Ever since I have met him, I have been better. A lot better. But now he's gone."

Friends as supporters are mentioned as much as family members. Friends are talked about as serving both near and far, recent and old. One stateside wife in 2004 confided: "I don't think, if I had not met Korinna, I would have gone back home to North Dakota, or I would have stayed here by myself and seen a psychiatrist."

Notably, spouses identified exceptionally close friends and even extended kin, in Europe, during the deployment. Friends usually resulted from associations via other assignments at other times, noting that handfuls of spouses interviewed are senior in rank. Extended kin ranged from family members such as siblings in uniform in Europe or family close to their stateside post to parents retired in the region or abroad. Family members are also critical as a source of informal social support. For spouses, family is parents, siblings, and in-laws. Some family members lived nearby but only among those stateside. Others lived farther away and came for short- or long-term visits.

In some cases, the family served as essential sources of support, but they could not get away from their day-to-day lives. Reasons for not coming comprised the inability to leave jobs, finances, fear of flying, and medical and physical reasons, among others. A pregnant wife in 2003 acknowledged, "I talked to my mom, and she is really scared of flying. She is like, you have to tie me up to get me on there. She talked to my dad, and my dad said that it is not really a good time because he doesn't really have a set job, so they are not going to be able to come . . . my older brother was going to come, but a lot of things are going on with him familywise too. I don't know. It is really hard to tell."

After families, essential sources of social support buffers are coworkers, friends, and neighbors. As a multitude of spouses do not work outside the home, they are less likely to mention coworkers. Some spouses resigned from jobs during the deployment, mainly to be hyper available for their children. Neighbors could be military, civilian, German, or American. A sergeant's wife from a military family with a husband having twenty-seven of thirty-six married months deployed under his belt said, "My brother came out for a week. I have nice neighbors and I have had a lot of help."

The next largest group mentioned but in smaller numbers are military chaplains and church groups. Church-related groups are both on and off the post. However, chaplains have the unfortunate burden of symbolizing the worst news about soldiers, bringing terrible news from the front about their husband. In instances, spouses chided chaplains as "too religious" for spouses. On the positive side, a brigade commander's wife shared a story about a chaplain's wife running a women's support group: "The chaplain's wife, Regina, I spoke with her last night. She runs this program. She has eighty somewhat spouses, and they do some fun things. They meet once a month, and she has a few outings planned in December for the families to go to a tree farm and go out to lunch. It is a wonderful bonding."

In sum, while it may be common sense that one's primary source of support for married military spouses is their husband or wife, research contravenes this notion, showing that relying exclusively on one's spouse can backfire.[21] Extended family members can be relied upon, but geographic distance is a significant challenge, especially for overseas families, and sometimes they can exacerbate problems.[22] All forms of friends are great sources of social support.[23] Neighbors are social safeguards for military family members.[24] Reserve and National Guard service during the recent wars benefitted from the protective measures found in social support before, during, and shadowing deployments.[25] Active-duty spouses draw on social support as a buffer during deployments, and for both service members and military spouses, a lack of social support relates to mental health issues.[26] Undeniably, psychologist Stacy Ann Hawkins and her research team concluded that social support helps with coping and readiness, protects marriages, and can buffer everyone in the military family.[27]

## Conclusion

Army grass widowhood comes with advocates and helpers. Supports can be a burden and blessing. The U.S. Army has long provided a range of formal support services for soldiers and their families. These human service organizations are available both in peace and wartime. In abundance, most kick into high service during deployments. In addition to formal support services, spouses and other military family members deepen some of their informal social supports. Evaluations show that U.S. Army services have long been successful in fulfilling a critical need, but with some, there is limited participation, such as the FRG.

The formal support services identified by the spouses here working the best for them are the FRG, ACS, CYS, and FMWR. Support services receiving mixed reviews include the DoDEA and the CDC. Spouses seemed hesitant to complain during interviews about programs—a subcultural norm in the military not to be critical or negative—a "Negative Nancy."[28] Nevertheless, individual-specific issues emerged with a range of services, counting among them medical, dental, WIC, and the post office. Moreover, no one had good things to say about the Finance Office—to their credit (pun intended), they never provide anything extra and are crucified for providing less. There was attention on specific programs such as RDC and ERD. I only had concerns about one specific situation for the RDC but comments came from multiple spouses. Other RDCs appeared to work well. ERD complaints came from spouses that did not ERD. No spouses who'd ERD'd provided insights to their collective journey. ERDing in cohesive and shared community creates new issues especially given the role and perception of social media to relativize a sense of place. I anticipate that in an increasingly mobile and electronically mediated world, EASYs and ERDing will increase.

The spouses mentioned their informal support less often. When they did, they responded as we would expect in terms of significance and proximity.

Notably, a multitude mentioned being lonely as their primary source of social support—the spouse—is away. Again, constant, immediate, and real-time social presence could magnify the need and ability to communicate with informal supports. Although, new media brings with it new hitches and quandaries as I feature in the coming chapters.

Finally, a new generation of army spouses has made a kind of presence (an absence). They are emancipated army spouses that I call EASYs. These are women and men that consciously resist patronizing the support services provided by the army either in toto or selectively. They embrace a rugged but not hyper individualism where they are self-reliant, autonomous, and independent entities that are working, parenting, recreating, and surviving within or on the fringes of the military community. They are not loners or lone wolves. They are formally resisting stress, greediness from different sources, and militarization. They do so by necessity, privilege, choice, or in concert with their military spouse. The army could go a long way to learn from the sagacity of these free-spirited, autonomous, and emancipated spouses. But first they'll need to be found.

# 5

# "They Take the Brunt of the Deployments"

## ARMY CHILDREN AND ADOLESCENTS

My husband talks about wanting to have kids, and I don't know if I want them. People will be gone half the time the way that the deployments are now.
        —1LT West Point graduate's wife in Germany in 2008

As we entered the 2020s, uniformed members of the U.S. military including active duty, Guard, and Reserve had 2,582,001 military institutionally recognized spouses, children, and adult dependents.[1] Typically about two-thirds of these are children—they may comprise more not claimed administratively. Active-duty U.S. Army members had 401,179 children in 2020.[2] This number leaves out U.S. Army Reserve and National Guard children.[3] Because military members are disproportionately young, their children are young—typically, about half are under five years of age (revisit the table in the introduction). Increasingly, innumerable, like their civilian peers, are growing up in reconstituted dual-job/career (military), LGBTQ+, and single-parent families.

Between 2001 and 2015, two million U.S. uniformed military members (not counting DOD civilians and contractors) deployed to Iraq or Afghanistan at least once, leaving countless children at home. In both wars, 7,038 American uniformed members died, 53,117 were physically wounded, and more than 400,000 suffered psychological and emotional scars of war by 2020 year's end.

Scholars examined the numbers of children of deceased service members between September 11, 2001, and September 11, 2011.[4] They identify 15,938 uniformed service members that died during the period, and the deaths are associated with a range of causes such as accidents, combat, suicides, murders, and illnesses. The leading cause of death is accidents (34%), followed by combat deaths (31%). Just over half were both married at the time of their death and had children with their partner. The average age of the child at the time of their military parent's death was just over ten years of age. Ten years after September 11, 2001, deceased service members left behind a total of 12,641 children, where significant numbers were under five years of age. With this, the younger the child, the more likely the service member (he or she is also younger) died a violent, hostile death such as in combat or a nonhostile, accidental death.

In this chapter, I briefly introduce the reader to children from military families and follow with the voices of U.S. Army spouses commenting on their children and adolescents growing up in the shadows of deployments and redeployments in the GWOT.

The spouse interviews group into themes in two sections: (*a*) 2003 and 2004; and (*b*) 2008 and 2018. For 2003 and 2004, children and adolescents are not directly the focus of interviews with spouses, but the topic impelled the spouses in the interviews. The five major themes of these periods included sex, gender, and age of military children; adjustments; assuming new responsibilities; R&R; and subgroups among both children and adolescents.

By the 2008 and 2018 interviews, it became increasingly apparent that a new generation of children, tweens, and teenagers had endured multiple deployments across their short life course—entangled with separations like their at-home parent.[5] I began asking pointed questions about children and adolescents in interviews. Similar themes above emerged, but new themes surfaced too, chief among them the army as a kid-friendly organization; deployments; mobility; deviance and needs; reenlistment decisions; social comparisons to civilian family life; and evaluations of military family life for children and adolescents.

## Graswaisen—The Grass Orphans: Background of Military-Raised Children

Historically there has been little research interest in children from military families. They are silent voices in the backseat, seen but not heard. Researchers only began studying them—boys exclusively—in the human aftermath of World War II. Known as "military brats" or "army brats," they comprise the largest group of an organization's family-affiliated children among Third Culture Kids and Global Nomads because one or both parents are in an occupation or profession, often with time abroad including military, foreign service, missionary, and international business.[6]

Historically, researchers, policymakers, and people working with military families assumed "go the mom, so go the children." However, children confront military needs differently than mothers. Children and adolescents navigate the demands of military family life differently from their parents (although the parents themselves might be adult military brats). In addition, siblings sharing the same parents and household encounter the military demands differently. First, they are from different generational cohorts. Second, children go through military family life as a developmental experience while growing up compared with their parents, who likely underwent a localized, stable, and less mobile upbringing.[7] Third, the military lifestyle elements exist for children and adolescents the same as for parents/guardians, yet, are encountered differently. Beyond these is the potential for a predisposition toward military generational occupational linkages—soldiers making soldiers.[8] In this last case, sons and daughters of career military members are a reliable occupational pool of potential recruits—and while the numbers are significant, they are not as large as people might expect— but their numbers are growing. The number increases with military recruits of a parent or guardian with any military background—not necessarily career military—adding to the analysis that youth coming into the military today come from parents or guardians not drafted but who came in after the all-volunteer force instituted in 1973. The evidence all around suggests that the military imposes stresses, demands, and even militarizes generations of military-affiliated children and teenagers.

## The Spouses

### The Iraq War 2003 and 2004

The interviews over fifteen years evolved organically and specifically to children and adolescents. Initially, during the earliest phases of the war in Iraq in 2003 and 2004, military children and adolescents were not the focus of the interviews. Yet collectively their shared themes in the interviews became of import. Remember again that in 2003 and 2004, spouses (and indeed my interview team) are not anticipating long wars and the potential for two, three, or four deployments over two decades. The spouses in interviews during this time continued to have partners deployed for their first deployment in most cases.

### Sex, Gender, and Age among Army Brats

One new topic, specifically during deployment, is the role of a child's gender in coping with a parent's deployment. Historically, dating back to World War II, boys suffered because of the absence of men—their role models—off at war. In our interviews, however, mothers recounted how their daughters endure heavier than boys. In some cases, girls contrast with their stoic and adaptive brothers. A response in 2003 from Sara, a stay-at-home mother and spouse of an NCO with two of her children and caring for a six-month-old infant of a deployed dual-military couple, captures the theme well saying:

> Like my little boy . . . this is really their first [war]. My little girl, she is like, he needs to get out and I don't like him in the army anymore. She is daddy's baby. My little boy. He is just like, everything is just like, just shoot them. He says, "I would shoot them." I am like, "Don't talk like that." Then I completely just stopped them from watching the news. I wanted them to know what his dad was doing, some things were too graphic, but then there were some things, this is what your dad does, blah, blah, blah. He [the son] was just feeding on it. It was like a video game for him. Everything was just like, "I am going in the military, I am going to do this, I am going to get to go to war." I said, "It is not all about that." My little girl on the other hand is like, "Does my dad kill people?" I was like, "Well, I am quite sure that he did. But he was doing it, helping." She is like, "They have mommies and daddies." I was like, "You know what, they are doing whatever their president tells them to do, just like we are doing."

The gender topic reoccurs in detail in later years, where multiple deployments are the norm rather than the exception. I expound on this in the latter part of this chapter.

For differences in age, the spouses pointed to younger children coping the least well and adolescents coping better. One mother told us of how her youngest daughter reacted (again a girl having difficulty):

> My daughter. When my husband first left, for like almost a month, I could cry, because my daughter would go and knock on the door and say, "Da," like she would knock and ask for him through my other daughter. It got to the point for almost four months where we were not allowed to say "bye-bye." So, if Nanette was leaving, I would say, "You know, Julia, tell Nanette I will see you later instead of saying bye-bye." Because if you said "bye-bye" she would throw herself to the floor in hysterics. She did not like the word "bye-bye" for a while. She also stopped talking. She used to say twenty-five to thirty different words. After my husband left, she stopped talking. She just started talking again. When my husband came home for R&R she was a chatterbox. After he left, she stopped talking again. The doctor says it is normal. Every child deals with it [separation] differently. With her, that is the way she is dealing with it, she just doesn't want to talk.

While this younger sibling had difficulty with her father's absence, several mothers shared situations where adolescents did not cope adequately. One model comes from a Latinx/Hispanic mother of five, all girls, between two and thirteen and married to an NCO, who compared the children, saying, "The two younger girls, they really haven't shown too much, um emotion, or um even questions. You know, we sat down. And, of course, before my husband left and you know, went through it a little bit, and where he was going and what he was doing and um, but they were kinda, kinda like, 'Whatever,' you know? But the three older girls ask a lot of questions. 'What about this?' and 'What about that?' They are having trouble sleeping. The older two girls and my older daughter have been having problems in school."

Classic studies of military family separation during war treat children as an appendage—an afterthought.[9] Military studies in the mid-1980s compared military and civilian boys and girls and found that military girls suffered the lowest self-esteem among the four groups.[10] Recent work brings the children to the fore with the at-home spouse.[11] New research confirms past war separations—they are stressful and problematic for children and adolescents.[12] Reservist families prioritize boys (seven to eleven years of age) to be "little soldiers" during deployment and assume increased family responsibilities. In an interview for a documentary about military children, the late General Norman Schwarzkopf tells the story of his father "very ceremoniously" presenting him at twelve years old with his West Point sword and saying, "You are now the man of the house, take care of your mother and sisters" before he deployed to war.[13]

### Adjustments and Army Brats

Three unusual types of adjustments came out of the interviews regarding military kids. These comprised adjustments associated with longer separations, outgrowing the deployed parent, and difficulties with redeployments. Sharing her thoughts for mothering and children on long deployments, Sara, our infant caretaker mother, represented the first theme saying:

I guess, just talk to your kids more. You are going to have bad days— this time. Didn't have to do that last time. Be more understanding of their mood, not just hormones. There is separation anxiety, missing dad, not understanding. It took me a minute to realize. Just like I have bad days, kids have bad days. There are times I have told them, "Fine, go to your room. But after a day of it, you are coming out. You are not going to hang in that room 24/7." I guess there is a point. You still got responsibilities.

In terms of children outgrowing parents, a junior enlisted member's wife and mother told a heart-melting story:

> My daughter can talk and actually two weeks ago he [her husband] called during the daytime. So, my children were actually able to talk to him. My son, he acted like really nothing was going on. He talked, "Hey, how are you doing?" My daughter said, "Hey daddy." And she mumbled some words and then, "Hi daddy!" He just broke down [crying]. He was so sad because he hasn't heard her [speak yet]. She was saying, "da, da" [when he was here] and trying really hard to talk, but she didn't. And now she does. A lot. She says everything.

I informed spouses that I would be out-briefing the division commander about my overall impressions from the interviews. I asked what they wanted me to share regarding children and adolescents, and a brigade commander, colonel's wife stressed, "a re-integration class for kids." Full stop.

The above spouse represents what spouses did not know yet, but scholars would uncover. Communications Studies scholar Andy J. Merolla learned that children and adolescents serve as "a positive relational force for separated partners" even when they provide no instrumental support during military deployments.[14]

### Parentification among Army Brats

Based on the Schwarzkopf quote above and spouses at home taking on new roles, I expected to hear stories about individual resilience and children assuming adult roles—what military scholars call "parentification." However, those stories infrequently surfaced in the interviews. One reason is that fewer adolescents exist in military communities today compared to past years. While military families have children earlier than their peers, all Americans have children later in life. As a result, fewer teenagers are military brats today than during the days of the Vietnam War, the late Cold War, and even the First Persian Gulf War. For example, Googling images of soldiers coming home embracing at airports is different today than in past wars. A Vietnam-era American father coming home from war greeted by teenagers on the tarmac is different today with military mothers arriving to greet toddlers.

The below quote grabbed my attention representing adjustments. Asked if the kids had changed during her husband's deployment to Iraq, an African American mother of a newly minted teen and wife of a WO responded:

> I know that my son has definitely grown up and taken on, or tried to take over, for his father. And I think he tried to be, because he never showed any emotion through this whole thing, and I think that he tried to stay strong for me. He is 13. ["What is he doing different?"] He is taking over the yard work. Now that he is out of school, he calls me at work and asks if I want him to pick up Michelle [his younger sister]. If I come home with groceries, as soon as I open that door, he is out there trying to empty the car. These are things that he never did before. I asked him to pick up my daughter before, and he was like, "Oh mom." Now he calls, "Mom, do you need me to pick up Michelle. Do you need me to?" I hope he doesn't regress [when his dad comes home]. There is no way to tell.

Like children, once a little older, U.S. Army War College scholars Leonard Wong and Stephen Gerras discovered that active involvement, non-deployed familial support, and perceived American support for Iraq and Afghanistan significantly mitigated stress for military adolescents.[15] Importantly, military adolescents can be resilient, proactive, and cope well when a parent deploys.[16] Nevertheless, there are fewer teen and tween stories of assuming parental roles today than in past years.

### Deployment Rest & Recuperation

In the interviews, I learned of two new topics involving children and teenagers unique to the post-911 army family: the R&R and subpopulations in military families. Initially, the R&R (highlighted in chapter 2) came to light from spouses relative to their children. All praised it with some simple qualifications and adjustments. One observant senior FRL spouse shared her perspective representing the collective sentiment:

> I think that it [R&R] is a good thing. Honestly, when we went on our off-site,[17] all fifty of us in the division before the guys left, I was in a small group and I said, "No, they should not come home." Too many problems with the children, too many problems with the buildup and excitement when they come back and the horrible let down when

they go back. I was looking at it that way. I must tell you. Honestly, I have changed almost completely in my thought. I have seen different families, different people, talked to many people, and the bottom line for me, I have found some women who struggle with the good-bye again. Most children seem to do very well with it. Different ages, we are talking kindergarten through high school, it is really, okay, and they understand, or they just get into their lives and go on.

The above example shows how the village works in the post-911 military separated world. All in all, R&R is desired, necessary, and children and teens might do better with it than their parents or guardians do themselves and expect their children to.

### Subpopulations of Army Families

A second new topic that surfaced is subgroups—subpopulations. Subpopulations or unique groups in the military are not new in the broadest sense.[18] Soldiers are highly likely to have families in the post–Cold War era. But their diversity increases in the post-9/11 era. Several spouses came into the interviews representing a range of family formations comprising dual-military couples; pregnancies; instant, reconstituted families with nieces or brothers; non-married soldiers with children; adults from military families; children with special needs; spouses taking or sending children back to their hometowns; and seriously injured or deceased family members.

Subgroups are individually novel and extraordinary, sometimes seen as atypical or outliers in a military community. However, collectively they are a critical mass and constitute an ongoing broader picture of an increasingly diverse military family in the post-911 separation era. Further, the interviews suggest that the army, at the community and the soldier level, responded well to accommodating these subgroups routinely or even on the fly. In other words, the army is an increasingly diverse organization but needs to inclusively orient for families—especially when it comes to children. Numerous examples cropped up in the interviews. However, inclusion may come at a price: militarization.

One typical U.S. Army company had forty spouses in the unit, and fifteen had chosen to return to their hometowns. Returnees would take children out of school and repost at a different school. A company commander's wife shared a tragic incident. A unique situation arose—but where unique became normative—the child of deployed soldier died. She shared, "He came home for two weeks, emergency leave, and the battalion commander allowed him to stay an additional two weeks. They extended his emergency leave, so he was home for four months. That was appreciated by both the soldier and spouse, and their family as well."

Diverse military families are the norm today rather than the exception. Army families mirror their civilian counterparts in terms of diverse structures and representations.[19] So much so, even putting the traditional, two biological children, first-marriage heterosexual couple with a father military breadwinner in the minority. Diverse family structures and forms will have varied implications for separations.

### 2008 and 2018: Is the Army a Good Place to Raise Children Today?

U.S. Army spouses in Germany in 2008 had endured multiple deployments and in most of the interviews had an army spouse deployed to Afghanistan or Iraq during the interview. In 2008 I began directly asking about the status of children and adolescents. Specifically, to broach the topic, I asked, "Is the army a good place to raise children today?" I continued this line of questioning in the summer of 2018. Then, spouses of soldiers had one or multiple deployments relative to their years of military affiliation. The spouses I interviewed in Germany in 2018 had husbands regularly deploying to eastern Europe in support of Operation Atlantic Resolve.[20] All had previous separations associated with Iraq and Afghanistan.

Keep in mind that the U.S. was well into the GWOT in 2008—seven years in Afghanistan and five years into Iraq following a surge in troops and commitment there in 2007. It was unusual to find a spouse lacking a deployment unless they were newly married or married to a recently enlisted soldier or commissioned officer at their first duty station. Second or third deployments were typical. I asked them pointedly if they thought the army was a good place to raise children today. Half said, "Yes." Close to half said, "Yes and No." And just over 10 percent said, "No."

Of course, I then trailed with a query for them to explain their answer. When asked to share the positives, the spouses, with children but others without, cited a range of features counting a structured community; safety; activities and opportunities; resources such as free medical and dental care; tolerance of others; living abroad; and travel and exposure to diverse people and cultures. The three top oft-repeated themes are financial stability and plentiful resources, living abroad and travel, and cultural diversity. Consistent with what we know about army families, the first two themes are old hat. Cross-cultural and diversity exposure are new among parents. Although we know this from adults raised as military brats reflecting on growing up. Below is an instance of the army being an excellent place to raise children today. As one captain's wife from Laramie, Wyoming, highlighted, "Yes [the army is a good place to raise children]. I know that it's a great opportunity to teach your children about the world and teaches people to be culturally aware, not only of their own culture, but of other cultures . . . not only where you live but also the different demographics that the military can attract. You know in Wyoming, we've never had a neighbor from Guam, ever. But we do here. So, I think that's a unique experience."

Other spouses are less confident about the military being a positive place for children today. A private first class spouse, six months in Germany, with her husband deployed, shared, "Financially yes, emotionally not so much. With younger kids, I don't have a hard time because they don't exactly know what's going on. But when they get to be teenagers, they know what's going on and I'm sure it's hard."

A small group of spouses, representing both seasoned and new military spouses, commented that the military is not a good place to raise children today. The wife of a major with twenty plus years in service and three children flatly said, "No."

Really, we've been in the army before this [GWOT] all started. We've kind of split our time half and half. My kids have been without their dad. He's been gone one and one-half years of the last three years. Given a choice, would anyone want to raise their children like this? I don't think so. I didn't want to be a single parent, that's why we waited to have children. We waited eight years to have kids because we wanted that company command out of the way because he knew how much time it would take. Nobody could predict that this was going to happen. But I didn't want to be a single parent and now I've been a single parent for a while and it's very, very hard.

As I have noted throughout, spouses predictably shied away from appearing as complaining about military life—a subcultural norm in the military. When I asked about this, one spouse in Germany in 2018 labeled it coming across as "Negative Nancy." A prior service army spouse with two daughters and a human behavior degree felt observant and entitled, given her earlier service, to be critical of the military. However, she would often catch herself during the interview and apologize or soften her language. Sundry spouses would respond in this manner during interviews. After their initial rebukes of the army, the spouses would then soften contemptuous language with other forms of appreciation of army life. They referred to the advantages of army life for their children and tempered their responses to me. However, collectively, spouses continued to see the significant challenges of army life associated with the standout features of army life for their children, specifically in deployments, mobility, and separation. There was a group of unique challenges for overseas life, such as culture shock returning to the United States and interacting with local Germans, but clearly, deployments dominated the challenges.

A concern during deployment is the length of the separation and getting to know children. A Latinx/Hispanic wife of an LTC shared, "I think that separation is an issue. I see my friends and their children get very emotional when they see a soldier. We had high school graduation last Friday and there were four to five children that were on VTC on the big screen, so the kids are watching their daddy in Iraq [and vice versa]."

Finally, a captain's wife with no children exclaimed:

> Well, I ran into a kid at the PX. Was it a week and a half ago? A wife I know and their children and he's a major about to be lieutenant colonel and they were talking about a move that is going very differently from ours. And I was doing the spouse thing. I was comforting her and saying I'm sure it'll all work out and this is what you do in the army and she has her son who I think is about seven or eight. And he said, "Well, daddy said he's going to retire." And his mom kind of looked at him and said, "Well, so and so's husband has said he's going to retire for the last ten years, and he hasn't done it yet." And I saw the boy's face and it just broke my heart. He didn't want to do the move. He didn't want to leave his home. He wanted his dad out and there was no part of his face that didn't show that.

Next to deployments, frequent moves are a high-level challenge for children and particularly for adolescents. My previous research on adults looking back on growing up in the military confirmed this—but it is a paradox.[21] Living in a host of different places, especially abroad, is an awesome opportunity of growing up military; but moving is the worst—even crueler, looking back, than having a deployed father. Adult military brats loathed moving.

Much like spouses of previous generations, the spouses I interviewed also see moving as a double-edged sword. It has both positives and negatives. Living in exciting places around the United States and abroad are positives, but one must move there and leave someplace else—the negative. Commingled with moving are stability, relationships, and the educational system, further complicated for older children moving in and out of schools with diverse curriculums. Military adolescents undergo a significant amount of loss compared to civilian peers. A typical spouse comment comes from a mother of three teenagers with three tours in Germany: "I think that it made them well rounded, great kids. They are outgoing, and successful. I don't know how different they would be if they stayed in the same place the whole time." And a mother of both a six- and a seven-year-old living off-post in Germany said, "Well, again, moving around. So. They make their friends and then they have to leave their friends. So. First of all, if you have a shy kid, to make a friend may take a while to get a really good set of friends and then you have to leave them and then you have to do this again and again and again."

The role of children in the military will remain a dominant theme for recruitment and retention. Moving stress increases during times of separations, expressly war, and continues during peacetime, with frequent moves. The encouraging news is that past research has informed the present, and efforts are afoot to help support and cope with military deployments through both the family and school.[22]

In addition to asking about whether the army is a good place to raise children, I asked other questions. Among them, whether deviance increased in the community during deployments; what are the needs of children and adolescents in the community; positives and negatives of military family life; and whether being a military brat versus being a civilian is better, worse, or the same.

### Child and Adolescent Deviance in the Military Community during Deployments

I asked spouses if they thought children had been acting out in the community due to the deployments. Three-quarters of the spouses said behavioral problems had increased in the community. Nevertheless, they identified few to no specific incidents of deviance outside of rumor and hearsay. Mike commented: "I heard of a prank at the high school that turned into a major event from three kids who were normally very good kids. But you don't know if they were just seniors who were stupid."

Along these lines, spouses remarked on the degree of special tolerance of defiant behavior because uniformed parents in the community were indeed deployed. An SFC's spouse and mother of four children lamented, "There's a lot of graffiti on this post on the playground. We reported, I reported, it last summer because it had cuss words and I don't want my children on the playground even though they don't know what it says. No kid needs to be out there with that and the MPs come out and their excuse is, 'Well, we need all these children and everything because we know parents are having a hard time with their children because spouses are deployed.'"

Still others noted they saw nothing extraordinary among children and adolescents. Providing clarity of intolerance of extreme behavior, another SFC's German American wife with a three-year-old daughter suggested, "I don't think so. I think over here it's a little different. Because, what happens if a child does act out or behaves very badly? The sponsor [parent/ guardian] loses their command sponsorship. They have to ERD or return a dependent to the extended family [or friends stateside]. I am not seeing a lot of bad things like that."

Children enrolled in Department of Defense schools show "modest adverse effects" on their academic performance with a deployed parent.[23] Research on adolescents with a deployed parent shows that they had higher heart rates than their non-deployed parent and civilian parent peers.[24] Along these lines, children of a deployed parent showed a higher likelihood of engaging in some deviant behavior[25] compared with non-deployed others. Further, children of deployed parents have higher rates of psychological and behavioral distress.[26] Military brats also have less self-control than nonmilitary brats.[27] These results are consistent across several western nations with soldiers deployed to Iraq and Afghanistan.

## Needs of Army Children and Adolescents

When asked what army children needed, spouses provided a range of responses. The requisites included prioritized medical appointments, communication resources, better schools, and college tuition. Dominant responses fell into a category calling for stability and consistency indirectly related to mobility and parental separation in military families. A typical response came from a company commander's wife and mother of two toddlers:

The obvious things. They need family, they need family support and structure. My kids light up when their dad is home. They just can't wait for him to get home. Part of that is that they don't see him all day, but it's hard. The dad is just such a strong figure in the household. He's the head of the household if you will and they know that, they see that, and they look to him and delight in him and they find so much of their own security in him. If he's working fifteen-hour days or working on weekends all the time or deployed often, then it's hard on them because they have to find other sources. Moms cannot

always fill that [role] or one parent can[not] only fill that if you are
filling so many other roles. It's like they need both halves of that.

I noted at the beginning of the chapter that some of the earlier studies of
military children concentrated on boys with absent fathers off at war, to the
exclusion of girls. The military of today is not your grandfather's military.
The military community is an increasingly equitable space for gender socialization—less a masculine-dominated culture than in past years and perhaps
even demasculinized in places such as in military families. Ironically, the
military space is extra complicated and demasculinizes when deployees are
highest among men.

Historically, one of the demands of military life is being part of an organizational structure that is highly masculinized. However, at the turn
of the millennium, with an increased number of women in uniform and
moving into senior leadership positions in a traditional Military Occupation Specialty and army branches, masculinity is being oddly subverted.
Additionally, men in American society are becoming increasingly aware of
their gender roles and vanquishing traditional roles for desirable flexible and
fluid roles. At the same time, army wives may be less traditional depending
on some social factors such as partner rank,[28] moving into nontraditional
domains, and increasingly working for pay in or outside the home or having the desire to work.[29] The American civilian culture and structure have
spilled into the American military.

I asked directly about the need for equity between girls and boys in the
military community. Overall, spouses found equity in gender roles and the
treatment of children in the military community. Neither group seemed ad-
vantaged. I was not surprised by the finding, but readers might be. Spouses
with younger children perceived equity among the children but were not
sure about it among adolescents. However, the spouses with adolescents saw
equity. Spouses provide illustrative examples and descriptions including the
appropriate amount of opportunity, activity, and service for boys and girls.
An LTC's wife, Latinx/Hispanic with two children, said, "I don't think that
there is a difference. I really don't. I think, although some of it, males in the
family feel that daddy is gone, and they need to step up. It is the men's job to
mow the lawn, to fix up the house. But, I mean, there are girls that help as
well, so I don't think that there is a difference."

Only a few spouses noted that boys continue to benefit in the military community. A typical response came from another LTC's wife with two children:
"I think it does. I think it benefits boys more. Because in general the military
is more male oriented, and a lot of the benefits are geared towards males, and

you have your parents and even female soldiers are going to be harder and stronger than their males. It is more. I don't know how to explain that."

Several spouses said that girls benefitted over boys during the deployment. Sigrid, the wife of a wounded captain, speculated:

> I would say girls benefit more, at least my kids' ages, tend to. She's really close to her dad. But boys have to get really creative. Boys typically speaking are more sports orientated. Dad usually does that. Mom has got to pick up the slack [during the deployment]. You just have to. Like I taught my son how to ride a bike the year his dad was gone. During baseball season you can't just sit on the side. You have to get yourself moving because if dad's not there to practice with him and mom's not doing it. Mom has to pick up more of that slack. During deployment it's more the boy stuff. Girls, she's close, but it's not the same. She's got mom to paint nails with.

Again, Wong and Gerras found that active involvement coupled with non-deployed familial support and perceived American support for Iraq and Afghanistan significantly mitigated stress for military adolescents.[30]

### Positives and Negatives of Military Family Life

I asked spouses, "What are the big-time positives and negatives associated with military family life for children?" They offered innumerable positives over the negatives, as is the cultural norm of not explicitly or publicly criticizing the military. The few negatives mentioned centered on moving—specifically, separating from extended family and friends, stability in general, and school issues—most significant, parental separation from a parent for an extended and conspicuously non-recoupable time for children and adolescents. A typical heartfelt exemplar comes from another LTC's wife with three sons—one with a learning disability: "I think that one of the negatives is that they don't necessarily get to grow up with extended family, with cousins, grandmas and having what they call 'where is your home' that other kids have. Well, you are a military brat. They have moved all their life. They really don't have a place to call home. Whereas my oldest son still calls Savannah his home. That is where he lived for the first twelve years of his life." In terms of absent parents, a 1LT's wife said,

> When my husband talks about wanting to have kids, and I said I don't know if I want them, because that is essentially what it means.

People will be gone half the time the way that the deployments are now. That means that he has either got to miss the pregnancy, the first year of the child, or the second year, pregnancy and second year. That makes me seem alone. To me, a job is very important that helps me feel fulfilled and you know, make friends and feel like I do this more than just a job. I need to be out in the community doing things. I am a teacher, that is kind of my thing.

Isolated responses came from spouses highlighting a group of negative features roping in too much handholding; bullies; struggles in school; AAFES; and a lack of opportunities for preschool-aged children and younger.

In terms of the positive aspects of military life for children, a kaleidoscope of responses ranged from economic security to DoDEA schools and child care to Child Youth Activities to patriotism to medical care to structured life. An SFC's wife with no children and close to completing her PhD in social sciences at a German university verbalized: "They get to see a lot. We have friends that have kids and since they were in Germany they got around. They went to Rome [Italy], they went to Athens [Greece]."

Positives fell into the traditional military life element of foreign residence and the quality-of-life aspects that brings, among them opportunities to travel, developing a worldview and greater tolerance of others, increased adaptability, and overall exposure to different cultures. Again, various spouses, particularly those living in Germany, offered the diversity of the military community itself and the living in a different culture as positive features of military life specifically.

### Army Brats: Better, Worse, or the Same?

When interviewing about growing up military, I saved a comparison question for the end. I would ask spouses whether they thought the military was the same, better, or worse for children and adolescents than their American civilian peers. Not a single spouse said "worse off." The vast majority said "better off," even with a parent deployed to a war zone!

The better appreciations manifested in learning about unfamiliar cultures, developing flexibility, adjusting to different situations, and successfully surfing the military structure. A typical sameness response came from a captain's wife with two young children: "I would say the same. I don't think that they are better off because they must deal with different issues, but I don't think that they are worse off either. The same, it just shifts a little bit."

In terms of being better off, a simple response is to say, "Personally I think they are better off with the experiences." Others went decidedly in-depth but still sided with better off.

A richer gauge is a propensity to remain in the army. I questioned the spouses about the practical matters of children being a part of their decision to reenlist or retire. Eighty percent of spouses said that children are a part of the decision. In other words, children play a vital role in job decisions. A typical response comes from an SFC's wife with three children under twelve: "Very big. Because my children are starting to get bigger, and I have to think about high school years now and in the near future and that is the one area that I don't think I will compromise on. I think that when my oldest starts high school, I want him to attend one for the four years. I've done a lot of talking to the high school kids here in Boxberg, Germany, and they have all expressed the same feelings. If you can let her, be in one, let her be in one. Don't move around."[31]

Decisions to retire or not are also central for some families. Pregnant with their first child, the wife of an Officer Candidate School officer with significant prior enlisted time confessed, "If they continue [deploying], I can see where we might say it's more beneficial for us to get out. Like I said, because we have the two other kids [from his first marriage], they don't live with us, he doesn't get to see them very often and now he gets to see them even less. I think no matter how long he's been in the military it always is something in the back of your mind, 'Would the kids be better off if I'd get out and find a civilian job and stay in one place?'"

Only a handful said, "No" or "Not sure" regarding the role of children in their career decisions. A PFC's wife with one son provided, "Yes, he's planning on staying in for the twenty years. I'm not really sure if the kids were a part of that decision or not. Like I wanted him to stay in just because I know financially it's better for both of us. And it allows me to do what I want to do because I wanted to stay home with the kids. With him staying in the military, I'll be able to do that."

Again, in my previous research, adult military brats overwhelmingly said they were "better off" than civilian peers.[32] Many had dads deployed to Vietnam and even Korea, suggesting separations can become normalized, militarized, for children and adolescents in the military.

## Conclusion

War has taken a toll on children around the world and American children specifically.[33] An unbelievable three thousand children had a parent killed in the 9/11 attacks in New York; Washington, DC; and Pennsylvania. Millions of American children have grown up in military families. Because troops associated with Iraq and Afghanistan are likely to be older than troops from the recent past wars (not World War II where the average age was twenty-six), they are likely to be parents. Jake Spann has been identified as the first child to have an American military parent killed in Afghanistan.[34] Tens of thousands of children have had a parent killed or wounded in Iraq or Afghanistan since 9/11. Also in the tens of thousands are children and adolescents of U.S. troops deployed to Iraq and Afghanistan who have sought mental health services and inpatient visits and have suffered maltreatment, abuse, and neglect.[35] Further, coping strategies have emerged to support parent-child separations in the military.[36]

In my interviews, army spouses shared their perspectives on military children and adolescents. Their voices help us contextualize and understand what children and adolescents undergo, at least from the vantage point of grass widow parents and nonparents.

Dynamic, compelling, storied, and new themes surfaced in our interviews. Military children and adolescents face challenges with deployments. They are graswaisen—grass orphans. Tensions arise in the social contexts of sex, gender, age, family adjustments, limited parentization, subgroups, and the two-week R&R window when the parent comes from and returns to war. More broadly, children and adolescents in military families are influenced by the larger society. They wedge between their parents' work, immediate family and extended kin, their neighborhoods, the surrounding community, school and leisure activities, mass and social media, and the broader cultures—American, German, and others. I uncovered few examples of "parentification" in our interviews with spouses. I suspect this theme would have been prevalent with a more direct focus. Case in point, Canadian sociologists Deborah Harrison and Patrizia Albanese describe the phenomena in their book titled *Growing Up in Armyville: Canada's Military Families during the Afghanistan Mission*—spending years in a military community among the schools.[37]

Nevertheless, despite the above elements, most parents continue to perceive the military as a relatively kid-friendly institution, particularly relative to their civilian peers, despite, as one spouse told me, "They take the brunt of the deployments." Notwithstanding significant deployments during the GWOT, the military remains a healthy but challenging place to raise children. Learning thus persists about how socialization in a military family and a military community militarizes children and adolescents. They are less "little soldiers" and more "little veterans." Will these children—the graswaisen of GWOT—follow their parents' footsteps into the military or will they become enduring civilians? America needs to ask herself if she wants a warrior class and the long-term implications for this civilian-military imbalance.

Additionally, the army is less of a masculine-dominated organization, at least in the military household. In other words, rather than militarizing military family members, the inverse occurred. Neoliberal society has positively feminized the military in military families. Girls and young women achieved equity within military families, more so during deployments. Usually men deploy out of a military community, leaving it in the hands of women and their children—half of whom are girls. Army wives and their daughters expanded their role repertoires, increasingly adding masculine activities and feeling emboldened by the experience. They often did not want to relinquish them easily once a deployment ended and the uniformed spouse returned home. Nor did daughters. As Canadian military brats did.[38] Once a daughter mowed the lawns and took out the garbage, it became hard for them to return exclusively to the kitchen and painting nails. Alternatively, they can do both. It is unclear the degree to which military fathers embrace this newfound feminine empowerment in their homes. However, evidence from daughters joining the military from military families shows that militarization has leapfrogged over gender and come into male-headed military families. A paragon is the first female cadet leader of the Corps of Cadets (first captain) at West Point in 1989, Kristin Baker, who came from a career military family. The first woman to achieve the rank of three-star general in the U.S. Army—Lieutenant General (retired) Claudia Jean Kennedy—was the eldest daughter of a service member born in Frankfurt, Germany, during the earliest days of families joining in on the U.S. and allied nations occupations. Women are now exempt from combat exclusions. It should be interesting if a disproportionate number of the pioneering women into newfound military roles will be women firsts from career or veteran military families.

# 6

## "He Has a Laptop"

### SOCIAL NETWORKING BETWEEN WAR AND HOME FRONT

> I mean, they are not being charged diddly-squat. If anyone is complaining, they are insane.
>
> —Army wife

Smartphones are du jour and taken for granted. Mediums to communicate electronically permeate virtually every aspect of human activity. They are ubiquitous in our lives and have unprecedented interactivity and processor power. Yet, only a few short years ago, human electronic exchanges lacked such diffusion and efficiency. Landline telephones had become ubiquitous by the outbreak of World War II in family and community life but lacked mobility.[1] By the 1990s cellular phones could travel but the limited number of cell towers complicated connections and texting was only in its infancy. At the turn of the millennium, one in three U.S. households had a personal computer.[2] Today, the computer, TV, and telephone have all but converged into a mobile device usable from virtually anywhere on the planet.[3]

Social media is the current popular term that refers to applications (apps), websites, and various platforms such as Facebook, Twitter, TikTok, and Snapchat, which allow people to share information electronically between users. Social media facilitates telecommunication devices such as phones, computers, and tablets that permit social networking. Social networking eases personal, professional, and business relationships.[4]

Although social media is becoming a generic term in popular culture and largely tied to handheld devices, this chapter focuses on the mediums used to socially network rather than social media platforms. We know that 90 percent of military families are on social media today.[5] But how they have used and are gratified by mediated communication during our recent war separations is only beginning to surface.[6] This chapter shares the themes around mediated communication that emerged from interviews with spouses and deployments. I have written elsewhere on how deployed soldiers experience the home front via communications.[7] Soldiers and families have always communicated during war. But over the past twenty years, communication has astonishingly varied, regularized, and real-timed.

Management professor Ariane Ollier-Malaterre and her colleagues argue that technology crisscrosses at the intersection of work and family boundaries so pervasively that management is all but futile and the development of digital cultural capital is a great necessity.[8] In the military community, taken for granted and ubiquitous communication media in everyday lives easily transfers to wartime separations. Communication devices are clearly desired, available, and used habitually on the war and home fronts. More so, there are heightened individual and concerted efforts to overcome the separation of deployment through communication to fill the desire for informal social support.[9] There is spillover facilitating the home into the work of war and war work into the home and perpetuated through the uses of different modes of transmission.[10]

Human electronic linkages between the home and the war front directly connect to soldier and family member satisfaction and well-being.[11] To say stress magnifies during a wartime separation is a radical understatement. Such separation facilitates institutional greediness by breaching the boundaries of time and space. But not just between work and family. It enables and expedites bringing others in, among them extended and fictive kin, friends and coworkers, the community, and the larger society. Finally, communication media control militarizes by usurping one's autonomy as a free agent to engage with loved ones, friends, and even less significant others.

Survey data collected from army spouses early in the GWOT found they managed to link up with their soldier "downrange."[12] Mediated communication is salient but no less sparse in the early phases of the deployment and continues deep into the deployments. Instant, private, and regular communication becomes pervasive and prevalent over the deployment and across the wars. Connected or not, communication precipitates a host of practical issues such as access, costs, technical difficulties, real versus lag time, and long waiting lines.[13]

This chapter provides personal insights into the remarkable events associated with spousal and family member communication activity on the home front. I begin with soldiers rolling into Iraq in March of 2003 as their families had limited to no contact with the service members—but an invasion carried live on television with select soldiers. Within one year, connections between the home and the war in Iraq became ubiquitous through a host of both old and new devices. By 2008, the arch of quantity and quality communiqués had increased markedly. They had become a normative feature of the wars in both Iraq and Afghanistan. And certainly by 2018 instantaneous and continuous communications had become nothing but normal. In some cases, communication even became extreme.

Social networking matured, moved unfettered, and permeated in the boundary between home and war fronts in terms of accesses and users. With it came contemporary issues and challenges for families across the wars. The chief themes from the interviews included access and rank inequities, the timing of exchanges, costs, security, casualty notification, children and social networking, and self-regulation.

## Communication and the Iraq Invasion in 2003

During the Iraq invasion, U.S. wives and soldiers had no methods of mediated communication. Details in the next chapter cover television and the war, but CNN broadcast portions of the prewar Iraq environment and later showed isolated aspects of the invasion itself—live. Looking back at the Vietnam War, families would strain in vain to see their loved ones on one tape-delayed, fleeting, small-screened, boxed in on nightly TV segment news broadcast.

Years later, the U.S. and coalition forces participated in Operation Desert Shield followed by Desert Storm in 1990 and 1991—a six-month buildup in Saudi Arabia preceding the eventual one-hundred-hour war known as Operation Desert Storm that liberated Kuwait from the Iraqi army. CNN did feature surgical segments of American soldiers in that prewar desert. While the military leadership could have allowed for showing some soldiers, they opted to stream senior leaders' briefings showing air to ground bombing known as Shock and Awe on their twenty-four-hour news cycle.[14] While Vietnam was the first TV war, Operations Desert Shield and Storm is called the first live TV war with soldiers, family members, extended kin, community members, U.S. society, indeed, the world, watching the war unfold. This set the new precedent for war—where the war would (or could) be televised.

As I described in the pre-deployment chapter, spouses I spoke with watched their loved ones' units roll across the desert toward Baghdad. In some cases, the war was televised live in the background as I interviewed wives. Soldiers had limited telephonic accesses before the invasion as the soldiers prepared in the Kuwaiti desert for two months before crossing over into Iraq headed for Baghdad. In that prewar environment, they could make what the army refers to as "morale calls" from telephone banks. Soldiers typically stood in line to make brief calls home during opportune times that family members might be at home and awake. A pregnant wife of a junior officer noted: "Well, he left two weeks early, so he was calling me about once a day because there wasn't anybody else there. But once everyone else got there, it was once every few days he was able to call." In addition to phone calls, letters continued. An NCO's wife shared her pre-invasion communiqué over a two-month period:

> Let me see, I've gotten three letters from him since he's been gone, and two phone calls and that's it. We're actually, you know, writing fifteen to twenty letters and I know that he's really busy, so I don't expect much. I just want the reassurance that he's okay. Yeah, I understand [they are busy], that's the part of me that understands, but as much of communication [as they have], it's hard. He's a platoon sergeant so his soldiers have to come first. They get to call, they get the time to write, you know. That I, that he, puts everyone before himself. Which makes him a good leader, I guess. But it's hard for me, you know . . . But I, I think that a lot of what keeps me going is that I write. I write to him three, four, five times a day.

Connecting is a social and psychological need, but one that conflicts and requires a balance with the tactical, operational, and strategic demands of war.

### Access and Inequity

Inequity with communications became a dominant issue during the preinvasion. Equity involves access but also senior leaders forgoing calling home so their soldiers could, as the quote above relates. The wife of a Kiowa helicopter pilot in 2003 stressed: "No email. It is horrible. It is frustrating. I know that he has waited sometimes two to four hours in line to make a call home and the phone lines would go out. If they do, he will get a 'Hello' then out, a 'How are you?' or something, and then that is it. It is just not him. That happens to tons of people."

An officer's wife and mother of three noted, "There is a speech time delay [on phones], I guess the troops are sharing one. But there is no email, although some people are finding ways to email."

Once the invasion kicked off, communication with the home front ceased. A pregnant junior officer wife quipped that she did not hear from her husband for weeks: "When the war kicked off, I had nothing for five weeks. I got a call on April 9th; it was a phone call at 5:15 in the morning. [It lasted] about two minutes. Just, 'I'm safe, wanted to let you know. I'll try to call you later.'" A young 2LT's wife, Brigit, noted a novel mode of sharing messages that we might not expect from a millennial—a Cold War communication relic similar to soldiers pressing albums of vinyl during World War II with their voice and mailing those albums home from war.[15] The 2LT spoke into a microcassette that held mini-tapes and did this during the war's duration (note this is 2003). Now iPhones have voice-recording apps and I would be curious to learn how these are used today in separations. Brigit said:

> I think that it was in late March, early April, something like that. It was after all of the big, huge stuff was going on. My husband had sent me a tape. He had a little mini-cassette thing, just like that one [referring to my mini-recorder] and he recorded some audiotapes, and I had one, a cassette at home so that I could listen to it. I got it in the mail, and it was about an hour's worth, a little on this day, a little on that day. Some of it was from right before, like maybe a day before the war started. That was very interesting. I had a different perspective of it with him being a troop commander. He had recorded a rumor control session that he does with his soldiers. He does it every week. He does that every week and he recorded one of those sessions for me to hear. It made me feel better. It made me feel more confident. He was very confident when he was talking to the soldiers, and he was kind of waylaying their fears. Then he sent me another tape from after the war started and I got that, maybe about a week after the first tape. That one was him in a convoy. I could hear the vehicles in the background, and I could hear him stop talking and say, "Hey, move that vehicle over here." So, it really felt like, okay, he is busy, he is doing okay. That made me feel really good. That was the only communication, just those tapes.

After the initial invasion, Brigit continues to hear less from him. She went on:

> Not as much [after the mission]. Maybe every two weeks. I will get either a phone call or an email. Now it has been almost three weeks since the last time that I heard from that email. I also know that a lot of the other spouses are hearing from their soldiers more often and I know kind of why. My husband, he will let all the other soldiers use the phone or use the email whatever, before himself, unless he has some business. At the same time, he told me a couple of times, as things were going on, he would say, I am sorry that I am not writing you in person. He would send a letter back to the FRG and then nothing, not even to say hi. It was all just like, "Hi ladies, your husbands are doing great." He told me that he was doing that on purpose to

save his own sanity, kind of. I think that he went into this, some of those tapes that he sent me before, he was almost like, almost kind of like crying when he was talking, and he was saying, "I don't know if I can lead these soldiers, I don't know if I can do it. I am scared that I am not going to be good enough for them. I am not going to take care of them well enough." I think that having him see how he did, I think that will raise his confidence a little bit. He had one of those talks with me before he was commissioned when we were engaged, and he was about to graduate from West Point, and I remember us being in his room and he started crying. He was like, "I am about to be commissioned and I am supposed to lead soldiers." It is kind of sweet to me to see that in him. I think that this will raise his confidence. I think that he is going to really look back on this command as just one of the best times in his life.

Access continued to be an issue after the initial invasion. The army set up phone lines, but communication unavailability and poor connectivity reigned. A mother of three said, "Yeah, we have a lot more. It took a while. Some of the husbands started calling and then some of them weren't [calling. There's] conflict with that. Oh, my husband called me. It was just by chance. They still have to stand in line and the connections are still really awful. There are times, like when they took the DSN [a Department of Defense communications network] away, now it is back, and then it goes away again." One other wife with a career officer husband in a senior leadership position shared, "With my husband being in the position that he is, he has a laptop. I get emails. I email him back. I have gotten more emails than letters or phone calls. I don't let the ladies know. It is not fair. I just happen to be in a position. My husband is in a certain position."

Hearing a voice early and in real time during a war is an unrelenting desire for spouses of deployed soldiers. They drove this time-honored point home in innumerable interviews. A wife married for ten years tried to express herself forcibly relative to her appreciation for family versus military security conflict: "That's what's getting aggravating. I mean, I know, I know you don't want things to leak out. That's fine. But these are their wives. We are, you know, it's you know just, we don't. We're not just little people that are off on the side. We're their wives and we need to know what's going on, you know. Not just when it's convenient for whoever. We need to know."

The major desire for wives (and again, these are exclusively wives married to men in combat arms units in 2003) is a strong need to hear their husband's voice in a timely way to assure them of their relative safety. They understood the situation and context. Yet, these wives and soldiers could not foresee the long war that awaits the U.S. and other militaries and the Iraqis and Afghanis through the remainder of the first two decades of the twenty-first century. An army wife of a career soldier, raised in a military family whose father had served in Desert Storm in the early 1990s, and naïve of the coming persistent deployments, said, "Very little communication, but I knew, my husband. I knew he didn't have the time. So, it was like I said. I have to type the letters. I got a phone call like the beginning of March. So, he said, 'I won't be calling for a while.' I said, 'Okay.' I knew something was going on, they were all antsy and they went over there to do something. So okay, let's do it and come home. You gotta do your job and then you come home." All came home eventually. Thousands went back again, again, and again.

## Communications and Full-Spectrum Operations in Iraq in 2004

By 2004, the U.S. military mission had evolved from capturing Iraq's Saddam Hussein to counterinsurgency operations, training local nationals, providing essential services, promoting governance, and creating economic pluralism.[16] However, several perceived in early 2004 the effort in Iraq to be a peacekeeping-type mission rather than a combat operation.[17] Just over a year after "securing" Baghdad and other parts of Iraq, U.S. forces had significant electronic infrastructures in place for soldiers to contact others in and outside Iraq. Enter me. I spent the summer of 2004 in Baghdad, Iraq, and observed and surveyed about communicating home.[18] The prominent sources of communication are regular letter mail and packages, cellular telephone, email, instant messaging, cameras mounted on computers, and video teleconferencing. The most used and preferred are telephone, email, IM, and mailed letters and packages. I watched military postal clerks working daily twelve-hour shifts in Iraq to process mail. The massive postal facility at Camp Victory North in Baghdad, Iraq, got named after U.S. Army SPC Frances M. Vega who was killed in Iraq on November 2, 2003.[19] Fewer soldiers had access to computer-mounted cameras. The army sponsored VTCs sat idle, little used. We learned long ago that VTCs—the public version of the private Zoom—left soldiers and their families demoralized after using them.[20]

### Timing of Communications

In 2004 in Iraq contact between home and war front ranged from irregular weekly to several a day calls, emails sitting in inboxes, and letters in mailboxes. IM required both parties to have their computers on. Wives would leave their computers sitting idle all day and night with the volume turned to maximum. A chime sound indicated someone had just gotten online and wanted to engage. Some soldiers had computers in their shared trailer rooms. Some Forward Operating Bases sponsored and provided Internet cafés, in the mode of trailers with banks of dusty computers, dotting a base. I used them myself to send communiqués home but mostly observed and eavesdropped on soldiers doing the same—all while stepping around and over their temporarily discarded battle helmets, flak vests, and loaded M4 carbine rifles.[21]

I returned to the U.S. that summer and later that fall and interviewed spouses of deployed soldiers. A company commander's wife involved in the FRG said IM is popular as "a lot of people just leave it on all day and whenever they chime in," they can jump online. An animated brigade commander, colonel's wife excitedly stressed before I could even finish asking her about communications, "Emails, cell phones, it is amazing to me because when this began, the second month we got into it, I got copies of meetings [meeting minutes] and such, [and learned] I was the only one who was not in contact with their husband. To this day, I never call him. I know a lot of the other ladies call. I don't."

A pregnant tanker's wife shared that she communicates every other day—an atypical occurrence in 2004 but forecasting the wave of communication to come: "He has a cell phone and since I am nearing the due date, he carries a cell phone with him." One wife said, "I could call him every day, but I don't." A mother of two who worked at a media outlet: "Oh yeah. We make big boxes, but I don't do it every week. I get a box and as I see things, I throw it in there. I think that is pretty good in a war zone. We also send lots of handwritten letters." Another wife said she writes a letter every night and mails it the next day.

Given the unprecedented access to both real and lag time platform services, one would expect a great deal of satisfaction. The social reality however is that access does not alleviate crises. It simply magnifies old and creates new quandaries. And this is the case with army families. The major topics revealed in the interviews with the wives are: relative communication; cost; access; connectivity; avoidance; Operation(al) Security and internal threats; and casualty notification.

First, senior wives discussed what I call relative deprivation of communication. They stressed how their friends and acquaintances in the large military division they had replaced the year before had virtually no electronic exchanges. Family members in that division—like the 2003 spouses I interviewed—could not connect with their loved ones in Iraq and the communication infrastructure proved nonexistent. Several spouses, chief among the senior wives, had a big-picture perspective on what others had undergone in Iraq and their familiarities with previous deployments. They qualified their remarks via social comparisons to others noting how privileged and lucky they felt regarding any access to their spouses. They wanted the younger spouses to feel the same. But the opposite happened.

Undeniably, the high degree of connectivity led some spouses to mention the overabundance of talk. A mother of two who worked in media captured the sentiment well:

> Yeah. For a while, he wasn't [communicating] at all and then I com-
> plained, and then he was calling me every day. That is too much.
> Let's find a happy medium because they do have access especially
> where he is located. There is a phone on his desk and all he has to do
> is pick it up. So, I wasn't understanding while all these other wives
> were hearing from their husbands. I complained and he went over-
> board until I told him to stop. Now I talk to him maybe about once or
> twice a week. That is a good amount of time.

Second, with increased access comes a higher price. Cost of communi-cation surfaces as an additional key concern among our spouses. For some, notably, early on, the costs seemed excessive. And this is dramatic for junior enlisted troops. Overall, however, the costs of calling cards, cell phones, and bills seemed inexpensive and worth the price. One sergeant's wife said, "Yes. It is costing me an arm and a leg. The pay phone. We would have to send him phone cards to use, and that is just as much and the time of him getting there and the fact that mortars keep hitting the phone, the phones are always down from people getting hurt, blown up, or whatnot, so. I don't know what he is paying. From my end, I use phone cards. I am spending many dollars every other day." I can confirm the access but not the cost from a summer in Iraq. In contrast, a first sergeant's wife gave a perspective from that of the soldiers, "Yeah, they like that, they want that. Most of the barracks where you can have Internet connections in their rooms, they have to pay for it. It is minimal. I mean, they are not being charged diddly-squat. If anyone is com-plaining, they are insane. If you have two guys in one room, it is costing them maybe ten bucks a month. That is no big deal out of their budget."

Third, in past deployments, spouse and soldier access varied and stood out as a foremost theme. In Iraq in 2004, access to communication media in various forms seemed almost limitless—the desired modes lacked but forms existed. Leaders in Iraq and on the home front tried to assure affordable and regular availability to communicate. A senior spouse commented:

That is one of the things that I ensure that we do as a battalion before our husbands deploy. I felt that in the land of automation that [email] is the best form of communication. We used to do newsletters [hard copy]. We cut back to stuff like that and not to mention who has time to do it. So, it is easier to put information out via email. A couple of months ago, Dell computers was giving away free computers. In our entire battalion, we had one spouse without a computer. One out of the entire battalion. ["Did she get a free one?"] She got a free one. Dell is about to do the same initiative in another battalion. We have one spouse. We even said, if you don't have email, guess what, Yahoo, Hotmail, AKO is offered. We will get you an email address. It has worked for us.

Inconsistency in communication perpetuated in the war zone. There seemed to be a disjuncture by locale, unit, timing, and experience in terms of access, resulting in perceived or real differences in cost and access and perceived inequities. The contradictory comments from spouses reflect the differences.

Fourth, access links to connectivity. Glitches, brownouts, and complete blackouts on connectivity occurred regularly for military forces in Iraq in 2004. Connectivity varied throughout Iraq and even on a FOB with different modes of communication from cell phones to email. One spouse became fed up with military-sponsored email and found an alternative. "The email, they had problems with their Internet. I finally got him a laptop and sent it down there. He never has any time. What he does, that is usually once a month [that he writes], I write him a letter every day explaining what's going on."

Fifth, sundry spouses and soldiers opted for avoiding using certain devices or discussing issues given the abundance of communication activity. They chose not to share types of information. One spouse FRL said about soldiers, "Some of them don't even mention anything to their spouses, but they will get a phone call from the rear detachment [detailing events on the ground in Iraq]." A tanker's wife, lashing back against the needs of her husband, confessed, "They have Internet. They are spoiled. When he asked me for a phone, I said, 'Why don't you think about the fact that I got to cook dinner. I got to change diapers, I got to go and pick up kids from school. She [referring to her daughter] has got tutoring. I got things to do. Sorry but you are not my world right now. There is a lot going on here.'" A sergeant's wife, pushing back against learning too much information about the realities of war, unwrapped, "My husband is not so actively involved in the missions and patrols. He doesn't tell me as much information, and it is probably better that he doesn't. When they first got there, they had some attacks and problems and he told me a couple of things and I then told him that I didn't really want to know because it was too stressful."

Sixth, OPSEC is a major feature of military missions and deployments. The old navy adage "Loose Lips Sink Ships" refers to a military idiom from World War II highlighting unguarded talk about anything associated with the military activity or movement that could jeopardize the mission and cost lives. The enemy could be listening. In the age of communication and social media, this idiom is hyper pronounced. Numbers of spouses, for obvious reasons, did not reveal in the interviews with us if their husbands violated any OPSEC issues. I don't blame them. But hearsay surfaced. A first sergeant's wife emphasized: "Some wives get replay word for word what is happening right in front of them while they are sitting on the cell phone calling and that is not always a good thing." If this is real or not is irrelevant. It suggests the tangible potential for operation security information harvests from military family members on the home front.

In addition to external operational security enemies, there are internal threats. These internal threats resulted from electronic devices leading to violating cultural decorum. As an example, the army's casualty notification process inextricably links to communication media. By the time of our interviews in the fall of 2004, 7,459 American soldiers had been injured and 2004 became the second-deadliest for American forces in Iraq with 849 fatalities.[22] The U.S. Army's Casualty and Memorial Affairs Operations Division is designed to provide face-to-face notification following a fatality by a designated Casualty Notification Officer within twenty-four hours of the death. "Serious Injuries" and "Very Serious Injuries" require an official telephone call within twenty-four hours to designated primary and in some cases secondary next of kin. All soldiers and deployed civilians have an emergency data form used to determine people to be notified, the disposition of pays and allowances, and designated beneficiaries in the event of death or SI.

The senior leadership in Iraq established a formal blackout of communication immediately learning of any unit experiencing casualties, either injuries or fatalities.[23] Ironically called a "kill switch," all cell phone and email transmissions would be shut down for a period in Iraq, usually localized to that unit, in the city of Baghdad, Taji, or Fallujah. The system lacked universality, so it became an understood cultural norm that soldiers should not share any information with the home front about a casualty in a unit. However, communiqués of various sorts got through, and contemporaneous rumors spread. Indeed, the kill switch or the absence of communication resulting from it, contrarily symbolized the likelihood of actual casualties and impending official notifications coming to families on the home front. A company commander's (army captain) wife shared an event following a significant combat event that resulted in U.S. casualties, "It was right after the deployment, and it caught all of us completely off guard. What we realized is that soldiers were calling home a lot of time before the rear detachment could make that official notification, which is destructive on our end because they are getting the information before we are. Basically, so when they call us, we are a lot of time caught off guard and don't really have any information to give them."

Unfiltered and freestyle communication is a two-sided coin. It on the one hand usurps the dignity and decorum of the official casualty notification process for directly impacted families. On the other hand, it simultaneously relieves the emotional terror and turmoil for families where the soldier is alive, safe, and less impacted. Casualty affairs and the notification process need to better account for the immediate, decentralized, and ubiquitous role of communications between home and war.

## Communications after the 2007 Surge

In January 2007, President George W. Bush controversially increased the number of troops in Iraq by 20,000—the strategic effort is known as The Surge. By 2008, U.S forces in Iraq had come off the deadliest year with 961 fatalities in 2007—almost three per day. That number of deaths reduced by two-thirds by the end of 2008, but the risk, fear, and concern for soldiers and families persisted. Fatalities in Afghanistan swelled as well, with the highest number of 295 in 2008 although Afghanistan would suffer innumerable American deaths before the numbers receded in 2016.

Again, of the dozens and dozens of U.S. Army–connected families living in Germany in 2008 that I interviewed, the majority had fulfilled multiple deployments. Yet, during their recent deployment, they lived far from home, away from the support of extended family and friends and American society. Interviews found soldier-spouses deployed to Iraq or Afghanistan when we sat down and talked. Communication media use and satisfaction in a military context had expanded and matured mightily by 2008. New devices—in particular, webcams and Skype—seemed to fold organically into our communication repertoires. For the spouses I interviewed, they seemed to move effortlessly into embracing the new modes while holding on to old modes. This facilitated pervasive, broader, wider, and even regular and normal exchanges between war and home. Yet, the major themes continued to be access, types, and abundance of interactive activities in 2008. Additionally, while connections with children and adolescents certainly occurred in the earlier deployments in '03 and '04, it did not warrant any standout discussion from the spouses in our interviews. But by 2008, parent-child communications emerged and became a dominant theme to addressed more explicitly. I have already said a good deal of these two groups in chapter 5, but some of their electronic uses are described below.

### Children, Adolescents, and Communication

Three-quarters of the spouses had a positive response regarding communication between their children and adolescents and the deployed parent. Majorities found the resources to be plentiful and diverse enough on both ends to meet needs. The types of modes mentioned continued to be email, telephone, and IM, but webcams and Skype appear and became popular. Regarding webcams, an SSG's wife from Arizona with a husband on his second tour to Iraq said, "Communication is the biggest thing. I feel that the webcam thing, for some reason, just seems like the ultimate thing that they [the children] can have—webcam Internet access. You can see daddy while you are talking to him. For kids, that is huge. For us too. I mean, even as a wife, I love when I watch it. When the kids are sleeping, we will turn it on, we are just sitting there but it feels like we are having an actual [face-to-face] conversation."

Four issues associated with communication stem principally from the children. They are divergent styles between siblings; mode preferences for specific children and adolescents; the inability of small children to verbalize or write; and timing, that is, time zones. First, representing the first theme of sibling uses, an LTC's wife from Savannah, Georgia, with a husband on a second tour in Iraq and also counting deployments to Bosnia, Somalia, and Kuwait, noted the difference between her two sons of the same age group. "[Johnny] doesn't really want to do the email thing. He does talk on the phone when his father calls. That is how my twelve-year-old is. The eleven-year-old does not want to talk on the phone, but that has a lot to do with his disability. He can, and occasionally he will. If he is watching TV, he is too busy. We know that is how he is. My husband does not take it personally."

Second, spouses pointed to different social media preference uses within families. For example, siblings simply have different interaction styles that may be gender or age based. Mike in Germany provided a contrast between his male and female children:

You know my son is at the age where he is like, "Hey mom. You're gone, I love you, talk to you later." He is really short. "Hi mom, I love you mom, good night, bye." My daughter, she likes the webcam, and we have it set up so that you can actually do voice now over the Internet. Her and my daughter will sit and play silly little word games on IM chat. They will sit there for hours since they can see each other. The other night they were playing pool. They can sit there and communicate while they are playing a game of cards or checkers like they were sitting in front of each other. It's a spontaneous thing . . . As good as technology has gotten. There are still quirks and sometimes it takes a few minutes to get everything working to where you can hear each other and see each other. Mostly because I think the internet system over there is not 100 percent. But once that's going it's spontaneous. My wife will call and say, "Where is Melissa? I want to play games." They can sit there for two or three hours and just communicate and talk and play.

Third, children are simply too young to communicate in writing. Thus, telephonic communication becomes the default means and hence tricky. A German national and wife of a U.S. Army captain said, "[We communicate] very little. My daughter [eight years old] tried to write a couple of emails but since she is still fairly little, it is not really going that well. On the phone, he doesn't have enough time. He doesn't have much time. He can't stand in line and wait an hour for the phone. When he does call, usually my kids are not there, or we have only so many minutes to talk. I try, but it is not working for the kids."

Others do cope with email in novel ways to overcome the shortcomings of the children. A couple of officers' wives with husbands in leadership positions shared their uses. Maggie with three daughters in Germany stated:

For my five- and four-year-olds, they will come into the office, sit on my lap and I will say, "Let's send dad a note." I will sit there and type whatever it is they say and hit send. [Marvin] will write back to them. The next day I will let them know that dad sent them a note and we will go in there and I will read it. We have a picture of him [father] on the refrigerator that is kid level, and they can go and talk to the picture any time that they want. They tell the picture hello, goodbye, good night, good morning. That works really well with [Precious]. The first time he deployed she knew who he was when he came home.

Another German national wife from Bavaria—married to a captain commanding a company and with prior enlisted service on his third tour to Iraq with a deployment to Bosnia—talked about her son. She said: "He [four-year-old son] usually will send a picture, 'This is my big truck' or 'This is me with Lex Luther' [comic book character] or whatever. So, he sends pictures." A mother and wife of a senior leader with two small children shared, "At that stage, they didn't really want to get on the phone. They didn't want to talk to Daddy too much. It was more, 'What did Daddy say?' And I would have to relay back and forth a lot because they were only three and five."

Last, in terms of timing, a prior servicewoman and wife of a staff sergeant with four children pointed to the nuance of the time difference (between Germany and Iraq) that her husband could not call at an appropriate time to catch the children, declaring, "With all of the people there, it is easier for him to get online while they were in school. There are lines."

I asked the spouses what their children talked to their deployed parents about. This questioning often required probing and prodding. They genuinely thought no one would be interested in what kids and a deployed parent shared. I assured them that readers and I would be fascinated by what they talked about. Collectively, their responses centered around everyday activities with occasional discussion of personal matters. The overall sentiment from the interviews suggested that in countless cases the communication is long, frequent, rich, and significant. Below are three exemplars of what got talked about. The wife of an LTC shared, "It's kind of funny. At first, it's kind of awkward. My kids actually got very comfortable and talk about their whole day and my daughter especially she talks and talks and talks, it's like, wow. My other daughter writes. She's hearing impaired so it's easier for her. She can't hear on the phone as well. She would write to him, and we do have a webcam that we use as well to communicate that way." The wife of a male MSG with seven children noted, "[He talked about] everyday stuff. He was very quiet about his job. One thing, he's MI. He doesn't talk about his job at all. So. I really had no idea what he did while he was there. It was always more support. I don't have a clue what he does, so he's a good soldier that way. No. It wasn't about his work, very little. It was more what was going on with the family and what we've been doing, how we all are, stuff like that." Finally, the husband of a woman senior NCO on her second deployment with a thirteen- and six-year-old said, "[My son would talk about] what he did in school that day or what he did outside or what he did on the video game. He would just tell her everything and she would listen. And that is what made him happy. And with my daughter, she would talk to her about the things she was afraid to talk to me about, like female issues."

Returning to access, not all perfected with communication. About a quarter of spouses in 2008 shared challenges with me. One specialist's wife from Texas who had multiple devices and platforms said, "His email is not good. There aren't Internet connections, I mean he can't use his personal computer, so he goes to MWR [services that provide Internet cafés] which is great but after being out all day, he is tired, I don't expect him to wait in line to get online. The first time he was there he got instant messenger. A webcam would be better for more, for him to see Jackson [six-month-old baby]; but we are fortunate he has a cell phone. I can reach him."

Overall, children and adolescents communicate with their deployed parents but do so with and in unique and novel ways. Exchanges are typically about authentically mundane yet building blocks of everyday life. Older children are articulate and can write their text and engage. Young children have different interpersonal needs. They need real-time voice and face-to-face communication. Toddlers with the assistance of someone at home need something visual to communicate with their deployed parent. Families are creative in their use of a range of devices and platforms to buttress their communication needs. By 2008 communication between partners and children had taken on a normative dimension. Exchanges across time and space with a separated partner or parent began to become a regularizing part of military family deployment life.

Family members also had begun to assert a level of agency in their uses of communication media—something not seen in previous years and certainly not in previous wars. With the pervasiveness of communication devices, they began self-regulating their communiqués. U.S. Army spouses had developed their own styles of digital competence across individual deployments and then multiple deployments. Norwegian spouses of soldiers deployed to Afghanistan have revealed similar examples of normalization.[24] It is unclear if the uses are the direct result of familiarity with deployments or that the availability of varied mediums facilitated the agency. What is clear is the devices are quickly adopted—they are picked up like language immersion—and families adapt or don't connect. These are not cherished, onesie or twosie, novel-type engagements with a loved one deployed to a warzone as in World War II, Korea, Vietnam, or post–Cold War deployments such as in Haiti and Somalia. Today's family members normalize the practices of war separation communiqués—at least at the level of settling in and interacting. Military children and adolescents, grass widows, and soldiers came to view their loved ones at home or on the war front as only a chime, inbox ding, or ringtone away by email, IM, DM, or Skype.

## Communication and Eastern Europe in 2018

By 2018 mobile phone ownership had become ubiquitous in the U.S. and even the planet. According to Pew Research, in 2020 over 95 percent of Americans owned a cell phone, up 35 percent from 2011.[25] Similarly, habitual communication existed between U.S. soldiers deployed to eastern Europe. I interviewed wives whose husbands deployed to eastern Europe out of Germany—although umpteen had combat patches sewn on the right shoulder of their uniform representing deployments to combat zones at earlier times with other units from the GWOT. A typical response came from a senior NCO's wife—a sergeant major's wife in 2018 who said: "Communication is readily available. It helps because they can stay in touch." Relative self-regulation continued. Particularly, spouses can afford to be discriminating in their sources of messaging via smartphones. The wife of a 2011 West Point graduate and a captain in 2018 said they preferred to do text and phone calls on military deployments and training exercises. She even likes two-minute phone calls. She tends to share her everyday life. Similarly, another captain's wife from Ohio said she "doesn't like talking on the phone." She prefers to text.

Markedly, soldiers I visited even a year later in eastern Europe in 2019 carried smartphones everywhere as did we.[26] I interviewed a captain in a café outside a shopping mall. I later spotted him casually walking, talking, and shopping on FaceTime in the mall with his wife back in Kansas[27]—as though they were both casually window-shopping on Main Street USA on a Sunday afternoon. It gave me the idea to call my wife as I shopped for some specialty pottery. She haggled with the owner (as I distanced myself by rolling my eyes). She insisted on supervising the packaging of the bowls for my flight carry-on baggage because I had a three-country layover flying home. So much have mobile phones changed the conditions of family separation.

## Conclusion

In sum, the experiences shared by the spouses are consistent with what scholars have found in studies on spousal communication during recent deployments.[28] The themes across the home-front side revealed significant increases in exchanges over the wars, varied access, connectivity difficulties, costs, family member use variance, the casualty notification process, restrictions due to OPSEC, and self-regulation. What is new and nuanced are features from the home front such as the role of timing between the two fronts, connectivity, self-regulation, and uses and gratifications differing within a household among different members of a family.

Psychologist Sarah P. Carter and her research associates summarized the findings from seventeen articles that focused on exchanges between home and war fronts. Consistent with the spouses here, they found an increase in communication prospects over time, both across and within deployments, variation in access, different media facilitating different communication intentions, military restrictions on communications, and soldier distraction from home-front communications.[29] Psychologist Stacy Ann Hawkins and her team of social and behavioral scholars in another review of several studies found that the ability to contact and communicate with a deployed soldier has increased yet rank and component continued to vary.[30]

Overall, communication is not a simple matter during deployments.[31] An overall conclusion of a special issue of the *Journal of Family Psychology*[32] dedicated to the topic of soldier-family communication during deployments holds that constructive communication during the deployments correlates with lower anxiety for at-home spouses but destructive communication during the deployment increases anxiety for both[33]—a kind of soft technological determinism. Military spouses of nations around the world have adopted social networking for communicating with others, among them the UK[34] and Slovenian soldiers.[35] In the Dutch navy, texting is pervasive and positive communication between partners is conveyed as healthy for well-being.[36] Sociologists at the Dutch Royal Military Academy, René Moelker and Manon Andres offered some practical considerations on dating while at a distance incorporating making a screensaver with pictures of two lovers and learning to say, "I Love You" in several foreign languages and writing those to each other.[37] Library scientist Edward A. Benoit III at Louisiana State University is preserving soldier communications during the war for future scholars to examine.[38]

A new direction in military family research demands the direct examination of how family members use devices during military deployments and offers new ways of thinking about how the family integrates such mediums into their lives. Communication media in this way facilitates the greediness of the intersection of the military and the family during a time of greatest separation and potential stress—a war deployment. The uniqueness of the military family is as an institution with a collection of demands that are distinctive to the military but found throughout work and family life. The electronic encounters shared in this chapter should begin to fill our understanding of the new gap between military families specifically and meditated communication but also separated families more generally. Further, devices may increase the militarization of spouses as they fold deeper into military affairs. The ongoing erasure of time and space via devices facilitates immense, ongoing, and deeper military indoctrination. It is a hope that other professions, in other contexts, and other times, might glean lessons on how the strohwitwe and graswaisen used and attempted to minimize the separation between home and work fronts through mediated communication.

This chapter gives a voice to army spouses and their children and how they connected with their deployed spouse over almost fifteen years of deployments. It focuses on an arch of invention and outcomes from the old to the evolution of the new communication media and platforms. These practices will need to keep pace with the consistently evolving and fickle nature of commercial communication devices invented and adopted by soldiers, spouses, children, and extended family and fictive kin.

Further, there is an added risk of being passé already. Twitter, Instagram, Snapchat, Jodel, and related "socials"—the current term for social media platforms—are potentially obsolete at this writing with others such as TikTok capturing the market. Undergraduate students tell me new apps could be dispersing the big-name market, creating subgenres of social networking more broadly. A popular culture mash-up. But two things are clear. First, new devices will likely not displace older modes but simply complement them and people will have an even greater need to self-regulate what, when, where, and how they preference devices. Second, new devices will surely alleviate old challenges but be mindful of the invention, creation, and adoption of new ones.

Thus, communications remain a double-edged sword. They have both positive and negative outcomes for soldiers, spouses, children, and adolescents associated with a deployment; yet in the final analysis, early and frequent communications during a deployment attested to beneficial outcomes for the families during and after a deployment.[39] Rather than controlling mediated communications, leaders, soldiers, and family members should educate, train, and inspire one another to self-regulate around their interpersonal communication needs. All should do so in a healthy, proscriptive way that does not exacerbate old or create new catches. The next chapter further describes the self-regulatory notion via the role of television in the lives of spouses and their family members from their perspectives during the GWOT.

# 7

# "Wolf Blitzer Doesn't Talk to Me Anymore"

## WAR ON TELEVISION

Like, they [TV news] said helicopter pilots have died. Well, every single
wife of every single helicopter pilot is probably going crazy right then.
                                        —Army captain's wife in 2003

A formidable feature of war today is the ability to watch portions of war unfold live on a screen. Scholars argue that facing the realities and implications
of war, at least visually, repels us from the likelihood of engaging in war.[1]
Unfortunately, bringing wars live into living rooms has not seemed to abate
the world's appetite and need for war. Rather, we take sides. Scholars have
studied the various constituents and consumers of war coverage, including
journalists, service members, and the public.[2]

Innovative advancements in satellite and internet technology have dramatically increased the ability of the media outlets and increasingly individual service members to transmit and report the war to immediate family
members—military spouses, children, and others. They, in kind, can react
in real time to real-time events on the ground on the war front. While social
media for networking is one form of communication, mass media is another
compelling feature of deployments today. Both are prevalent during the
early and more dramatic, controversial, or contested times during the war.
Exposure and satisfaction with mass media emerged for army spouses during the deployment and dramatically during the earliest phases of the wars
in 2003[3] and 2004,[4] when the wars in Iraq received impressive and wide
national and international coverage. For perspective on the rapid adoption
of technology, note that the spouses of soldiers deployed to Bosnia in the
mid-1990s received their information about that deployment primarily from
the daily *Stars and Stripes* newspaper.[5] Mass media changed precipitously
over the past thirty years. The mass media in Japan focused on the Iraq War
participation and provided both support and critique from the standpoint
of their military family members.[6] Similarly, Dutch and Canadian military
spouses reported that the media coverage of the deployment to Afghanistan

contributed to their anxiety.[7] Mass media likewise impacts the individual to the group, community, institutional, societal, and global levels.

The present chapter describes the personal contentions of spouses, children, and extended family and friends' use of mass media during their loved ones' deployments. The chapter begins with a brief social history of televised war. Next, wives provide descriptions of viewing their husbands live on television during the height of the invasion of Iraq known as Operation Iraqi Freedom in March of 2003. The wives responded by managing the media into three types of viewing: "Compulsive," "Controlled," and "Constrained." The chapter concludes with how mass media coverage of both the wars waned, spouses gained expertise with news coverage, and the concomitant movement toward and increased use of social media.

### Previous Wars and Television

Today soldiers can blog, phone, FaceTime, and text from the war front with instantaneous real-time engagement anywhere on the planet. In the 1860s, Civil War reporting came from letters written by soldiers with considerable lag time between war front events and home front reading of the event. Reporters roamed the battlefield unimpeded during sundry early American wars, including the Spanish-American War, World Wars I and II, and the Korean War; however, censorship was routine. Reporters and editors self-censored in a paternalistic manner. Censorship lifted during the Vietnam War as reporters roamed and informed freely on all aspects of the war and soldiers. The lag time between fronts existed. Vietnam became the first TV war, and army families used this medium to learn about Vietnam's happenings.[8] Beginning with U.S. invasions of Grenada and Panama, forward reporter access became skillfully restricted with limited censorship.[9] The Persian Gulf War is the first "CNN War" connected to the "CNN Effect."[10] The CNN Effect means that the twenty-four-hour news cycle played and plays a crucial role in U.S. foreign and domestic politics—images of the war came directly into homes—often live. These images circumvented policymakers going to the global public, and as a result, sociopolitical strategy decisions had to account for public reactions. Of course, war correspondents and embedded reporting from a war zone are not new; the newness is real-time coverage viewed and read by the public.[11]

By the invasion of Iraq in 2003, some fifteen to sixteen hundred unilateral reporters covered the war from outside of Iraq and six to seven hundred American and international reporters from both televised and print media served as "embedded press"—"they traveled with the troops in their units, ate with them, and were billeted with them; they saw what soldiers saw, were under fire when troops were and endured the same hardships."[12] Research comparing 2003 television broadcast stories of either embedded or unilateral reporting found the former to be "jingoistic."[13] In the same study, 2003 war-related stories found the five American dominant networks—ABC, CBS, NBC, CNN, FNC—and Al Jazeera to be relatively balanced. The one exception was FOX, with a stated strong bias for and favoring the American-led war. By May 1, 2003, President Bush declared the primary combat operations to be over, and the U.S. military lifted the formal embedding of the press. The debate continued.

One argument is that journalists are independent professionals, allowed to freely roam the battlefield documenting war, sometimes with a critical gaze. Whereas others see them as propaganda tools serving as mouthpieces for the sociopolitical needs of the administration or even the perspective lens of their audience.[14]

On the surface, all indications are that embedded reportage will continue in the future.[15] There is legal precedence for maintaining press access on the battlefield.[16] Media executives praise the system—requesting added military-style training and preparation for reporters.[17] Public approval appears to exist.[18] Journalists are killed and injured in war zones.[19] Soldiers are critical of coverage.[20] What, however, does live media coverage mean for U.S. military families?

Military families and their circle of significant others have an apparent personal stake in the mass media emanating from the embedded media with their soldiers. For example, family members can attach themselves to the dispatches of a correspondent embedded with their soldiers' unit. A case in point is Katherine M. Skiba, a reporter for the *Milwaukee Journal Sentinel* and attached to the 101st Airborne Division in the spring of 2003. The paper's editors were astounded by the increased readership and letters from new readers worldwide.[21] However, a significant gap exists in the social and psychological research literature on key constituent groups associated with and impacted by embedded reporting.

This chapter takes up one constituency in this war and television process: the home base of the soldiers informed on—particularly their spouses and children—and the relationship to the rear detachment and their circle of others, extended family members, friends, and the broader society. The spouses share experiences that describe the relationship between military families, the mass media, and the larger society associated with their loved ones' deployments to Iraq and Afghanistan. Three types of television viewing come into view. Each is associated with stress mitigation and a waning of coverage that converges with greater media savvy and a pivot toward social media consumption. The media has joined in as a critical player in the military family–greedy institution bifurcation. Further, mass media narrows the so-called civilian-military divide, militarizing viewers on aspects of the military institution and potentially repelling them from the horrors of war.

## War Live: The 2003 Iraq Invasion

The twenty-four-hour broadcast television news services such as CNN, FOX, and MSNBC carried the Iraq War invasion and aftermath live. Family members closely monitored their soldiers on television via embedded reporters traveling with specific American units. Wives I spoke with, on average, shared anywhere from not viewing at all to watching fifteen minutes per day to as much as twenty-four hours with the television coverage remaining on while they slept. They recorded the news as well (prior to DVRing), where some 30 percent of wives taped the television news ranging from thirty minutes per day to taping the entire day. Just over half allowed their children to view the television news coverage. CNN and FNC are the most viewed.

The television coverage of the Iraq War in 2003 was pervasive throughout the military community, both on and off the military installation I visited. Limitless common neighborhood areas on the military installation tuned into the war coverage, including the PX food court, the Red Cross office, numerous office environments on the post, including the Army Community Service center, Casualty Affairs, and military dayrooms.

Several spouses shared how media exposure related to their well-being. Well-being declined, specifically during the early phases of the invasion when media attention laser-focused on the event, and public attention remains riveted to the conflict developments. A Red Cross worker in the community offered her observations on the "combat stress" at home with CNN and FNC windows into the war, stating, "Too much caring—the care providers are tired. Furthermore, this is related to the ebb and flow of media coverage. A father heard on television that his son took injuries and then received SNOK notification. Rear people are working fourteen-hour days and have been doing so for about four months in the TV spin cycle, and everyone is in crisis mode. There is so much negativity and emotional exhaustion."

In addition, off-post restaurants popular among soldiers and families, such as Ruby Tuesday's, had continual coverage of the war on multiple televisions as soldiers and families dined, drank at the bar, and conversed. Brigit provides a description of commenting on TV viewing: "My mom came down from New York. I picked her up at the airport. She wanted to stop at Apple-bee's [a chain restaurant]. I saw on one of the televisions that the soldier had been killed. I got up, stood next to the salad bar, and watched the TV. I started to flip out. We had to go home."

Once at home, from the interviews with the wives, three patterns of live television viewing emerged that I labeled "Compulsive," "Controlled," and "Constrained." *Compulsive Viewers* are anyone who watched television coverage of the war for six hours per day or greater. One-third of wives fell into this category. The family members monitored the news north of one hour at a time, viewed at any hour of the day or night, and in some cases slept with the news on, waking periodically during the night to monitor reports. A mother of three small children represented compulsive viewing and shared, "There are certain things like if I hear Walt Rodgers's [reporter embedded with husband's unit] voice. I will be like, 'Hey, my husband's unit is on.' I wake up when I hear his voice. Like every hour." Similarly, the pregnant wife of a private shared this comment concerning her temporary roommate during the deployment, a pregnant wife of a combat medic in a different unit: "Last night it was two o'clock in the morning, and I was up watching it. My eyes were hurting. I went to her room to turn the TV off, and she automatically wakes up. Her husband calls from Iraq and tells her to stop watching TV all night. She was so ecstatic to finally hear from him . . . she didn't even get to tell him they were having a boy." She goes on about herself:

When they first declared war, [I watched] all day, every day for five days. Watched it all day, every day. Then I realized that, okay, like my mother-in-law watches it all day, every day, and she has no idea, like the military or anything and she would call me and say, "I don't understand this." "What is going on?" I have kind of stopped watch-ing it. It is very hard. I do fear I am going to be watching and I will see his tank or whatever he is riding in now, blow up and I don't want to find out that way. But then, when I don't watch it, she calls me and she says, "Oh, I saw his profile, he was eating." I'm like, "Dang it, I didn't see it, I didn't." And, whenever she calls me and she says, "Oh. His unit blew up something," or "They are doing so good," or "When they had the missiles come in and they were standing around their vehicles, and they scrambled in and went in." She was like, "Oh. They are doing so good." I am like, I got to watch, I got to see what is going on. Every time the phone rings, I am like "Okay" [and she exhales] or the doorbell rings. Have you seen that movie *We Were Soldiers Once . . . and Young* [about Vietnam and features casualty notifications of wives via telegram]? "Whoa, I am like uh-huh." If anybody comes up to my door, a chaplain or an officer, I am like, "No." I am not opening up the door.

In comparison, *Controlled Viewers* made a conscious and systematic attempt to monitor news coverage of the war with a prescribed formula—for example, one half hour in the morning, one half hour in the afternoon, and thirty minutes to a few hours in the evening, watching only at specific times and usually for only one to four hours per day. Two-thirds of the wives recounted this strategy. A wife entrusted, "I didn't realize the TV coverage would be every day. I saw the captain [husband's commander] on TV, and my first thought is that I know him. He [my husband] must be safe. Then I felt pride; they must be good if the news chose them. So, I wake up every day and turn on the TV." The wife of a specialist who works full-time as a special education teacher confided:

> I watched again. I taped it all day that Friday. Friday night I watched it when I went home, but I kind of realized I had six hours, eight hours, worth of tape, I am not going to go back and watch this. I want to watch now when it is happening. That was when I kind of backed off. You know, it is going to happen whether you are taping it or not, it really doesn't make a difference. They are with [husband's unit]. You are probably not going to see him. What I have done now is when I get up in the morning, I will watch just to see if anything new has happened and before I go to bed. I am not really watching it that much anymore.

Again, the local Red Cross worker on the post and a girlfriend of a deployed soldier provided observations: "The media is too specific. They provide too much detail about a specific unit. I suggest to women that they turn off the TV. CNN and FOX News focus too much and I always suggest that wives limit the TV. Some wives do heed this advice."

The third group of spouse interviewees comprised *Constrained Viewers*.[22] This group represents roughly 10 percent of the interviews. They refrained completely from viewing any television coverage. A nineteen-year-old wife of a PFC opined: "I don't watch TV at all, I get too upset. I don't want to use the computer or Internet because it might block his call. I get information from other people." A female soldier, non-deployable because of pregnancy, offered a two-sided point of view—as both soldier and army wife. She asserted, "I try not to watch [TV] . . . it would drive me crazy. I have mixed feelings about the embedded reporters. The media needs to be careful about what they say. For example, one reporter said on the air, referring to soldiers firing on a tower, 'We'll have to give them a hard time for missing that tower.' I would not want to find out something happened to my husband from TV. This is a huge fear for most wives. The coverage is okay, but I would prefer if it were not live. They go into details that scare me."

Most wives confided that they watched extensive coverage—meeting the definitions of *Controlled* or *Compulsive Viewers*—though only a minority remained compulsive by day ten of the invasion. In addition, FRLs soon recommended that wives unremarkably limit their viewing—adopting elements of our Controlled or Constrained Viewer strategies. A wife of a sergeant with three children confided, "I watched it the first week and then I stopped because I got high blood pressure, and I was getting sick. I said, 'What is the use of watching it?' I have a life back at home. I can't stay home watching news. I used to watch it all day when the first, the start of the war, and after that, I just stopped because my blood pressure was going sky-high. I was worried about him over there." One more medically non-deployable soldier and wife of platoon sergeant related:

> I have mixed feelings about the embedded reporters. It is good to see what the conditions are like but sometimes it is bad to see. Reporters shouldn't say anyone is killed, a POW, or MIA until afterwards. The coverage makes me mad, the slant the reporters use make it sound like we are bad soldiers. During the first week I watched eight to ten hours per day—I wasn't living—just watching. Now I watch four to six hours and watch the last half hour before going to bed. Seeing the army generals [retired] on TV doesn't make me feel better. They are not a good representation because they are not down in the trenches.

A sergeant's wife, married for three years with a toddler and infant, remarked on the community:

> For me, it is good. I did watch them sometimes. For [our unit] it was good. But I knew sometimes every single report was not accurate. On the other hand, for some of the ladies, because every single thing that happened, they took to heart. Anytime they made a mistake, you would get a phone call after phone call after phone call. It was

horrible. Parents [of soldiers and in-laws] were worried to death and
that is another reason—don't watch TV all the time. But, once you
started watching it, you would get hooked. It is hard for them not to
watch it. I would still catch the occasional; I would be at Wal-Mart
shopping, and they have the big TVs in there and you would hear,
"Attention Wal-Mart Shoppers." I mean, you would still see it and
people would be standing there. I just stopped watching TV, even in
Wal-Mart. I would stand and watch as well, but it is just something
I just could not watch all the time because I could see how it would
make you scared.

In addition to viewing habits, teeming numbers remarked on their satisfaction with the coverage. Legions of wives commented about concerns of
media exploitation and manipulation. To gain access to the "human interest
story" of the war, media outlets increasingly contacted family members directly to coordinate interviews rather than using the on-post Public Affairs
Office sources. Wives off the post had increased difficulties if they could not
be anonymous. Journalists from print and televised media at international,
national, and local levels frequented a popular café immediately outside the
back gate of the army post, shared information, and had extra-accessible access to army families. Their presence and behavior created a paradox. Wives
perceived them as predatory. Nevertheless, they seemed to both relish the
media attention and calculate their use of it. A private's wife represented a
handful of critical views and protested, "The media definitely needs to tone
down by CNN coming here to Fort Young. I feel like they exploit the wives
that are left behind—'Oh, well, what does your husband do? What does your
husband say?' I am like, 'Look, can I just do an interview and tell my husband that I love him, I don't really want to answer any questions or nothing,
I just want to tell him that I love him.' I think that they exploit the situation
to the point that it is almost sickening."

We returned to the post a month later to conduct follow-up interviews
and check in with the Rear Detachment Command. A mother of two children interviewed a month after the initial invasion and reflecting on the
month said:

Some of the stuff they were showing, I thought was too graphic.
Even me, I am like, "Good Lord, I don't want to see it. I don't, I don't
want to see it." And that one time they showed where these guys,
I think it was either the Marines or the 101st [Airborne Division],

went into the house. They kept zooming in on this little kid. I know it was terrifying for this child. The kids, they made them come inside and they searched the house and they had to get down and they had their hands up like this, and they were crying, and I am just crying. I am like, "Oh my God." It makes our guys look so bad. When you are looking at those soldiers' faces, they are terrified. But, also, you know, the camera keeps looking at that little boy and I am just like, you know, his heart [my husband] is probably just breaking. I am doing this to a child. I said, you know, you know I look at that, that is what my husband is going to have to remember, I terrorized a child. Even though he had to do it . . . That kind of stuff. That was just too much.

A junior officer's wife with two children provided some critical angles noting:

CNN had an embedded reporter with us, and as soon as the action stopped, they dropped us like a hot potato. We felt used. Many wives, we talked about it. We felt used. We were really ticked off. It was like one day he [embedded reporter] was there and the next day, boom, nothing. We kind of like got addicted to hearing where the guys were and what they were doing. It was like we needed our fix, and it just wasn't there. That is how I felt. So, I must say, days go by, and I don't even watch the news.

Again, the mass media is a mixed blessing at the intersection of twenty-first-century war and the home front. Wives, in this case, developed viewing habits falling into one of three categories—compulsive, controlled, and constrained. Further, these categories proved dynamic as wives migrated from less to more healthy modes of consumption over time—they become savvy media consumers.

Complicating mass media coverage are two factors. One, increased coverage increased others of relative significance to the soldier, and his family caught wind of the story worldwide. Mass media vastly expanded the definition of the military family in terms of others significant to them. Two, others, often out of heartfelt concern, in turn, contacted the soldier and his family for supplementary information. Increases in mass media begat increases in social media use.

For example, think about the AMC television series *The Walking Dead*—a television drama that first aired in 2010 about a postapocalyptic world with a few human survivors and millions of zombies (the walking dead) and aired new seasons until November 2022. If the show had originated in 1960, it would be exclusively a mass medium—a gross one, but a mass one, nonetheless. Thus *TWD* could then be comparable to the Vietnam War news broadcasts watched across the country. However, *TWD* first aired in 2010 coming through global mass media. It now has a global community audience following it via social media communication such as Twitter, Snapchat, Facebook, and blogs linking viewers, cast members, critics, and a host of others directly and instantaneously. As the TV series and wars continue, the attention span of viewers may fade into the background as other shows and news capture viewers' attention. By 2004 mass media coverage of Iraq and Afghanistan had faded, dramatically.

## Mass Media Lite: Iraq in 2004 and Post-Surge Iraq and Afghanistan in 2008

By 2004 and certainly by 2008, television coverage of the wars in Iraq and Afghanistan had waned significantly. Because of a smaller active-duty force compared to past wars, service members began doing second, third, or fourth tours in Iraq or Afghanistan. Estimates are that 40 percent of military service members had been deployed more than once in 2009.[23] In 2004 approximately 15,200 U.S. troops had boots on the ground in Afghanistan.[24] The number had practically doubled in 2008 to 30,100. Iraq held steady over time but with added troops—130,600 in 2004 and 157,800 in 2008.

April of 2004 proved particularly deadly for American forces and 2004 the second-deadliest for Americans from 2003 to 2017. During the surge, in 2007, U.S forces in Iraq had come off the deadliest year, with 961 fatalities in 2007. That number reduced by two-thirds by the end of 2008, but the risk of injury and death remained an everyday reality. Fatalities in Afghanistan had been increasing as well. Deaths of those killed received coverage—often providing a photo image, their name, age, and hometown—but the battles not so much.

Compulsive television viewing among army wives had all but waned and pivoted by 2004 but monitoring continued. The technology evolved too. Wives moved from TV to online. They began learning lessons. From personal backgrounds with previous deployments, then through friends or vicariously via other units, they also pivoted to social media. Personal communications with their spouses began to improve exponentially and dramatically. A senior officer's wife who worked for a print media newspaper represented the lessons learned: "I often think about the [previously deployed] Fourth ID people who had nothing. Their wives only watched TV and how scary that must have been. I am very grateful for email and everything else."

When high-profile events get reported and televised when they happen—such as deaths—if it bleeds, it leads is the adage. Moreover, political scientists Ross A. Miller and Karen Albert at the University of Nebraska-Lincoln found a relationship between international disputes going public in the *New York Times* and a rise in fatalities.[25] The home-front leadership seemed increasingly savvy about managing the news media, information overload, and the rumor mill fallout it appeared to generate. A company-level FRL and wife of a captain and company commander informed us: "We put out there [to spouses] to be careful of what you watch on the news, but some watch it, some more than others. It is both the news and what their spouses tell them." In general, most wives fell into the constrained mode regarding TV viewing—they avoid it. Below are three exemplars, with the last one about children and news. A pregnant sergeant's wife said:

> I don't want to know [what is going on over there], as long as my hus-
> band is alive, if he isn't dying or getting hurt, I don't need to know. I
> don't watch the news. I don't watch the news. I don't want to know.
> My mother and I talked about it and my father and I talked about it
> and he thought that I am very paranoid. I get really scared very easily
> with that kind of stuff and we decided that since I was having a baby
> it would be easier for me that if anything happened with him, he
> would tell me, or they will tell me. I don't need to know.

The wife of a captain with two children said:

> They try to be really specific about what the guys are doing and if
> they have had soldiers performing excellently in their areas or doing,
> single people out or whatever, but still, I can't count how many phone
> calls I receive. I don't watch the news. I deliberately stay away from
> it because they, say Baghdad, it is hard for me to be, okay. I just saw
> him today on the web camera. I know he is fine, let's see. Baghdad. I
> am like, "Oh my God." So. I don't watch the news. I get these phone
> calls [from spouses]. "Oh my God, did you hear about the explosion.
> I haven't heard from my husband." You try to explain to them. "They
> want us to wait forty-eight hours." [They say] "I can't wait that long;
> I need some information." Okay, well. Then they start going to look
> trying to find information [on the Internet]. When they find some-
> thing, they try to pass it along.

The wife of a sergeant major with two boys, eleven and nine, amid a second long deployment shared:

> I don't let the children [watch television]. I try one time a day to sit down, I time it in the morning when I get him in the shower, I catch the news brief. Other than that, I don't leave it on. Wolf Blitzer doesn't talk to me anymore. It used to just run, and I would wake up every time they would do the "Bom-Bom" [sound of breaking news on CNN] with the news flash. So, every time a soldier breathed, they had a news flash. So, this time, I make a specific amount of time that I know, and I catch the news when I know Iraq stuff is going to be on. Then of course, through roundup, and then other people will call and say something. I will make an effort to watch the news if someone that I know will be on TV. Other than that, and if I miss that, it is not like my life has stopped. I will go three, five days and someone will ask me about something that is headlined in the news, and I am shocked by it. Especially since I found out that what we see is such a small negative portion, no matter how they try to spin it positive, it isn't. Also, I ask all of that. I know when they come back from R&R, what is the difference between . . . They don't show anything of the [positives]. They show a very small amount of the good things. And, if it isn't sensational or really nasty, it doesn't make it.

Mass media coverage of the wars in Iraq and Afghanistan moved to the back pages of newspapers in the mid-2000s. Television coverage provided casualty counts and, with exceptions, provided the names and photographs of the fatalities. *PBS News Hour* impressively and consistently remembered and honored U.S. service members killed in Iraq and Afghanistan through to the last American soldiers to lose their lives in Afghanistan, including the thirteen killed during the U.S. exit on August 26, 2021. Again, they provided photographs, names, ranks, age, and hometowns.[26] Likewise, compulsive television viewing for spouses ended. Their curiosity did not wane, and they moved their monitoring of the war to online sources and social media.

### Mass Media Avoidance While Abroad

By 2008 and living abroad, wives could avoid the war in the U.S. popular press with ease. First, fewer cable news networks followed the war, and second, they did not have access. A wife of a captain with four deployments by 2008, four children, and two years in Germany expressed on watching the news:

I watch the weather channel. I didn't watch them again. It's like you can't do that. Some spouses sit at home and watch every news report. That's not a good thing. Just watch the weather channel. Their news is like for five seconds. You know I go to expatriots.com and I read about what's going on in Germany. I know this sounds crazy, but I kind of left the United States. I mean I was kind of glad to leave the United States because of the political stuff. It was just too painful. You know my husband's in the army and they're taking that and twisting it for the benefit of the one side or the other. It comes from my sister-in-law . . . Like Skype . . . I quit skyping with them because her son would get on and say, "Why does Uncle Luke carry a gun?" and "You know that's bad." And I just don't like those attacks, those political attacks, and it was just so . . . I just felt very, I don't like hearing all that stuff on the TV day in and day out and it's all just so, what do you call it, not united. It's very [pregnant pause] divisive. Very divisive and not helpful at all and my kids don't need to hear, you know, things like that. They don't need to be getting in a political debate at the school. We don't have that as much here but back in the States we had kids fighting on the playgrounds and, oh, "You should be a Republican" and "You should be a Democrat" or "You should vote for this and that and if not, you're bad." Or we did have that, I guess, we did have that here. But it's teaching them to deal with conflicts, but I don't know, you know, I can kind of get away from that over here and it's slower paced. I do like it.

We see a concerted effort here to exert control of TV and other media sources in numerable ways. Controlling one's situation appears a healthy compromise between compulsive and constrained uses of social and mass media.

## Conclusion

In sum, mass media in the U.S. has always communicated war home. Live TV with embedded journalists with troops is new. Spouses early on developed three patterns of television news coverage about the war in Iraq: compulsive, constrained, and the moderate controlled. They might practice all three, gravitating from one to another throughout the deployment. They migrated from the extremes of compulsion and constraint to more moderate control. TV news coverage and monitoring by spouses decreased across the decades of war. TV coverage of the war waned. The role of TV became increasingly less significant; however, high-intensity moments during the war brought television coverage and army spouses and the others significant to them to monitor the news. Journalist Martha Raddatz describes the spin of events in the book *The Long Road Home* where TV and radio news reports about a firefight in the Sadr City "neighborhood of Baghdad left four U.S. soldiers dead and at least forty wounded."[27] The news brought illustrious attention to American forces in Iraq but again, subsided sometime later.

Last, the CNN Effect and global television coverage see policymakers vying for public reaction to war news. Nevertheless, on the home front where the spouses are, we see the impetus for the role definition of the military to expand out to the larger society and create additional strains and greediness on the part of everyone affiliated with the deployment—a kind of Walking Dead Effect. An expanded definition of the significant others to the soldier includes her leaders to the Rear Detachment Command to the Family Readiness Group and other formal supports on-post to the wives and children to the broader community of blood and fictive kin and others of significance and even to those insignificant to the soldier and her spouse.

Over time, spouses traversed an arch of TV coverage to new sources to moderate and verify events through multiple sources, including TV, social media, the Internet, and increasingly, actual and lag-time contact with their spouse deployed downrange. By 2018, there is little coverage of soldiers and families in Iraq and Afghanistan. Wives made mention of less media coverage of their husbands regularly deploying to eastern Europe.

Television and social media are greedy. TV coverage created profound and palpable stress and anxiety for wives either through monitoring it or avoiding it. Mass and social media are greedy institutions vying for the time and emotions of family members. TV coverage of the live war, rather than repelling families from the horrors of war, did the opposite. It contributed to a step-by-step process of socializing spouses to become de facto spokespersons about the military war engagements of their soldiers. TV accounts had to be viewed, captured, reexamined, and verified. This gradual process intersected with the well-being of spouses. The more they viewed war, the more they became militarized, even desensitized, and with increased militarization became the normative vibe of accepting and being strohwitwe. Live war became pervasively cultural on multiple social levels. Richard J. Pinder, a military health researcher, and his research colleagues at King's College in London, England, found that mass and social media coverage rattled members of the British Forces during the Iraq War to include how their families viewed the war.[28] American feminist scholar Cynthia Enloe argues that militarization bakes into American society—probably more during war.[29] TV is added to the recipe of war and reifies militarization as reporters, unambiguously those embedded with troops, are de facto similarly and summarily militarized. Journalists should court and establish relationships with military families during times of peace in anticipation of war.[30]

# Conclusion

Do you think I wanted this life? This husband that disappears without any kind of warning. Do you think that anyone would want that? Who would want that?

—Clare in *The Time Traveler's Wife*

The 2009 popular film *The Time Traveler's Wife*[1] is a metaphor for separated families generally and military families and the wars in Iraq and Afghanistan during the 2000s specifically. Considered an instance of the time-displacement romance film genre, both the film that grossed almost double its cost and the bestselling book of the same name have Henry DeTamble, the time traveler, and his wife, Clare, the non–time traveler.[2] The film moves back and forth across their life course from small children to becoming parents, both separated and together. After miscarriages (spoiler alert), as the embryos time travel out of the womb, they finally have a daughter named Alba. Interestingly, in the book, Alba is born on September 6, 2001.[3] She inherits her father's genetic primary status of time travel. The beat of separation drums forward with the intergenerational genetic master status. She shares the proclivity for time travel with her father, but she travels unexpectedly far less. As a next-generation time-traveler, she has keener control of when and where she goes. Perhaps this speaks to the military recruitment shortfalls of the 2020s.

Henry separates from Clare seventeen times across the film. Ultimately aware he will die and fearing his demise, Henry, like thousands of soldiers in Iraq and Afghanistan, is shot during one of his travels and dies at the young age of thirty-three years.

One argument is that the film represents pathologized and traumatized masculinity in contemporary culture.[4] In this sense, mental time travel is what Henry suffers from, not mechanical time travel.[5] Anne Demers, a professor of health science and recreation at San Jose State University, highlights the subtheme of "time-traveling" as the immediate after of returning from a war zone.[6]

Like army spouses I interviewed, Clare develops and grows accustomed to her husband's travels. She learns eventually to simply go about her everyday activities when he leaves at a moment's notice. For example, he disappears sitting down to dinner. Clare cleans up the plate he dropped and continues with her dinner, alone. Clare is a fictional strohwitwe across her childhood, teens, and early adulthood. Ultimately, she becomes a Witwe—a permanent widow. However, Henry does return once after he dies and encourages her to move on with her life without him. If only.

In the author's note of a new printing of the book, novelist Audrey Niffenegger shares comments from readers she had received over the years since the first edition. One of them is an army wife who says, "My husband is in the army, our relationship is like the DeTambles', he's always leaving."[7] A *Slate* magazine article highlights that "Clare's plight is that of an army wife times a thousand."[8] Although I have no evidence, I suspect the book, film, and TV series would likely lack any popularity minus the wars and separations of Iraq and Afghanistan seared into America's psyche.

Around the same time as the subtle popularity of *The Time Traveler's Wife*[9] comes an army-specific, explicit, pedestrian, and top-rated situational drama TV series called *Army Wives* that aired on the Lifetime cable channel.[10] It ran seven television seasons from 2007 to 2013, featuring the lives of four wives and one husband of army service members of various ranks located on a fictional army base in South Carolina known as Fort Marshall.

*Army Wives*, like *The Time Traveler's Wife*, emerges from a book, but a nonfiction one by Tanya Biank, an army brat, army wife, and former reporter for the *Fayetteville Observer*—the local paper for the surrounding community of Fort Bragg (now Fort Liberty), North Carolina—originally titled *Under the Sabers: The Unwritten Code of Army Wives*.[11] Biank also served as a consultant on the Lifetime television series.[12]

*Army Wives* commingles the range of demands imposed on military families and traditional American values. Demands again include, among others that I have highlighted throughout this book, overseas living, normative constraints, a masculine-dominated culture, long work hours and shiftwork, the risk of injury and death, and separations for deployments. At the same time, the show provides subtle reinforcement of traditional American values such as individuality, to appease, perhaps, the civilian viewer. They include individualism, arduous work, equality, and upward social mobility.[13]

Indeed, the first episode captures the major elements and diversity of army families.[14] The young PFC that marries the single parent of two relocates to a new base and encounters military-specific rules—a citation for having high grass on the new base quarters where they have just arrived. Similarly, she salutes the first officer she encounters, not knowing the customs. There are intergenerational occupation linkages with an officer, father, and son. In addition, there are parental abuse, PTSD, and the military community monitoring the war on television. Other features of the first episode are a white military spouse surrogacy for African American twins; military-speak and jargon; gossip; a hegemonic male culture; army wives forgoing nursing, police, and legal careers; officer-enlisted wife conflicts; and army brats. All of this occurs with the backdrop of active deployments in the first episode: An African American LTC returns home from a two-year deployment and is greeted by her husband. A later scene has a white major deploying with his troops as families see them off.

Rather than art imitating life, the story I weaved here is from actual U.S. Army wives and husbands and their families during war deployments. Army spouses have shared their deployment separations and related experiences during the GWOT. Based on interviews of 199 different spouses over fifteen years, I have covered an arch of their singular experiences during the invasion of Iraq in 2003 to settling in for the insurgency a year later, on through the decade and fighting in Iraq and Afghanistan in 2008, to old hat, new, and novel deployments in eastern Europe in 2018. The breadth of their militarized entanglements is compelling and rich, and I hope there are lessons here for private and other public sector families as well.

In summary, I have rooted the army spouses here in studies of military sociology, building on a long history of scholarly studies dating back to World War II. Military sociology is a subfield of sociology not unlike medical sociology and other institutional studies such as the sociology of sport, criminal justice studies, or the sociology of religion. Military family studies are a subfield of military sociology. Research began in earnest in the U.S. during and immediately after World War II with the groundbreaking study by Reuben Hill—the now-classic 1949 work titled *Families under Stress: Adjustment to the Crises of War Separation and Reunion*—providing a multi-method undertaking involving 135 Iowa families with an active service member deployed to war. Likewise, work and family studies began in the context of industrialization that first compartmentalized home and work life and burgeoned in the aftermath of World War II as women's labor force participation changed and as men returned home from the war.

Today, the claims of work and family on members are unprecedented, cross-cultural, and global. Couples are parting physically but not emotionally. One separates from the home because of work-related exigencies creating strohwitwe(r)—grass widow(er)s—and they are global. The occupations of separation are airline pilots, long-haul truckers, professional athletes, and soldiers, among others. Such spouses and partners share being deployees, and countless have a spouse or partner and other family members remaining back home.

Army spouses during the GWOT faced what civilian separated spouses encounter regularly in the postindustrial world—separation due to work and institutional requirements and impositions. Army spouses are an integral part of the garrisoned military community and institutional requirements of a military that has become increasingly isolated and painstakingly hyper normative in the world since 9/11—one that had melted away prior to 9/11. Military spouses experience this ambiguous civilian-military gap as they are physically, socially, and culturally both detached and virtually ubiquitous via social media in the dominant socioculture. I have used stress theory, binary greedy institutions, triadic institutions, and critical studies to frame the struggles and victories of the spouses, and the research shows these army spouses to be both isolated and integrated. They are in a dynamic, negotiated dance across the military deployment cycle. The dance emerges within and betwixt the family, work, the state, and the larger society to the tunes of relative accommodation, militarization, and even resistance.

The U.S. Army is one of the largest employers in American society, and I've sought to show how during the GWOT, military spouses, their children, and in some cases, their extended kin, the larger military community, and U.S. society are baked into and exploited as a two-plus-person, one-career entity. They are both near and far from the front lines. Yet, spouses serve as a combat service support domestic element on a home front that intimately binds soldiers, families, the state, and society together. They are free labor—"voluntariats"[15] or "volunteerpriots"[16]—volunteering to help their country starting with their spouse and children. What some have labeled "The Incorporated Wife."[17] Voluminous numbers of spouses wholly submit to the position and wait. Others shared how they struggle with their role but respond accordingly with purpose. Still others are unaffected, and a whole other group, which I identify as EASYs, are emancipated army spouses resisting military indoctrination selectively or altogether.

*Army Spouses* began with chapters about deployment: before, during, and after. A novel chapter features the impact of live war coverage and families and another on communications between the war and home front during the deployment. *Army Spouses* also includes chapters on children and adolescents during the emotional cycle of the deployment and informal and formal support services available to army families.

The military is a bona fide social institution. Like other social institutions such as education, sports, and leisure, the military touches the common genres of popular culture, from books to TV to video games to comics to social media. YouTube videos of returning soldiers surprising family members have tens of thousands of views—including during the 2020 State of the Union Address.[18] Mass and social media bring increased attention to military families during the GWOT, with detailed reporting via broadcast and social media, the emergence of not-for-profit organizations, film, and music.

Army families from the GWOT can be an exemplar for military and other occupational separations now and in the future. Pre-deployment shows to be a complicated emotional phase of deployment for army families associated with various psychological and social outcomes. Loads of spouses surrendered to the impending deployment. Submission happens in weeks, months, and even a year out in cases.

The overall deployment is the most consuming occurrence for the strohwitwe. A battery of social and psychological encounters reveal in the deployment phase including mainstays such as loneliness and adopting new roles and responsibilities. Thinking about the nuclear army family in the context of others significant to the family provides a broader, contextual understanding of how families endured and managed deployments.

The post-deployment is a celebratory bargain where spouses, soldiers, children, leaders, others significant, and the military community engage in a gambol of reintegration with phases highlighted by events, rites, and setbacks, and then snapping back to a new but different normal. The institution-provided classes and training sessions add value, but resentment is pervasive.

Grass widows have formal and informal supports at their disposal, but the supports are a double-edged sword. Scores of formal support services work for spouses, and some receive mixed reviews. Army spouses are inclined to say nothing in the absence of something positive to say—silence is loud. In interviews, complaints about programs usually came from spouses not utilizing them, such as ERD. The ironic twist of deployments is that the spouse's support person needed, trusted, and wanted most during a deployment is their deployed spouse.

EASYs are a new and quiet faction of army spouses. They emancipate from military militarization and the imposing elements of military life. They are a new human element of the U.S. Army that resist perceived patronizing support services and embrace individualism, self-reliance, autonomy, and independence. They do appear in other societies around the world, such as Norway. In the U.S. Army, they may be male or female civilian spouses—and we should learn about them.

During the wars with a deployed parent, military brats are graswaisen—grass orphans—well, sort of, one parent is still home if they come from coresidential two-parent families. Military children fall into three groups—children, adolescents, and adults. I focused on the first two[19] and they vary wildly across sex, gender, age, family adjustments, limited parentization, and subgroups—sometimes in the same household. Overall, teams of kids are all right, and most parents think they are fine. Notably, though, it is not your father's army. Girls and young women have achieved equity within military families. In addition, the increase occurs during deployments with deployees—generally large segments of men leave a military community and place it in the hands of primarily women and their children—half of whom are girls. Army spouses told of expanding their role repertoires as volunteer-priots, leaving jobs and careers to do so, increasingly taking on masculine activities and feeling emboldened.

Further, they resisted relinquishing roles easily once a deployment ended and the husband and father returned home. Moreover, so did their daughters. Once a daughter is liberated (if she is not already), like their mothers, it becomes even harder for her to return to traditional roles. Do military brat girls share an emancipation with the daughters of civilian deployees?

Communiqués between home and war front are as old as war. Speed and decentralization are new. Today, the tempo of technological innovation changes not merely across wars but even within them. Thus, there is varied access, connectivity obstacles, costs, family member use variance, casualty notification disruptions, security breaches, and self-regulation. What is new and nuanced are features from the home front, such as timing between the two fronts, connectivity, self-regulation, and uses and gratifications differing within a household among different family members. Thus, exchanges remain a double-edged sword. They have both positive and negative outcomes for soldiers, spouses, children, and adolescents associated with a deployment, yet early and frequent communications during a deployment attested to beneficial outcomes for the families during and after a deployment.[20]

Finally, television and social media carry war live. Coverage waxes and wanes, as do viewing habits of military spouses and their children. Notably, the CNN Effect broadens from the policymaker orientation and the use of force to that of the military community. Coverage now expands the range of the military family and community as others significant to uniformed and civilian deployed families become privy, instantaneously, to the war via live television and instantaneous Internet coverage—a Walking Dead Effect.

## Recommendations

Given both the old and bold, new struggles and victories of army spouses, I offer below some recommendations for military family members, the army organization and leaders, and broader policymakers that oversee the military based on what is known about army families and the experiences of the spouses I encountered over fifteen years. These are out-of-the-box ideas generated from the spouses but based on my insider and outsider orientation. As a sociologist, I see big-picture perspective changes. Growing up military but also living as a majority member in minority neighborhoods have both shaped my outlooks. Thus, my personal and professional background as an outsider—someone a part of but progressively often apart from different in-groups and enclaves—allows me to challenge the status quo. Thus, I offer here a few proposals based on the shared happenings of my interviewed spouses and my own views. The recommendations certainly have direct application to the army and the military more broadly. Leaders of civilian organizations with deployees might want to check themselves against their organization as well. Are you doing all you can to support workers and their families?

### *Educate to Self-Regulate*

Years ago, while studying how soldiers and families communicate, a respected colleague, U.S. Army social worker colonel, and now professor emeritus of social work at Bryn Mawr College, James A. Martin, coined the term for me: "educate to self-regulate." It is a catchphrase. Nevertheless, it has a deeper meaning. In this case, a socially healthy way to communicate in the information age. It provides a middle ground between self, leader, and institutional imposed censorship and sanctions. First, it implies the organization does not need to create rules and sanctions about communicating. Second, it holds that families and soldiers can be culturally savvy about the impact of sharing information from them up through the organization to the broader societal and larger culture. Rather than controlling mass, social, and mediated communication, leaders, soldiers, and family members should educate, train, and inspire themselves and one another to self-regulate around their interpersonal information age needs. All should do so in a healthy, proscriptive way that does not exacerbate old or create new problems. For example, fisher(wo)men can now communicate with their families while at sea through various platforms, but the lines need to be regulated because they serve as a source for distress calls and Maydays should the need arise.[21]

The idea of educated self-regulation could be expanded to television and Internet use and monitoring. Spouses can learn to develop an understanding of the features of the emotional phases of the deployment cycle and the relationship to children and adolescents and apply them to their technology uses. Support can become a controlled media consumer. And they could educate their extended families on self-regulation.

### Diversify Service

U.S. Army–provided services meet the specific needs of soldiers, spouses, and immediate family members. This ain't no revelation. Given the organization culture of vetting how organizations come into being and the constant monitoring by practitioners and consumers, programs are in constant flux and change, hopefully for the better, as missions change. If anything, there should be a consideration for expanding formal services beyond the immediate traditional family. Military families are increasingly diverse, and families counter to the traditional nuclear family of biological children with a first-time-married heterosexual couple are the minority relative to all the others, including single soldiers with girl and boyfriends. Services should be more widespread beyond soldiers and immediate families. International businesses have long had family-friendly policies and programs with benefits increasing with seniority, rank, and status in the company. Rank-and-file deployees in all jobs could receive similar considerations, benefits, and programs based on their demographic profile and needs, increasing inclusions, equity, and sense of belonging. As the slogan goes: "One Team, One Fight."

### Experience Matters

The Global War on Terrorism lasted twenty years. In no other war have U.S. service members deployed and redeployed so often to a singular broader campaign. Much like soldiers describe the war in Iraq as akin to the highly and increasingly esteemed 1993 film *Groundhog Day*,[22] so too do military family members relive a deployment separation again and again and again. In the film, the Bill Murray character gradually develops insights and learns from each new day, and eventually escapes his quarantine. So too do military spouses develop a deployment cycle acumen over time. Each subsequent one becomes less of a struggle. It is clear from the interviews that older military spouses or those with practical contact and observations of a range of events outside the military cope better with deployments than those with less. Thus, there should be considerations on exploiting this rich acumen to serve families better to cool out and overcome crisis during deployments.

One way is to continue instituting a buddy system where all spouses provide additional support to look out for people at the individual level. Buddy systems seem to work for some already in the military community.[23] They work in Canada for military reservists who are isolated.[24] Additionally, companion-type systems should be socially engineered and implemented for the full range of the deployed family—from children to spouses to parents to include others that are significant to soldiers. The buddy system is a formal system that facilitates informal support. As informal support is desired over formal supports, it would alleviate stress on the formal systems and better serve spouses at their comfort level of support. Introduce buddy systems early and nurture them often, far before, during, and long after deployments.

## Diversify Military Housing

The housing of troops and their families has consistently varied over the history of the U.S. military. Privatized when the U.S. Congress passed the Military Housing Privatization Initiative on February 10, 1996, the program was called the Residential Communities Initiative. Additionally, this began to facilitate department-level civilians and retirees who could live in on-post housing. However, traditionally, military housing served the segregation of ranks—officers lived in one area and enlisted in an alternative one. In more cases, even within these ranks, segregation is based on senior officers and enlisted living in one area and the juniors elsewhere. Civilians and military retirees will reinforce military neighborhood stratification based on income.

To the contrary, homes should be built and housed based on family needs, not rank and interspersed. Once segregated by race and later desegregated, military housing should also desegregate by military rank. This way, extra-savvy spouses can engage with spouses of less acumen, helping to facilitate informal social supports. Fort Belvoir, Virginia, has provided a framework for military housing known as "new urban mixed-use" that socially engineers equity, inclusion, and diversity.[25] This social engineering could alleviate everyday troubles at the neighborhood level. Such housing would create "flying buttresses" to facilitate and support the buddy system. It would also bridge social class divisions that exist between officer and enlisted spouses by narrowing their officer-enlisted spouse divide. Take this recommendation even further and consider eliminating on-post military housing altogether and integrating service members deeper into local communities.

*Marriage Causes Divorce*

The comedian Groucho Marx is famous for saying, "Marriage is the chief cause of divorce." Indeed, so I begin each semester with this quote in our Marriage and Family course at West Point. I tell students that the relationship between marriage and divorce is 100 percent. All divorces involved people who were once married. It is not exclusively tongue in cheek. Family demographers tell us that just under half of marriages end in divorce. Contributing here is that the earlier one marries, the more likely divorce occurs. Compellingly, nearly 60 percent of people who married between the ages fifteen and twenty-two divorced before their midforties.[26] The logic here is that marital problems are normative. People divorce because of marital complications and young people deal with troubles less readily and divorce sooner. Knowledge and experience prevent divorce. Magnifying this is that military people tend to marry earlier than their civilian peers—a group that is currently marrying for the first time around thirty years of age for males. Additionally, deployments contributed to divorces during the GWOT in the U.S. military.[27]

My recommendation is radical but practical. I suggest that the U.S. military prohibit service members from being married and having legal-sanctioned dependents including a spouse, children, or other family members during their initial enlistment—typically their first three to four years. Moreover, they must reside in the barracks on the post during this period. This idea is not radical or without contemporary precedence. Cadets and midshipmen at U.S. military academies and military preparatory schools domiciled in the constituency of academies cannot have child dependents or a spouse. For a minimum of four (or five) years, this is stipulated by the U.S. Congress—or as stated, "Dependency. Any person for whom an individual has a legally recognized obligation to provide support, including but not limited to spouse and natural, adoptive, or stepchildren."[28] A military marriage delay (for active-duty service) would alleviate time, money, and resource stress on formal and informal support services and allow soldiers to better, exclusively, and laser focus on gaining training, education, and inspiration in their first tour in the profession of arms. Because they are more likely to marry people their own age, potential partners would have also gained some real-world independent living skills in the civilian (or military) sector. A longer courtship allows for development of social skills necessary to navigate military family life including a deployment.

Nuns and priests are prohibited from marrying. Prisoners can marry, including same-sex couples in the same or other prisons, but while conjugal visit privileges exist for all couples, they have been declining by state.

Civilian organizations might educate their deployees to self-regulate their courtships in an analogous way to gain a more professional foundation and develop oneself more holistically.

### The Fortified Nation-State

Political scientist and communication theorist Harold D. Lasswell published an important article on the garrison state in the *Journal of American Sociology* in 1941.[29] He held that the country should mobilize toward war following and during declarations of war. Not only must military service members muster for war, but the larger society should obligate to organize and share in the coming sacrifice. Unfortunately, in the rubble of the attack on the World Trade Center, the Pentagon, and a field in Pennsylvania, President George W. Bush encouraged Americans to "go shopping" and continue their normal activities, ultimately not sharing in the sacrifices of war.[30] In a more Lasswellian move, First Lady Michelle Obama and Second Lady Jill Biden leaned in and established Joining Forces with the mission "to support those who also serve: military and veteran families, caregivers, and survivors"— essentially encouraging and celebrating service families.[31]

While it is too late to legislate the past, we can learn from the spouses. What about the next time the army deploys from a post, vanquishing the military community and the accoutrements of barracks, dining facilities, and all the other services available. We could deploy college student interns to the military post. They would be students in early childhood education, recreation and leisure, family therapy, psychology, sociology, social work, etc. They could provide direct services to spouses, children, and adolescents in the community. They could serve as modern-day camp followers for a semester or a year—a gap year or semester but still earn practicum credit— as in combat service support serving those that directly serve their country. Additional housing avails if the community supports ERDing. Here we could encourage, support, and allow families to move to where they feel supported the richest. Short of universal national service (of which I am a proponent[32]), allow everyone an opportunity to oblige themselves to serve the common cause during times of major conflicts. Civilian companies might consider similar internship opportunities for their deployee families.

### Take It EASY

Make military family life accommodating for EASYs. Umpteen of the spouses I interviewed had interests in a range of areas outside the military community. Legions work in jobs and have careers. EASYs are women but can be men too. Innumerable civilian husbands opted not to be interviewed when I showed up in their community. Probably because they are seasoned and selfless and not in need of the formal services provided by the military. Scores are prior military service members. Much of this is an outgrowth of a larger percentage of career women professionals in the military. The military could use more EASYs—more women like these men and increasingly spouses like the EASYs interviewed in this book. EASYs emerge with employment opportunities for military spouses on or near military communities, more so if they are fulfilling enough to hold even during a deployment with children. The increase in working from home and not being colocated with coworkers in the post-COVID world seems deliberately conducive for military spouses.[33]

Along these lines, army posts are mostly located in rural communities away from the largest portion of the U.S. population centers. The army should establish or move army posts to urban areas and create dwell time in specific communities. EASYs are people who extricate themselves. But the community also extricates their skills, resilience, and grit to serve as a source of informal social support for others. The army should desire, encourage, and validate these free-spirited, independent, and emancipated spouses.

Civilian deployees in contrast have far more agency in how they live. Some may live in a shared community such as commercial fisher(wo)men or spouses of incarcerated people if they live near the prison facility. While others such as businesspeople, pilots, professional athletes, or migrants may not. Either way, their neighborhoods are less normatively restrained than that of the military and develop a different but shared sense of community.

## Institutional Responses

Social institutions outside of the military should share in the sacrifice of war deployment as part of garrison state. Religion, education, legal, economic, sports, transportation, mass media, and education should accommodate spouses during deployments and other forms of separation. I already noted above how college students could mobilize to help military communities during a deployment. University scholars have a history of being second or third responders. During World War II, sociologist Samuel A. Stouffer at Harvard and a bevy of social scientists mobilized to study the American soldier and the American home front.[34] Other institutions should channel their strengths, people, and resources toward the common cause and share in the sacrifices. Other countries such as Norway and Denmark have adjusted well, and their military spouses seem to fare better for it. The garrisoned state should include all her institutions not only the military.

### (De)Militarize

All the recommendations share speaking directly to militarization. Feminists have long recognized how women in and around the military become militarized.[35] In the post-9/11 military, scholars are identifying militarization among military spouses in Canada[36] and the UK,[37] including children.[38] The U.S. military needs to account for militarizing spouses and children—for relying on the free and (in)visible labor of these voluntariats and volunteerpriots. On the one hand, many spouses want to be fully committed and contribute to their service member military spouses' career and become full-fledged institutional citizens in the military organization and culture—they welcome militarization as an individual and a family. There is much evidence here that spouses wanted, desired, and did this. On the other hand, there are EASYs that resist militarization completely and still others that selectively resist. In this case they pick and choose what elements of the organization they submit to and what features they want no part of. Spouses and children do not formally swear an allegiance to the Constitution as do service members and government employees. Yet they provide a tremendous amount of in-kind service to the organization. They are de facto public servants to the military. Seeing spouses and children through the critical lens of militarization will better inform their experience. The same can be said for other occupations that create strohwitwe.

### Emulate Martha Washington at Valley Forge

Finally, consider returning to our birth as a nation. Allow spouses to visit and spend time on forward deployments. Visits might overcome loneliness and allow spouses access to their most crucial support source—the partner. My wife visited me in Europe during my sabbatical teaching and researching abroad—it recharged me to complete my projects. Army spouses and partners that met for R&R in the middle of a deployment in neutral places such as Dublin, Ireland; Berlin, Germany; or Perth, Australia, seemed as or more satisfied than when spouses came home from war. In my collaboration research with fellow sociologists Remi Hajjar and Jacob Absalon, both at West Point during the time, we found that the spouses visiting their partners in forward-deployed places such as eastern Europe seemed genuinely pleased and fulfilled with the deployment.[39]

Again, there is precedent in other separation occupations. Prisoners have visitors including conjugal visits. Long-haul truckers take their family members along.[40] Pilots fly accompanied by their family members.[41] Cruise ship workers marry one another and work the same ship. The 1.5-million-person global commercial seafarer industry could support family members aboard cargo ships but often sell the limited accommodations to travelers.[42] And of course athletes such as Olympic skiers bring their loved ones along as they traverse the planet to find snow and compete at the highest levels.

The above recommendations laid out here aside, strohwitwe are an undeniable feature of the future. The future of military and other occupational work is bipolar in terms of locale—more working from home and more concomitantly working away from home. Either way, separation is a new normal. It is my hope this book helps the reader gain a deeper appreciation for army families during an unprecedented and challenging twenty years and that it informs current and future military and civilian deployees and strohwitwe about separations.

APPENDIX

# Methods

This section provides the methods background for the study. It begins with the deployment settings of the three major overseas missions of the spouses interviewed for this book. This enables the contextualization of the military communities my research teams and I visited. Then I describe my sample of spouses followed by the research procedures, my researcher positionality and racial/ethnic, social class, and sex/gender considerations, and some study limitations. I conclude with notes on data editing, coding, and the presentations of the findings.

## Deployment Locales

On October 7, 2001, following the September 11, 2001, airplane-commandeered terrorist attacks on the World Trade Center and the Pentagon and the downing of a third flight in Pennsylvania by passengers, President George W. Bush initiated Operation Enduring Freedom as the moniker for the U.S. forces deployed to Afghanistan to locate and capture Osama bin Laden—the architect of the 9/11 attacks and who was thought to be living and hiding in Afghanistan under the Taliban. So began the GWOT. The coalition forces came to include the U.S. and the United Kingdom among roughly twenty-eight nations providing deployed personnel and another thirty including Ukraine that supplied additional forms of support. The U.S. suffered 3,590 military-uniformed fatalities in Afghanistan by the official U.S. withdrawal on August 30, 2021.

Operation Iraqi Freedom officially began with an announcement by President George W. Bush from the White House Oval Office at 10:15 on the evening of March 19, 2003. On May 1, 2003, from the deck of the aircraft carrier USS *Abraham Lincoln*, he declared the major combat operations in Iraq to be over. The war however continued with thirty-seven coalition forces providing personnel or other forms of support. By late summer 2020, the U.S had suffered 4,902 service members killed and thousands more wounded. Like Afghanistan, government-hired civilian contractors from around the world including the United States have lost their lives or were wounded in OIF and its later derivatives. A small contingent remains in Iraq at this writing.

Military exercises, training, maneuvers, and joint exercises increased quantitatively and dramatically in eastern Europe.[1] American troops for the first time since the end of the Cold War began increasing their presence in the Baltic region including Lithuania, Poland, Estonia, and Latvia and other Baltic countries.[2] Thousands of U.S. and other multinational forces began moving in and out of these countries with deployments ranging from two weeks to one year. Soldiers with more than one term of service (three to five years typically) had deployments supporting GWOT missions. Now they and their spouses pivot toward other missions requiring separations. In March 2023 the military permanently assigned the first U.S. soldiers in Poland, a year almost to the day following the unprovoked Russian invasion of Ukraine.

## Spouse Interview Sample Participants

Both alone and heading up small three-to-seven-person research teams, I visited three geographically salient regions and specific military posts army spouses lived on or near with their uniformed husbands (see appendix table 1). In most cases, the latter had deployed or were deployed to Iraq and/or Afghanistan at the time of the interview: (a) twice to a large army post in the southeastern United States in the spring of 2003 (n = 35); (b) a large army post in the southwestern United States in the fall of 2004 (n = 20); (c) five military communities in Germany during the summer of 2008 (n = 83); and (d) a military community in Germany in the spring of 2018 (n = 11) totaling 149 formal transcribed semi-structured interviews across seven military communities in two countries over fifteen years. Another 50 informal, unstructured interviews occurred during all the study locales and buttress the findings (n = 199). These latter 50 are not included in the table. In addition, I or my team members met with key people in each locale including commanders, schoolteachers, casualty affairs leaders, Red Cross workers, and other people familiar with the community.

From the appendix table 1, rank of the military spouse and if and how many children were asked directly. Most of the ranks of the soldiers are enlisted (n = 77) but officers are overrepresented at just under half (n = 67) although they comprise 15 percent of the U.S. active forces. Typically, the difference between an officer and enlisted soldier is a four-year undergraduate college/university degree and training such as ROTC or a military academy attendance prior to first enlistment. Ranks range from privates to colonels. Officer spouses are overrepresented because officers and their spouses serve as gatekeepers and guides to military units and provide access to the spouses of the rank and file. Further, they lead FRGs and are thus more available and visible during the research-team visits.

More than half of the sample had more than one child. Number of children ranged from none to seven and from pregnancies to college-age children. Military couples tend to have slightly more children and have them earlier than U.S. civilian peers. All the other interviewee demographics originated from the interviewer identifying the spouse by race/ethnicity or sex, hometown, prior service, and a paid or nonpaid employment role. These emerged organically during the interview either directly from a prompt or given freely by the interviewee. I did find asking about hometowns of spouses living in Germany often broke the ice best and built rapport in the early phase of each interview.

Spouses are typically white women representing the overrepresentation of white men in the combat arms. Yet, spouses of color represent roughly 20 percent of the sample—a respectable but slightly underrepresented group—and there may be more but we sometimes did not ask. Again, I identify the sex/gender and race/ethnicity of the spouse if their quote represents the theme more than adequately. A notable number were in mixed-race marriages and there are likely more (I don't want to identify any to protect their anonymity).

Ages were not asked or recorded but ranged from late teens to midfifties. Only a handful of wives reported having no deployment experience; some reported as many as ten deployments.

Overall, spouses interviewed come from all over the U.S. and abroad and some are military brats. Some wives had never lived overseas, and others had not yet been to the U.S. as an army wife living in Germany. A handful of wives had sons in the active army or reserves. One mother and wife had both a son and a husband deployed at the time of the interview. Some grew up in rural communities or large urban areas while others come from military families. Others are not U.S. citizens. Some worked for pay full- or part-time, others volunteered full- or part-time, and others said they were "stay-at-home" wives and mothers, or men with prior military service. A handful mentioned leaving paid or nonpaid part- or full-time employment to accommodate or dedicate to the deployment. Others had done combinations of some or all these statuses. Not in the table, but education levels ranged from less than high school to one staff sergeant's wife working on her PhD at a German university. Others used the deployment to work on degrees. One was active-duty army and non-deployable. Some had prior military service including

**Appendix Table 1. Sample: Formal spouse interview participants (*n* = 149)**

| Rank of spouse soldier | No. of children | Hometown | Race/ethnicity | Prior service | Sex | Other |
|---|---|---|---|---|---|---|
| Southeastern United States, 2003 | | | | | | |
| Specialist | None | Unknown | White | | F | |
| Captain | 2 | Unknown | White | | F | FRL |
| Chief Warrant Officer 2 | 2 | Military Brat | Unknown | | F | |
| Sergeant | 2 | Maine | White | | F | |
| Unknown | 2 | Unknown | Unknown | | F | |
| Captain | 1 | Florida | White | | F | |
| Specialist | Unknown | Unknown | White | | F | |
| Private First Class | 1 + pregnant | Alabama | White | | F | |
| Captain | Pregnant | Unknown | White | | F | |
| Junior Enlisted | 1 | Unknown | White | | F | |
| Senior NCO | 2 | Unknown | White | | F | FRL |
| Sergeant First Class | 2 | Unknown | White | | F | FRL |
| Private | 1 | Military Brat | White | | F | |
| Junior Enlisted | 3 + pregnant | Unknown | White | | F | |
| Senior NCO | 6 | Wisconsin | White | | F | |
| Specialist | 2 | Unknown | Latinx/ Hispanic American | Yes | F | Military |
| Major | 2 | Unknown | White | | F | FRL |
| Chief Warrant Officer 2 | 2 | Unknown | White | | F | |
| Second Lieutenant | None | Unknown | White | | F | |
| Second Lieutenant | None | Unknown | White | | F | |
| Sergeant | 2 | Unknown | White | | F | |
| Captain | 1 | Unknown | White | Yes | F | |
| Staff Sergeant | 2 | Unknown | African American | | F | |
| Staff Sergeant | 1 | England | White | | F | |
| Private First Class | None | California | White | | F | |
| Warrant Officer 1 | 4 | Unknown | White | | F | Teacher |
| Senior NCO | 1 | Unknown | White | | F | |
| Warrant Officer 1 | 4 | California | White | | F | |
| Warrant Officer 1 | 1 | Florida | White | | F | |
| Staff Sergeant | 3 | Unknown | White | | F | |
| Captain | 2 | Trinidad | African American | | F | |
| Specialist | 2 | Germany | White | | F | |
| Sergeant | 3 | Unknown | White | | F | |
| Specialist | Pregnant | Unknown | White | | F | |
| Unknown | 1 | Unknown | White | | F | |
| Southwestern United States, 2004 | | | | | | |
| Sergeant | Unknown | Unknown | White | | F | |
| Master Sergeant | Unknown | Unknown | African American | | F | |
| Captain | None | Unknown | White | | F | |

| Rank of spouse soldier | No. of children | Hometown | Race/ethnicity | Prior service | Sex | Other |
|---|---|---|---|---|---|---|
| Unknown | Unknown | Unknown | White | | F | |
| Sergeant | Pregnant | Military Brat | White | Yes | F | |
| Specialist | None | California | White | | F | |
| Master Sergeant | 2 | Georgia | White | | F | |
| Captain | 2 | Unknown | White | | F | |
| Specialist | Unknown | Unknown | White | Yes | F | FRL |
| Staff Sergeant | 2 | New York | White | | F | FRL |
| Enlisted | 1 | Unknown | White | | F | |
| Enlisted | 1 | Germany | White | | F | |
| Sergeant | 1 | Unknown | White | | F | |
| Captain | 2 | Unknown | White | | F | FRL |
| Colonel | 2 | Unknown | White | | F | Teacher |
| Sergeant Major | 2 | Military Brat | White | | F | |
| Lieutenant Colonel | 3 | Unknown | White | | F | |
| Master Sergeant | Unknown | Unknown | White | | F | |
| Enlisted | Unknown | Unknown | Latinx/ Hispanic American | | F | |
| Lieutenant Colonel | 3 | Unknown | White | | F | |

## Germany, 2008

| Rank of spouse soldier | No. of children | Hometown | Race/ethnicity | Prior service | Sex | Other |
|---|---|---|---|---|---|---|
| Lieutenant Colonel | 3 | Georgia | White | | F | |
| Lieutenant Colonel | 2 | Connecticut | White | | M | |
| Enlisted | 2 | Louisiana | White | Yes | F | |
| Sergeant First Class | 3 | Military Brat | Puerto Rican American | | F | |
| Staff Sergeant | 2 | Arizona | White | | F | |
| Senior NCO | 2 | Arizona | White | | F | |
| Specialist | 1 | Texas | White | | F | |
| Captain | 2 | Germany | White | | F | |
| Lieutenant Colonel | 3 | Washington | White | | F | |
| Sergeant First Class | 3 | Texas | White | | F | |
| Lieutenant Colonel | 3 | New Zealand | White | | F | |
| Senior Officer | Unknown | Unknown | White | | F | |
| First Lieutenant | None | Kentucky | White | | F | |
| Sergeant | 1 | Illinois | White | Yes | F | |
| Lieutenant Colonel | None | Texas | Mexican American | | F | |
| Captain | 1 | Wyoming | White | | F | |
| Second Lieutenant | 1 | Texas | White | | F | |
| Staff Sergeant | 1 | Germany | Latinx/ Hispanic American | | F | |
| Private First Class | 1 | Virginia | White | | F | |
| Lieutenant Colonel | None | Michigan | White | Yes | F | |
| Specialist | 2 | Hawai'i | Native American | | F | |

*(continues)*

Appendix Table 1. Sample: Formal spouse interview participants (*n* = 149) (*continued*)

| Rank of spouse soldier | No. of children | Hometown | Race/ethnicity | Prior service | Sex | Other |
|---|---|---|---|---|---|---|
| Staff Sergeant | None | Military Brat | White | | F | |
| Specialist | None | Romanian | White | | F | |
| Sergeant | None | Portugal | White | | F | |
| First Lieutenant | None | California | White | | F | |
| Staff Sergeant | None | California | White | | F | |
| Staff Sergeant | 3 | New York | White | | F | |
| Captain | 2 + pregnant | Germany | White | | F | |
| Staff Sergeant | 2 | Philippines | Filipino American | | F | |
| Master Sergeant | 7 | Washington | White | | F | |
| Warrant Officer 1 | None | Scotland | White | Yes | F | |
| Sergeant First Class | 2 | New York | White | | F | |
| Lieutenant Colonel | 2 | South Dakota | White | | F | |
| Chief Warrant Officer 2 | 3 | California | African American | | F | |
| Lieutenant Colonel | 2 | Texas | Latinx/ Hispanic American | | F | Counselor |
| First Lieutenant | None | Illinois | White | | F | |
| Sergeant First Class | 2 | Washington | White | Yes | M | |
| Sergeant First Class | 1 | Military Brat | White | | F | Gov't Svs. |
| First Lieutenant | None | Louisiana | White | | F | |
| Sergeant | 3 | Wash., DC | African American | | M | |
| Colonel | 2 | Georgia | African American | | F | |
| Second Lieutenant | None | Illinois | Latinx/ Hispanic American | | F | |
| Captain | 1 | Pennsylvania | White | | F | |
| Specialist | 2 | Alabama | White | | F | |
| Specialist | 1 | New Mexico | Native American | | F | |
| Lieutenant Colonel | 1 | Texas | White | | F | |
| Sergeant Major | 3 | Michigan | White | Yes | F | |
| Lieutenant Colonel | 2 | Maryland | White | | F | |
| Captain | None | Illinois | White | | F | |
| Captain | 1 + pregnant | Ohio | White | | F | |
| Specialist | Pregnant | Kentucky | White | | F | |
| Sergeant | 1 + pregnant | Georgia | White | | F | |
| Warrant Officer 1 | 1 | New Jersey | Latinx/ Hispanic American | Yes | F | |
| Sergeant | 2 | California | White | Yes | M | |
| Captain | 2 | Colorado | White | | F | |

| Rank of spouse soldier | No. of children | Hometown | Race/ethnicity | Prior service | Sex | Other |
|---|---|---|---|---|---|---|
| Unknown | 2 | Arkansas | White | Yes | F | |
| Staff Sergeant | 4 | California | White | | F | |
| Staff Sergeant | 2 | Indiana | White | Yes | F | |
| Major | 4 | Kentucky | African American | | F | |
| Corporal | 3 | Texas | White | | F | |
| Master Sergeant | 1 | Florida | White | Yes | F | |
| Sergeant | 2 | Tennessee | White | | F | |
| Captain | 4 | New Hampshire | White | | F | |
| Captain | 1 | North Carolina | African American | | M | |
| Sergeant | 1 | Ohio | White | | F | |
| Junior Officer | 1 | Oregon | White | | F | |
| Warrant Officer 1 | 2 | Military Brat | Asian American | | F | |
| Sergeant | 1 + pregnant | North Carolina | White | | F | |
| Sergeant | 1 | Oregon | Latinx/ Hispanic American | | F | |
| Captain | 2 | Florida | White | | F | |
| Sergeant First Class | 2 | Germany | White | | F | |
| Major | 3 | Military Brat | White | | F | |
| Major | 2 | New York | White | | F | |
| Master Sergeant | 3 | Tennessee | Unknown | | F | Nurse |
| Enlisted | 4 | Germany | Cuban American | | F | |
| Sergeant | 1 + pregnant | Indiana | Latinx/ Hispanic American | Yes | F | |
| Sergeant Major | 3 | Montana | White | Yes | F | |
| Captain | 3 | Military Brat | White | Yes | F | |
| Captain | 4 | Minnesota | White | | F | |
| Captain | 3 | Illinois | White | | F | |
| Captain | 2 | Military Brat | White | | F | |
| Senior Officer | 4 | Military Brat | White | | F | |
| Chief Warrant Officer 3 | 2 | Texas | Mexican American | | F | |

**Germany, 2018**

| Rank of spouse soldier | No. of children | Hometown | Race/ethnicity | Prior service | Sex | Other |
|---|---|---|---|---|---|---|
| Colonel | 4 | Florida | White | | F | |
| Sergeant Major | 2 | Military Brat | Puerto Rican American | | F | |
| Lieutenant Colonel | 3 | Florida | White | | F | |
| Sergeant | 1 | Pennsylvania | White | | F | FRL |
| Staff Sergeant | 2 | New York | Dominican American | | F | Legal Aid |
| Chief Warrant Officer 3 | 4 | Wyoming | White | | F | |

(*continues*)

Appendix Table 1. Sample: Formal spouse interview participants (*n* = 149) *(continued)*

| Rank of spouse soldier | No. of children | Hometown | Race/ethnicity | Prior service | Sex | Other |
|---|---|---|---|---|---|---|
| Captain | None | Kansas | White | | F | |
| Captain | None | Minnesota | White | | F | |
| Major | 4 | Utah | White | | F | |
| Captain | None | Ohio | White | | F | |
| Staff Sergeant | 2 | Maine | White | Yes | F | |

husbands of military wives. Family backgrounds varied. Still others were on second or third marriages and/or made up reconstituted families.

We did not ask about LGBTQ+ status as DADT lifted in 2011 and the transgender ban in 2016 only to be repealed in 2017 and lifted again in 2021. No 2018 wives shared their sexual orientation or gender status that year. We interviewed exclusively spouses who were recognized as legal dependents. I did this for a host of reasons including access and availability. Although, both non-married partners significant to soldiers could be as high as 25 percent of the force added to just over 50 percent married.[3] LGBTQ+ partners could comprise a high single digit percentage.

### Research Procedures

An opening to interview army wives (combat units prohibited women serving at the time) associated with the initial Iraq invasion presented itself as the U.S. prepared to invade Iraq.[4] We acted expeditiously in anticipation of a short war in Iraq not unlike the one-hundred-hour Persian Gulf War with Iraq two decades early. Spouses were contacted via telephone and email prior to our arrival and others once in the community. Subsequent interview locales involved a similar procedure. Interviews took place at the spouses' convenience. Recruitment rarely proved problematic, albeit recruiting spouses at the lower ranks required extra effort. A rental vehicle and living in the community on the post in guest quarters or with friends in the local military community provided around-the-clock access. I remained flexible for interviews and as a result was able to interview in homes on and off the military post, in cafés and restaurants on and off the post, using FRG facilities on the post, at work locations of the spouses such as the local high school or the on-post thrift store, in the military on-post library, at the community club bar, in unit barracks dayrooms, and in the military commander's offices associated with the military units. Most interviews had one interviewer. Some interviews included an interviewer and a note taker or child caretaker. Other interviews included multiple spouses, and some had children present either in the room or an adjacent room.

Interviews ranged from thirty to ninety minutes with most taking about sixty minutes to complete. Most interviews involved the use of audiotape or digital recording, but many utilized handwritten notes. All of the formal interviews have been transcribed, and original audio files and handwritten notes have been destroyed. Transcribed interviews were de-identified and collated into original Word document files for each of the military communities visited. The four periods of data collection in seven different communities (twice in the same community) yielded a varied number of single-spaced interview notes. The final project total yielded 2,015 single-spaced pages of interview transcriptions and notes at 736,125 words.

Each interview transcription includes the questions and comments by the interviewer and the responses of the interviewee. All the transcribed interviews utilize a semi-structured interview protocol. The remaining 50 informal, unstructured interviews result from impromptu tête-à-têtes—spontaneous situations. Each interview guide varied only slightly based on the time, experience, and locale of the community.

### Researcher Positionality and Ethical Considerations

I am a white, straight, cisgender male whose age varied from early forties to midfifties over the course of the study. I am not a veteran and received no designated research grants for the project.[5] But I am a military sociologist and grew up in an enlisted army family and thus I know my way around army communities. More notably, as a tenured faculty member with institutionally sanctioned academic freedom at West Point, the United States Military Academy in New York, during the study, I can pursue topics worthy of study and within the parameters of my discipline. I made no attempt to take the easier road of "good news" at the expense of the harder "bad news" as military family scholar Walter R. Schumm and colleagues refer to as dilemmas in our craft.[6] I did capitalize on substantial credibility and trust with many senior-level officer wives—many of whose husbands are West Point graduates and who themselves had met and dated their husbands at West Point. Further, members of my research team were affiliated with West Point as officers, officer spouses, and cadets, and this provided greater direct access and entry into the community.

This insider status offers a few important stratagems for conducting successful qualitative research in military communities including gaining access, developing rapport and trust, and possessing subcultural knowledge and experience of research subjects.[7] Further, I grew up in a military family and my intimate familiarity with Germany—having lived there as a child and in my youth and being fluent in the language, provided additional trust and credibility with my respondents. Finally, I have been to Iraq with deployed soldiers, adding even further insider social capital to my status—especially with the group whose husbands I had interviewed for another project in Iraq.

I recognize the contradiction here. What provided me access may inhibit interviewing. The hegemonic social capital I just noted can work in the reverse—once I gain access, I need to flip the switch to conduct the research—to subordinate my status with my people. As noted by Portuguese social scientists Helena Carreiras and Ana Alexandre quoting Joan Neff Gurney: "[T]he same characteristics which work to the researcher's advantage in terms of gaining access may become liabilities when the focus shifts to establishing and maintaining rapport with respondents."[8] I was cognizant of this bias.

On the other hand, my West Point status may alienate some spouses, especially working-class enlisted spouses due to my educational status or my insider rather than outsider status. I compensated by dressing down, wearing jeans or sport khakis and a button-down shirt with walking shoes. I wore reading glasses, have a low cropped beard, and carried a collegiate backpack—what my wife calls a "lumberjack chic" style reflecting more a stereotypical journalist-vibe than a stereotyped East Coast professor (liberal elite) or West Point–affiliated academic.

I was reflexive about my manners, attempting to be humble, approachable, and nonthreatening. I opened the interviews with small talk and explained my role, sociology, and the project. In a conservative organization such as the military, trust is exceptionally important at multiple levels—at the individual level, the unit level to include the chain of military command, the national level, and even the international level. Further, the military organization is gendered, and the gender of the researcher and the researched is likely to be more pronounced in these contexts.[9] The former protecting the subject but the latter hyper suspicious not only of compromising operational security but of the feeling that spouses represent the country to our international partners and enemies. The snowball sampling had an a priori dimension and helped filter respondents. However, being an older male may have fulfilled traditional gender role expectations for some women and fostered more openness than if I were a young woman or a person of color. Ironically, I suspect this might be the opposite when an interviewee is male.

One male subject with a deployed wife proved particularly hostile toward me and the research project, questioning my credentials and the research project more generally.

Finally, I consciously sought to interview in neutral, public spaces as a male interviewing primarily women—younger women, many of whom are separated from their husbands. At the same time, the public setting needed to be intimate enough to assure privacy and eliminate ambient noise while recording when possible. Some situations did not facilitate audiotaping or even interviewing. I would typically simply deep hang-out with a spouse or more often multiple spouses in situ and engage in our tête-à-tête. These group situations typically occurred in homes; before, during, and after FRG meetings; in parking lots and parks; at community clubs; and in restaurants, bars, and coffeehouses. Many spouses who did not want to be interviewed formally, feeling they had nothing unique to share, facilitated access to others, or simply wanted interview time given to others. In these cases, I took detailed notes later, each evening in my lodging quarters. In many cases, I had research associates and men and women assistants in the field and in the interviews functionally taking notes and/or accommodating children.

All the names used for subjects are pseudonyms and, in some cases, additional fictitious names are used for people, places, and things such as unit identifiers. Pseudonyms randomly represent and humanize spouses with a goal of providing a name that is easily recognizable and can be recalled for the subject throughout the book. The names do correspond to the sex of the respondent and their ethnicity should the name call for it. Military ranks and names of military support services remain the same as they are generic and not associated with any one post or another. The different studies received IRB clearance status from my host institution and when accessible, courtesy permissions from unit commanders to study the spouses of their soldiers.

## Limitations

There are limitations connected to this study. First, the study relies on a qualitative design. By such standards, the project orients toward a depth of understanding rather than generalization. Where quantitative studies seek commonality or integration around the mean of responses and similarity among respondents with an orientation toward generalization, qualitative research seeks out difference, indeed more fragmentation.[10] The reader should avoid generalizing beyond the units, the posts, the broader army, the military more generally, and other militaries around the world. However, the reader can focus on the depth of experiences, the voices of the respondents, and the windows to their world. Second, as I have noted above, there is an overrepresentation of voices of senior military officers and NCOs and fewer junior-ranked officers and enlisted service members. Moreover, there is focus on those more career oriented than noncareer oriented.

Third, women are overrepresented in the study. While there are a multitude of civilian husbands of military women (and men) in the military and the army specifically, few became available for the present study.[11] There are serious reasons for this underrepresentation. The bulk of interviews occurred before the full integration of women in combat arms units. As a result, most of the units I engaged with were almost exclusively comprised of men in the combat arms. And military-affiliated LGBTQ+ restrictions loomed large.

Because of the access via the FRGs, I learned anecdotally that many husbands traditionally do not participate in FRGs—and would not come into our research orbit. Many military husbands, in contrast to wives, are employed full-time outside the home, decreasing availability. Moreover, they tend to be older or have prior military experience. These latter features also contribute to less FRG participation. When I directly asked the men why so few participated, they said the ones they did know had no problems, at least not worthy of sharing. They saw "no need to participate in the research" about military families and their respective challenges.

And related but more speculative, many men do not feel they need military support services or resources and that they are self-sufficient. Indeed, they may be less likely to be or feel militarized than their female peers—a subject worthy of future study. Indeed, a sizeable number of these men might be EASYs—yet another compelling reason and benefit of increasing the number and proportion of women in the military.

## Data Editing, Data Coding, and Presentation of the Findings

To be cogent and readable yet transparent, I have done cosmetic editing of quotes and interviews throughout the book. Brackets have inserted words by me to provide more clarity and readability. In some cases I spell out acronyms and define military terminology for the nonmilitary-familiar reader.

The data analyses of the interviews followed qualitative data study methods long described by sociologists.[12] I created four separate complete and de-identified master files of interviews. I read all the data files. I used three levels of coding as outlined by University of Buffalo military sociologist Brenda L. Moore—open, axial, and selective.[13] Open coding involves reading the entire text. Fortunately, using a semi-structured interview format allowed me to focus on specific sections of each interview. These sections are cut and pasted into a separate open coded file that has some tentative thematic labels—for example, "pre-deployment" or "reintegration." Once in the separate open coded file, axial coding is used. Axial coding is a preliminary technique used to create categories and subcategories within the open coded files. Examples include "shock of" or "relief for" the eventual deployment during the pre-deployment phase of the deployment cycle. Finally, selective coding is used. Selective coding involves identifying a core category or theme. A core category might be the social construction of the situation, organizational greediness, or militarization during a specific phase of the deployment.

# Notes

## Introduction

1. Morten G. Ender, "Mom Wore Combat Boots: An Autoethnography of a Military Sociologist," in *Mothers, Military and Society* (Bradford, Ontario: Demeter Press, 2018), 157–87.
2. The terms "military" and "army" are used interchangeably. The Army is a branch of the broader military that includes the Navy, the Marines, and the Air and the Space Forces.
3. For reviews of the military family literature, see Karen Rose Blaisure, Tara Saathoff-Wells, Angela Pereira, Shelley MacDermid Wadsworth, and Amy Laura Dombro, *Serving Military Families in the 21st Century* (New York: Routledge, 2012); Bradford Booth, Mady Wechsler Segal, D. Bruce Bell, James A. Martin, Morten G. Ender, David E. Rohall, and John Nelson, *What We Know about Army Families: 2007 Update* (Alexandria, VA: U.S. Army Family and Morale, Welfare and Recreation Command, 2007); Lolita M. Burrell, Gary A. Adams, Doris Briley Durand, and Carl Andrew Castro, "The Impact of Military Lifestyle Demands on Well-Being, Army, and Family Outcomes," *Armed Forces and Society* 33, no. 1 (2006): 43–58, https://doi.org/10.1177/0002764206288800; Edna J. Hunter, *Families under the Flag: A Review of Military Family Literature* (New York: Praeger, 1982); Mady Wechsler Segal, "The Nature of Work and Family Linkages: A Theoretical Perspective," in Gary L. Bowen and Dennis K. Orthner, eds., *The Organization Family: Work and Family in the U.S. Military* (New York: Praeger, 1989), 3–36; René Moelker et al., *Military Families and War in the 21st Century*, and René Moelker, Manon Andres, and Nina Rones, eds., *The Politics of Military Families: State, Work Organizations, and the Rise of the Negotiation Household* (New York: Routledge, 2019).
4. "Word of the Week: Strohwitwe," https://www.dw.com/en/strohwitwe/a-17158817.
5. See various sources translated from Finnish, "Having a Military Career and a Family—Case Study in Finnish Defense Forces," https://puolustusvoimat.fi/documents/1951210/8529440/Sotilassosiologia_Anitta-Hannola/e5901d39 -23dd-49aa-9fa2-228498d68528?_ga=2.47240869.38137946.1578300310 -913803682.1578300310; Katri Otonkorpi-Lehtoranta, "Soldiers, Work, and Family" (PhD diss., University of Tampere, 2017), https://trepo.tuni.fi/bitstream

/handle/10024/101775/978-952-03-0475-1.pdf?sequence=1&isAllowed=y.
Hanna-Leena Autio, Minna Leinonen, and Katri Otonkorpi-Lehtoranta, *Work and Family Reconciliation of the Armed Forces* (University of Tampere, Finland: Labor Market Research Center, 2011), https://www.defmin.fi/files/1958/Tyon_ja_perheen_yhteensovittaminen.pdf.

6. Research in the UK shows work week away naval families share similar stressors as those involving a deployment. See Rachael Gribble, and Nicola T. Fear, "Living Separately during the Week: Influences on Family Functioning, Health, and Well-being of UK Naval Families," *Journal of Military, Veteran and Family Health* 8, no. 2 (2022): 82–93, https://doi.org/10.3138/jmvfh-2021-0062.

7. Manon Van der Heijden, *Women and Crime in Early Modern Holland*, trans. David McKay (Leiden and Boston: Brill, 2016), 98.

8. For a cultural description, see Rochelle Kopp, "Why Do Many Japanese Businesspeople Live Apart from Their Family? Tanshinfunin," *Japan Cultural Consulting*, February 11, 2012, https://www.japanintercultural.com/en/news/default.aspx?newsID=246. For research on the topic, see Yuko Tanaka and Jun Nakazawa, "Job-Related Temporary Father Absence (Tanshinfunin) and Child Development," in *Applied Developmental Psychology: Theory, Practice, and Research from Japan* (Greenwich, CT: Information Age Publishing, 2005), 241–60. For early insights comparing children of deployed Canadian service members to the Japanese Tanshinfunin, see Chok C. Hiew, "Separated by Their Work: Families of Fathers Living Apart," *Environment and Behavior* 24, no. 2 (1992): 206–25, https://doi.org/10.1177/00113916592242004.

9. Erella Grassiani, *Soldiering under Occupation: Processes of Numbing among Israeli Soldiers in the Al-Aqsa Intifada* (New York: Berghahn Books, 2013), 30–31.

10. There is no disrespect here to actual widows and widowers. Thousands of U.S. military fatalities occurred in Iraq and Afghanistan. Actual numbers are difficult to come by. Roughly half of U.S. Army service members were legally married, and approximately another 25 percent had others who were significant to them as partners. With 8,492 U.S. military fatalities in Iraq and Afghanistan as of Valentine's Day 2022, there were roughly 6,369 U.S. military—affiliated widows and widowers from these two wars alone. Their experience is real. New research by sociologist Brittany King and her colleagues shows that widows of veterans have some advantages compared to their civilian peers. See Brittany M. King, Dawn C. Carr, and Miles G. Taylor, "Loneliness Following Widowhood: The Role of the Military and Social Support," *Journals of Gerontology: Series B* 76, no. 2 (2021): 403–14, https://doi.org/10.1093/geronb/gbzq164. See also Erin C. Wehrman, "'I Was Their Worst Nightmare': The Identity Challenges of Military Widows," *Death Studies* 45, no. 8 (2021): 583–93, https://doi.org/10.1080/07481187.2019.1671540.

11. Karla Mason Bergen, "Accounting for Difference: Commuter Wives and the Master Narrative of Marriage," *Journal of Applied Communication Research* 38, no. 1 (2010): 47–64, https://doi.org/10.1080/00909880903483565.

12. Defined in Brian K. Williams, Stacey C. Sawyer, and Carl M. Wahlstrom, *Marriages, Families, and Intimate Relationships: Practical Introduction* (New York: Pearson, 2017), 239. See also Judye Hess and Padma Catell, "Dual Dwelling Duos: An Alternative for Long-Term Relationships," in *Couples, Intimacy Issues, and Addiction* (New York: Routledge, 2014), 25–32; and Karen Upton-Davis and Robyn Carroll, "Living Apart Together: Is It an Effective Form of Asset Protection on Relationship Breakdown?" *Journal of Family Studies* 26, no. 1 (2020): 92–105, https://doi.org/10.1080/13229400.2017.1333446.

13. Hanna Papanek, "Men, Women and Work: Reflections on the Two-Person Career," *American Journal of Sociology* 78, no. 4 (1973): 852–72, https://www.jstor.org/stable/pdf/2776607.pdf.

14. Nijole V. Benokratis and Cheryl Buehler, *Marriage and Families: Changes, Choices, and Constraints.* 9th edition (Boston: Pearson, 2019), 107. See also Meg Wilkes Karraker and Janet R. Grochowski, *Families with Futures: A Survey of Family Studies for the 21st Century* (Mahwah, NJ: Lawrence Erlbaum Associates, Publishers, 2006), 379–80.

15. Quenby Wilcox, "Trailing Spouse vs. Accompanying Spouse: Semantics or Principle?" *Huffpost.com* (April 17, 2014), https://www.huffpost.com/entry/trailing-spouse-vs-accompanying-spouse_b_5163777?guccounter=1&guce_referrer=aHR0cHM6Ly93d3cuZ29vZ2xlLmNvbVS8&guce_referrer_sig=AQAAAMMtBu6EFUS1jGb8WyXhoQ2ciup7jpR2AoKK-h1CDd2dAU5xfog83aWnPO03JA1xNGlb1AVgXHDnAKB2vCAkTlVB6M5Fr6Zkl3Hc7xblgoSA5tJ1zgY-uyVK_eIWJJFdgYCp7FHXnLILRVlJlEkPlId23bRuEC68AX2zuYGdoqRm.

16. See Morten G. Ender, ed., *Military Brats and Other Global Nomads: Growing Up in Organization Families* (Westport, CT: Praeger, 2002), 83–85.

17. Yvonne McNulty, "'Being Dumped In to Sink or Swim': An Empirical Study of Organizational Support for the Trailing Spouse," *Human Resource Development International*, 15, no. 4 (2012): 417–34, https://doi.org/10.1080/13678868.2012.721985.

18. Pooja B. Vijayakumar and Christopher J. L. Cunningham, "Impact of Spousal Work Restrictions on Expatriates' Work Life and Overall Life Satisfaction," *International Journal of Psychology* 55, no. 6 (2020): 959–63, https://doi.org/10.1002/ijop.12655.

19. See Katherine Charsley, *Transnational Marriages: New Perspectives from Europe and Beyond* (New York: Routledge, 2012) quoted in Williams, Sawyer, and Wahlstrom, *Marriages, Families, and Intimate Relationships*, 240. See also Anne Coles and Anne-Meike Fechter, eds., *Gender and Family among Transnational Professionals* (New York: Routledge, 2008), 5.

20. Jacob Mincer, "Family Migration Decisions," *The Journal of Political Economy*, 86, no. 5 (1978): 749–73, https://www.jstor.org/stable/1828408#metadata_info_tab_contents.

21. Thomas J. Cooke, "All Tied Up: Tied Staying and Tied Migration within the United States, 1997 to 2007," *Demographic Research*, 29, no. 30 (2013): 817–36, https://doi.org/10.4054/DemRes.2013.29.30.

22. Magdalena Krieger, "Tied and Troubled: Revisiting Migration and Subsequent Employment," *Journal of Marriage and the Family* 82, no. 3 (2022): 934–52, https://doi.org/10.1111/jomf.12620.

23. See Thomas J. Cooke and Karen Speirs, "Migration and Employment among the Civilian Spouses of Military Personnel," *Social Science Quarterly* 86, no. 2 (2005): 343–55, https://doi.org/10.1111/j.0038-4941.2005.00306.x; and Rick Cooney, "Moving with the Military: Race, Class, and Gender Differences in the Employment Consequences of Tied Migration" (PhD diss., University of Maryland, 2003), 243–44.

24. Tina Tessina, *The Commuter Marriage: Keep Your Relationship Close While You're Far Apart* (New York: Simon & Schuster, 2008), 2–3.

25. Danielle J. Lindemann, "Going the Distance: Individualism and Interdependence in the Commuter Marriage," *Journal of Marriage and the Family*, 79, no. 5 (2017): 1419–34, https://doi.org/10.1111/jomf.12408. See also Danielle J. Lindemann, "Doing and Undoing Gender in Commuter Marriages," *Sex Roles*, 79 (2018): 36–49, https://doi.org/10.1007/s11199-017-0852-x.

26. Danielle J. Lindemann, *Commuter Spouses: New Families in a Changing World* (Ithaca: Cornell University Press, 2019), 7. Earlier works include Marianne A. Ferber and Jane W. Loeb, eds., *Academic Couples: Problems and Promises* (Urbana and Chicago: University of Illinois Press, 1997) and Naomi R. Gerstel and Harriet Gross, *Commuter Marriage: A Study of Work and Family* (London: Guildford Press, 1984).

27. No author, "Geographic Bachelor-ing," *Military.com*, February 10, 2014, https://www.military.com/paycheck-chronicles/2014/02/10/geographic-bachelor-ing.

28. Rod Powers, "Military Puts an End to Geographic Bachelor Program," *liveaboutdo-com* (July 10, 2019), https://www.thebalancecareers.com/army-announces-end-to-geographic-bachelors-3353934.

29. Leo R. Chavez, *Shadowed Lives: Undocumented Immigrants in American Society* (Belmont, CA: Wadsworth, 2013), 29–33.

30. Chen Hong, "Left-Behind Children as Agents: Mobile Media, Transnational Communication and the Mediated Family Gaze," in *Mobile Media and Social Intimacies in Asia. Mobile Communication in Asia: Local Insights, Global Implications* (Dordrecht: Springer, 2020), 133–51; and Earvin Charles Cabalquinto, "[Dis]connected Households: Transnational Family Life in the Age of Mobile Internet," in *Second International Handbook of Internet Research* (Dordrecht: Springer, 2020), 83–103.

31. Pajarita Charles, Luke Muentner, and Jean Kjellstrand, "Parenting and Incarceration: Perspectives on Father-Child Involvement during Reentry from Prison," *Social Service Review* 93, no. 2 (2019): 218–61, https://doi.org/10.1086/703446.

32. Anisa M. Zvonkovic, Catherine Richards Soloman, Áine M. Humble, and Margaret Manoogian, "Family Work and Relationships: Lessons from Families of Men Whose Jobs Require Travel," *Family Relations* 54, no. 3 (2005): 411–22, https://doi.org/10.1111/j.1741-3729.2005.00327.x.

33. Martin J. Roderick, "An Unpaid Labor of Love: Professional Footballers, Family Life, and the Problem of Job Relocation," *Journal of Sport and Social Issues* 36, no. 3 (2012): 317–38, https://doi.org/10.1177/0193723512445283.

34. Faye McCarthy, Lucy Budd, and Stephen Ison, "Gender on the Flightdeck: Experiences of Women Commercial Airline Pilots in the UK," *Journal of Air Transport Management* 47 (2015): 32–38, https://doi.org/10.1016/j.jairtraman.2015.04.001.

35. Molly Dunigan, Kristie L. Gore, Katherine L. Kidder, Michael Schwille, Samantha Cherney, and James Sladden, *Civilian Post-Deployment Reintegration: A Review and Analysis of Practices across Federal Agencies* (Santa Monica, CA: RAND Corp., 2020), ix–xi.

36. Janice Marie Arceneaux, James LaVelle Dickens, and Wanza Bacon, "Commissioned Corps Deployments and Family Resiliency," *Online Journal of Issues in Nursing*, 25, no. 1 (2020): 1–5, https://doi.org/10.3912/OJIN.VOI25NO01PPT70.

37. David G. Smith and Mady Wechsler Segal, "On the Fast Track: Dual Military Couples Navigating Institutional Structures," in *Visions of the 21st Century Family: Transforming Structures and Identities (Contemporary Perspectives in Family Research)*, 7 (2013): 213–53, https://doi.org/10.1108/S1530-3535(2013)0000007011.

38. Karen L. Chiao and Mariellen B. O'Brien, *Spies Wives: Stories of CIA Families Abroad* (Berkeley, CA: Creative Arts Book Company, 2001).

39. I use "I" here and throughout instead of "we," recognizing I received considerable assistance over the years throughout the projects. However, I am solely responsible for the contents here.

40. See Sasha Khokha and Asal Ehsanipour, "'Haven't Hugged My Mom in a Month': Kids of Health Care Workers Feel the Strain," *KQED.org* (April 17, 2020), https://www.kqed.org/news/11812389/havent-hugged-my-mom-in-a-month-kids-of-health-care-workers-feel-the-strain.

41. See Jorge Casillo, "Even for Athletes with Family in Tokyo, Separation Remains Part of these Olympics," *Los Angeles Times* (July 30, 2021), https://www.latimes.com/sports/olympics/story/2021-07-30/us-baseball-families-in-tokyo-olympics-separation. See also Steven Zeitchik, "For NBC, the Covid Olympics will be a Feat of Strange Movements and Remote Mystery," *The Washington Post* (July 23, 2021), https://www.washingtonpost.com/business/2021/07/23/nbc-olympics-broadcast/.

42. See Chico Harlan, "In a War of Terrible Choices, These Are the Fighting-age Men Who Left Ukraine," *Washington Post* (March 9, 2022), https://www.washingtonpost.com/world/2022/03/09/ukraine-men-leave/.

43. Office of the Assistant Chief of Staff for Installation Management, "Military Family Month," *army.mil* (November 5, 2018), https://www.army.mil/standto/archive_2018-11-05/?s_cid=standto.

44. McCarthy, "Gender on the Flightdeck," 32–38.

45. See William Marsiglio, Kevin Roy, and Greer Litton Fox, "Situated Fathering: A Spatially Sensitive and Social Approach," in *Situated Fathering: A Focus on*

*Physical and Social Spaces* (Lanham, MD: Rowman and Littlefield, 2005), 7. Situated mothering is less prevalent in the literature. When it is found, "absence" takes on other meanings such as dementia and death. See Frances Greenslade, ed., *Absent Mothers* (Bradford, Ontario: Demeter Press, 2017), 1–7.

46. Jeremy P. Sayers and Greer Litton Fox, "The Haunted Hero: Fathering Profiles of Long-Haul Truckers," in *Situated Fathering*, 119–39 and Zvonkovic et al., "Family Work and Relationships," 411–22.

47. Beth S. Catlett, Michelle L. Toews, and Patrick C. McKenry, "Nonresidential Fathers: Shifting Identities, Roles, and Authorities," in *Situated Fathering*, 99–117.

48. Kevin Roy, "Nobody Can Be a Father Here: Identity Construction and Institutional Constraints on Incarcerated Fatherhood," in *Situated Fathering*, 119–39.

49. Eyal Ben-Ari and Yagil Levy, "Getting Access to the Field: Insider/Outsider Perspectives," in Joseph Soeters, Patricia M. Shields, and Sebastiaan Rietjens, eds., *The Routledge Handbook of Research Methods in Military Studies* (London: Routledge, 2014), 9–18.

50. See Benjamin R. Karney and John S. Crown, *Families under Stress: An Assessment of Data, Theory, and Research on Marriage and Divorce in the Military* (Santa Monica, CA: RAND Corp., 2007), 9–27; and Sarah O. Meadows, Terri Tanielian, Benjamin Karney, Terry Schell, Beth Ann Griffin, Lisa H. Jaycox, Esther M. Friedman, Thomas E. Trail, Robin Beckman, Rajeev Ramchand, Natalie Hengstebeck, Wendy M. Troxel, Lynsay Ayer, and Christine Anne Vaughan, *The Deployment Life Study* (Santa Monica, CA: RAND Corp., 2017), 70–74. See also Hamilton I. McCubbin, and Barbara B. Dahl, "Prolonged Family Separation in the Military: A Longitudinal Study," in *Families in the Military System* (Beverly Hills, CA: Sage, 1976), 112–44 and Cale Palmer, "A Theory of Risk and Resilience Factors in Military Families," *Military Psychology*, 20, no. 3 (2008): 205–17, https://doi.org/10.1080/08995600802118858; Gary L. Bowen, James A. Martin, and Jay A. Mancini, "The Resilience of Military Families: Theoretical Perspectives" in *Handbook of Family Theories: A Content-Based Approach* (New York: Routledge/Taylor & Francis Group, 2013), 417–36; Katherine S. Sullivan, "An Application of Family Stress Theory to Clinical Work with Military Families and Other Vulnerable Populations," *Clinical Social Work Journal* 43 (2015): 89–97, https://doi.org/10.1007/s10615-014-0500-7.

51. Reuben Hill, "Generic Features of Families under Stress," *Social Casework*, 39, no. 2–3 (1958) 139–50, https://doi.org/10.1177/1044389458039002-318.

52. See Blaisure et al., *Serving Military Families in the 21st Century*, 81–99; and Elaine Willerton, Shelley McDermid, and David Riggs, "Introduction: Military Families under Stress: What We Know and What We Need to Know," in *Risk and Resilience in U.S. Military Families* (New York: Springer, 2011), 1–20.

53. Michael D. Matthews, *Head Strong: How Psychology is Revolutionizing War* (New York: Oxford University Press, 2020), 86.

54. Mady Wechsler Segal, "The Military and the Family as Greedy Institutions," *Armed Forces and Society*, 13, no. 1 (1986): 9–38, https://doi.org/10.1177

/0095327X8601300101 and Mady Wechsler Segal, "Nature of Work and Family Linkages," in Bowen and Orthner, *Organization Family*, 3–36.

55. See Lewis A. Coser, *Greedy Institutions: Patterns of Undivided Commitment* (New York: The Free Press, 1974), 4.

56. See Amanda Barrett Cox, "Mechanisms of Organizational Commitment: Adding Frames to Greedy Institution Theory," *Sociological Forum*, 31, no. 3 (2016): 685–708, https://doi.org/10.1111/socf.12269.

57. See Booth et al., *What We Know about Army Families*, 24–28.

58. Karin De Angelis, David G. Smith, and Mady W. Segal, "Military Families: A Comparative Perspective," in *Handbook of the Sociology of the Military* (Cham, Switzerland: Springer, 2018), 341–57; Mady W. Segal, Michelle D. Lane, and Ashley G. Fisher (2015), "Conceptual Model of Military Career and Family Life Course Events, Intersections, and Effects on Well-being," *Military Behavioral Health* 3, no. 2 (2015): 95–107, https://doi.org/10.1080/21635781.2015.1009212.

59. Two examples are Lisa Ellen Silvestri, *Friended at the Front: Social Media in the American War Zone* (Lawrence: University of Kansas Press, 2015) and Michael Craig Musheno and Susan M. Ross, *Deployed: How Reservists Bear the Burden of Iraq* (Ann Arbor: University of Michigan Press, 2008).

60. René Moelker, Nina Rones, and Manon Andres, "Introduction: The Politics of Military Families and the Rise of the Negotiated Household—Tensions Between the State, Work, and Families," in *The Politics of Military Families: State, Work Organizations, and the Rise of the Negotiation Household* (New York: Routledge, 2019), 3–18.

61. See René Moelker and Manon Andres, "Epilogue: Dating from a Distance. Love and Separation in a Networked Society," in *The Politics of Military Families: State, Work Organizations, and the Rise of the Negotiation Household* (New York: Routledge, 2019), 324–32.

62. Karin De Angelis and Mady Wechsler Segal, "Transitions in the Military and the Family as Greedy Institutions: Original Concept and Current Applicability," in Moelker et al., *Military Families and War in the 21st Century*, 22–42.

63. Moelker et al., *The Politics of Military Families*; and Moelker et al., *Military Families and War in the 21st Century*.

64. Cynthia Enloe, *Maneuvers: The International Politics of Militarizing Women's Lives* (Berkeley: University of California Press, 2000), 3.

65. Roberto J. González, "Beyond the Human Terrain System: A Brief Critical History (and a Look Ahead)," *Contemporary Social Science* 15, no. 2 (2020), 227–40, https://doi.org/10.1080/21582041.2018.1457171.

66. Donna Alvah, *Unofficial Ambassadors: American Military Families Overseas and the Cold War* (New York: New York University Press, 2007), 81–82.

67. D'Ann Campbell, "Women's Lives in Wartime: The American Civil War and World War II," in *Life-Course Perspectives on Military Service* (New York: Routledge, 2013), 48–67.

68. Daniel Burland and Jennifer Hickes Lundquist, "The Best Years of Our Lives: Military Service and Family Relationships—A Life-Course Perspective," in *Life-Course Perspectives on Military Service* (New York: Routledge, 2013), 165–84.

69. See Cynthia Enloe, Anita Lacey, and Thomas Gregory, "Twenty-Five Years of *Bananas, Beaches, and Bases:* A Conversation with Cynthia Enloe," *Journal of Sociology* 52, no. 3 (2016): 537–50, https://doi.org/10.1177/1440783316655635.

70. See Cynthia Enloe, "Flick of the Skirt: A Feminist Challenge to IR's Coherent Narrative," *International Political Sociology* 10, no. 4 (2016): 320–31, https://doi.org/10.1093/ips/olw017.

71. See Alexandra Hyde, "The Civilian Wives of Military Personnel: Mobile Subjects or Agents of Militarisation?," in *The Palgrave International Handbook of Gender and the Military* (London: Palgrave Macmillan, 2017), 195–209.

72. Victoria M. Basham and Sergio Catignani, "War Is Where the Hearth Is: Gendered Labor and the Everyday Reproduction of the Geopolitical in the Army Reserves," *International Feminist Journal of Politics* 20, no. 2 (2018): 153–71, https://doi.org/10.1080/14616742.2018.1442736.

73. Cristina Rodrigues da Silva, "Military Families: Social Organization and Remote Basing Experiences for Brazilian Military Families" in *The Palgrave International Handbook of Gender and the Military* (London: Palgrave Macmillan, 2017), 211–26.

74. Kenneth T. MacLeish, *Making War at Fort Hood: Life and Uncertainty in a Military Community* (Princeton, NJ: Princeton University Press, 2013), 151–52.

75. See Harriet Gray, "Domestic Abuse and the Reproduction of the Idealised 'Military Wife,'" in *The Palgrave International Handbook of Gender and the Military* (London: Palgrave Macmillan, 2017), 227–40.

76. See Leigh Spanner, "Resilient and Entrepreneurial Military Spouses: Neoliberalization Meets Militarization," *Critical Military Studies* 8, no. 3 (2022): 233–53, https://doi.org/10.1080/23337486.2020.1815385.

77. See Gary L. Bowen, Todd M. Jensen, and James A. Martin, "Standing Strong in the Context of Organizational and Family Demands: A Measure of USAF Civilian Spouse Fitness," in Moelker et al., *Military Families and War in the 21st Century,* 211–30.

78. Emma Dalton, "Women as Helpmates: The Japan Self-Defense Forces and Gender," *Critical Military Studies* 8, no. 1 (2022): 39–57, https://doi.org/10.1080/23337486.2019.1707496 and "Normalizing the Japan Self-defense Forces via Marriage," *Journal of War and Culture Studies* 15, no. 1 (2022): 106–24, https://doi.org/10.1080/17526272.2020.1738680.

79. See Elin Gustavsen, "Constructing Meaning after War: A Study of the Lived Experiences of Norwegian Afghanistan Veterans and Military Spouses" (PhD diss., University of Oslo, 2017), 31. See also Anitta Hannola, "Relocating Military Families in Finland," in Moelker et al., *Military Families and War in the 21st Century,* 169–83; and Ann-Margreth E. Olsson and Sven-Erik Olsson, "Swedish

Families' Responses to Military Deployment," in Moelker et al., *Military Families and War in the 21st Century*, 253–66.

80. Elizabeth Ziff and Felicia Garland-Jackson, "'I'm Not your "Typical" Military Wife': The Construction of Gender and Agency through Stereotypes," *Armed Forces and Society* 46, no. 3 (2019): 376–96, https://doi.org/10.1177/0095327X1987548.

81. See Elizabeth Ziff, "'The Mommy Deployment': Military Spouses and Surrogacy in the United States," *Sociological Inquiry* 32, no. 2 (2017): 406–25, https://doi.org/10.1111/socf.12336, and Elizabeth Ziff, "'Honey, I Want to Be a Surrogate': How Military Spouses Negotiate and Navigate Surrogacy with Their Service Member Husbands," *Journal of Family Issues* 40, no. 18 (2019): 2774–2800, https://doi.org/10.1177/0192513X198628.

82. Lisa Leitz, *Fighting for Peace: Veterans and Military Families in the Anti-War Movement* (Minneapolis: University of Minnesota Press, 2014), 3–4.

83. Cited and discussed in Blaisure et al., *Serving Military Families in the 21st Century*, 48–49.

84. See Maren Tomforde, "The Emotional Cycle of the Deployment," in Moelker et al., *Military Families and War in the 21st Century*, 87–106; and Rachel E. Pye and Leanne Simpson, "Family Functioning Differences across the Deployment Cycle in British Army Families: The Perceptions of Wives and Children," *Military Medicine* 182, no. 9 (2017): e1856-e1863, https://doi.org/10.7205/MILMED-D-16-00317.

85. I also refer to the period as the Global War on Terror. I surveyed my cadets in classes, and they overwhelmingly prefer "The Global War on Terror" to "The Global War on Terrorism" for its simplicity.

86. Numerous books, articles, and documentaries are available on these groups and referenced throughout this book. For an exceptional documentary about both army reservists and their families, see *Off to War: From Rural Arkansas to Iraq*, directed by Brent Renaud and Craig Renaud (Kino International, 2005), 10 hours, https://www.imdb.com/title/tt0455986/?ref_=fn_al_tt_0.

87. For social history and demographics of the U.S. military, see David E. Rohall, Morten G. Ender, and Michael D. Matthews, eds., *Inclusion in the U.S Military: A Force for Diversity* (Lanham, MD: Lexington Books, 2017).

88. Meredith A. Kleykamp, "College, Jobs, or the Military? Enlistment during a Time of War," *Social Science Quarterly* 87, no. 2 (2006): 272–90, https://doi.org/10.1111/j.1540-6237.2006.00380.x.

89. Ziff, "'Mommy Deployment,'" 406.

90. See Aaron Belkin, *Bring Me Men: Military Masculinity and the Benign Façade of American Empire, 1989–2001* (New York: Columbia University Press, 2012), 42.

91. Kathrine S. Sullivan, Jessica Dodge, Kathleen McNamara, Rachael Gribble, Mary Keeling, Sean Taylor-Beirne, Caroline Kale, Jeremy Goldbach, Nicola T. Fear, and Carl A. Castro, "Perceptions of Family Acceptance in the Military Community among U.S. LGBT Service Members: A Mixed-Methods Study," *Journal of Military, Veteran, and Family Health* 7, no. 1 (2021), 90–101, https://doi.org/10.3138/jmvfh-2021-0019.

92. Current and past data are accessible online. See "Military One Source," *Military Community Demographics: Current Demographics Profile*, last modified October 9, 2022, https://www.militaryonesource.mil/reports-and-surveys /demographic-profiles. Typically, the DMDC lags two years in releasing data publicly—the current profile is for 2020.

93. Note that this number may not reflect "family members" not officially recognized by the military. For illustration, when I asked soldiers in 2004 their intimacy status with another person beyond the 50 percent reporting "married," another 25 percent indicated they were in an intimate relationship. See Morten G. Ender, *American Soldiers in Iraq: McSoldiers or Innovative Professionals?* (New York: Routledge, 2009), 10–11. Service members certainly have children, siblings, parents, or other next of kin or even fictive kin that are officially not recognized by the military yet under the service member's care.

94. See The Decemberists, "Sixteen Military Wives," track 7 on *Picaresque*, Kill Rock Stars, 2005, CD. For a modern film that cuts back and forth between the home and the war front and the role and emotions of the military wife. See also *American Sniper*, directed by Clint Eastwood (Warner Bros. Pictures, 2014), 2:13, https://www.imdb.com/title/tt2179136/.

95. Christie H. Burton, "Army Wives: Basic Training on the Tube," *Studies in Popular Culture* 35, no. 1 (2012): 71–89, https://www.jstor.org/stable/23416366 #metadata_info_tab_contents.

96. David Hinckley, "Married to the Army: A Routine Reality Show about the Lives of Servicemen's Wives," *NYDailynews.com* (November 10, 2012), https:// www.nydailynews.com/entertainment/tv-movies/married-army-routine-reality -show-lives-servicemen-wives-article-1.1199559.

## 1. "The Deployment before the Deployment"

1. See Leo Shane III, "Military Family Reunion Takes Center Stage at State of the Union," *Military Times* (February 4, 2020), https://www.militarytimes.com /news/pentagon-congress/2020/02/05/military-family-reunion-takes-center -stage-at-state-of-the-union/.

2. Wives are interviewed almost exclusively because of combat arms units, though husbands had wives deployed where women comprised roughly 10 percent of the boots on the ground in Iraq.

3. A "division" is an exclusive term to U.S. Army combat units. It refers to a specific echelon or size of an army unit. There are roughly ten combat divisions in the active army. Divisions are typically led by two-star generals.

4. The methods discussion in the appendix includes descriptions of the wars, the locales, and data collection procedures in more detail.

5. We assisted Dr. Munqith al-Dagher establish his Al Mustakella for Research Group (IIACSS), which conducts monthly polls of Iraqi citizens on a range of social and political issues, https://www.iiacss.org/. The group has consistently

collected data since the summer of 2004. See Munqith al-Daghar, "Iran's Influ-
ence in Iraq Is Declining: Here's Why," *Washington Post* (November 16, 2018),
https://www.washingtonpost.com/news/monkey-cage/wp/2018/11/16/irans
-influence-in-iraq-is-declining-heres-why/.

6. Steve Carlton-Ford, Morten G. Ender, and Ahoo Tabatabai, "Iraqi Adolescents:
Self-Regard, Self-derogation, and Perceived Threat in War," *Journal of Adolescence*
31, no. 1 (2008): 53–75, https://doi.org/10.1016/j.adolescence.2007.04.006.

7. Ender, *American Soldiers in Iraq*, 14–29.

8. For past and more recent reviews, see Blaisure et al., *Serving Military Families in
the 21st Century;* Booth et al., *What We Know about Army Families,* 1–9; Hunter,
*Families under the Flag;* Bowen and Orthner, *The Organization Family,* ix–xiv;
Moelker et al., *The Politics of Military Families;* and Moelker et al., *Military Families and War in the 21st Century.*

9. Family Readiness Group, or FRG, was originally known as Family Support
Group, or FSG. They serve a formal function, are command-sponsored, and
composed of family members, soldiers, and volunteers. They act most at the
company and battalion levels. A U.S. Army company is comprised of approximately 175 soldiers. Again, roughly half would be married, creating 90 spouses
per FRG. An army captain typically commands the company, and she typically
would have first lieutenants commanding the four platoons in the company—
these are the only officers with the remaining soldiers comprising the enlisted
ranks. Each company typically has a volunteer FRL. FRLs are further up the
organizational unit chart including battalion/squadron, brigade, and division
levels. Starting at the battalion/squadron level—comprising anywhere from
three to five companies, there are paid FRLs working alongside spousal FRG
volunteers. The FRG and the leader have several goals including fostering resilient families, providing a link between the unit command and each military
family, and educating families about benefits and entitlements, among others.
Paying an FRL further institutionalizes and militarizes the military spouse,
family, and family institution. FRGs are mostly face-to-face associations but
have become increasingly virtual as spouses are mobile and geographically di-
versified today. See Booth et al., *What We Know about Army Families,* 120; and
U.S. Army, *U.S. Army FRG Leader's Handbook* (4th edition) (Washington, DC:
Army Community Service, 2010), 11–13. See also Blaisure et al., *Serving Military
Families in the 21st Century,* 167–68.

10. See Amy Belasco, *Troop Levels in the Afghan and Iraq Wars, FY2001–FY2012: Cost
and Other Potential Issues* (Washington, DC: Congressional Research Service,
July 2, 2009), 9–13, https://fas.org/sgp/crs/natsec/R40682.pdf.

11. I use pseudonyms throughout the book for spouses and names that the spouses
themselves refer to in interviews such as the names of children, friends, coworkers, spouses, etc. I also use pseudonyms for places such as names of military posts.

12. Tomforde, "Emotional Cycle of the Deployment," 87–106.

13. Laura Werber Castaneda, Margaret C. Harrell, Danielle M. Varda, Kimberly Curry Hall, Megan K. Beckett, and Stefanie Stern, *Deployment Experiences of Guard and Reserve Families: Implications for Support and Retention* (Santa Monica, CA: RAND Corp., 2008), 251–52.

14. See James Hosek, Jennifer Kavanagh, and Laura Miller, *How Deployments Affect Service Members* (Santa Monica, CA: RAND Corp., 2006), 90.

15. See findings reviewed in Booth et al., *What We Know about Army Families*, 31–34.

16. See Stacy Ann Hawkins, Annie Condon, Jacob N. Hawkins, Kritine Liu, Yxsel Melendrez Ramirez, Marisa M. Nihill, and Jackson Tolins, *What We Know about Military Family Readiness: Evidence from 2006–2017* (Monterey, CA: Research Facilitation Laboratory, 2018), 99.

17. The size of a typical army brigade is three to five thousand soldiers—where brigades make up a division. About half are likely married.

18. See Blaisure et al., *Serving Military Families in the 21st Century*, 49–51.

19. Booth et al., *What We Know about Army Families*, 35–36.

20. See Rueben Hill, *Families under Stress: Adjustment to the Crises of War, Separation, and Return* (New York: Harper, 1949), 337–49.

## 2. "The Temporary Widow"

1. Booth et al., *What We Know about Army Families*, 29.

2. Ibid.

3. See Mark Thompson. "Here's Why the U.S. Military Is a Family Business," *Time.com* (March 10, 2016), https://time.com/4254696/military-family-business/.

4. The various branches of the military created a Battle Buddy system for troops. It is a comrade system where troops partner starting in basic training, encouraging team members to look out for one another's well-being. It later became applied to assist soldiers transitioning from military to civilian life. See Blaisure et al., *Serving Military Families in the 21st Century*, 104. It has since been adapted to military spouses on the home front during deployments.

5. Victoria Jennings-Kelsall, Lindsey S. Aloia, Denise H. Solomon, Amy D. Marshall, and Feea R. Leifker, "Stressors Experienced by Women within Marine Corps Families: A Qualitative Study of Discourse within an Online Forum," *Military Psychology* 24, no. 4 (2012): 363–81, https://doi.org/10.1080/08995605.2012.695255.

6. Leora N. Rosen, Doris B. Durand, and James A. Martin, "Wartime Stress and Family Adaption," in *The Military Family: A Practice Guide for Human Service Providers* (Westport, CT: Praeger, 2000), 123–38.

7. D. Bruce Bell, Jocelyn Bartone, Paul T. Bartone, Walter R. Schumm, and Paul A. Gade, *USAREUR Family Support during Operation Joint Endeavor: Summary Report* (Special Report 34) (Arlington, VA: U.S. Army Research Institute for the Behavioral and Social Sciences, 1997), 3–5.

8. S. Kerner-Hoeg, S. Baker, C. Lomvardias, and L. Towne, *Operation Restore Hope. Survey of Army Spouses at Fort Drum, New York: Survey Methodology and Data Book* (Fairfax, VA: Caliber Associates, 1993), cited in Booth et al., *What We Know about Army Families,* 31–32.

9. Survey data reported in Booth et al., *What We Know about Army Families,* 36–37.

10. D. Bruce Bell and Walter R. Schumm, "Providing Family Support during Military Deployments," in *The Military Family: A Practice Guide for Human Service Providers* (Westport, CT: Praeger, 2000), 139–52.

11. See C. J. Aducci, Joyce A. Baptist, Jayashree George, Patricia M. Barros, and Briana S. Nelson Goff, "The Recipe for Being a Good Military Wife: How Military Wives Managed OIF/OEF Deployment," *Journal of Feminist Family Therapy* 23, no. 3–4 (2011): 231–49, https://doi.org/10.1080/08952833.2011.604526. See also Booth et al., *What We Know about Army Families,* for a review; Jennifer Davis, David B. Ward, and Cheryl Storm, "The Unsilencing of Military Wives: Wartime Deployment Experiences and Citizen Responsibility," *Journal of Marriage and Family Therapy* 37, no. 1 (2001): 51–63, https://doi.org/10.1111/j.1752 -0606.2009.00154.x; and Gillian K. SteelFisher, Alan M. Zaslavsky, and Robert J. Blendon, "Health-Related Impact of Deployment Extensions on Spouses of Active Duty Army Personnel," *Military Medicine* 173, no. 3 (2008): 221–29, https://doi.org/10.7205/MILMED.173.3.221.

12. Reported in Tomforde, "Emotional Cycle of the Deployment," 87–106.

13. Christoper Dandeker, Claire Eversden, Catherine Birtles, and Simon Wessely, "The British Military Family: The Experiences of British Army Wives before, during, and after Deployment, Their Satisfaction with Military Life, and Their Use of Support Networks," in Moelker et al., *Military Families and War in the 21st Century,* 107–27.

14. Manon Andres and Julie Coulthard, "Children and Deployment: A Cross-Country Comparison," in Moelker et al., *Military Families and War in the 21st Century,* 177–90.

15. Philip Siebler, "'Down Under': Support for Military Families from an Australian Perspective," in Moelker et al., *Military Families and War in the 21st Century,* 287–301.

16. See the DMDC data reported in Blaisure et al., *Serving Military Families in the 21st Century,* 52–53.

17. Christopher H. Warner, George N. Appenzeller, Carolynn Warner, and Thomas Grieger, "Psychological Effects of Deployments on Military Families," *Psychiatric Annals* 39, no. 2 (2009): 56–63, https://doi.org/10.3928/00485713-20090201-11.

18. Emma Long describes the in-between state of liminality among UK army spouses. See Emma Long, "Living Liminal Lives: Army Partners' Spatiotemporal Experiences of Deployment," *Armed Forces and Society* 48, no. 3 (2022): 589–608, https://doi.org/10.1177/0095327X21995996.

19. I recognize there is a feminist distinction between "motherhood" and "mothering." I however allow my spouses to use the terms they prefer. For further

reading on these distinctions, I recommend the array of peer-reviewed scholarship on Motherhood Studies in Demeter Press—an independent press—at
https://demeterpress.org/.

20. See Segal, "Nature of Work and Family Linkages," 22–23. See also John P.
Hawkins, *Army of Hope, Army of Alienation: Culture and Contradiction in the
American Army Communities of Cold War Germany* (Westport, CT: Praeger,
2001). See also Alvah, *Unofficial Ambassadors*.

21. See D'Ann Campbell, "Women's Lives in Wartime: The American Civil War
and World War II," in *Life-Course Perspectives on Military Service* (New York:
Routledge, 2013), 48–67. See also Evelyn Millis Duvall, "Loneliness and the
Serviceman's Wife," *Marriage and Family Living* 7, no. 4 (1945): 77–81, https://
www.jstor.org/stable/347560#metadata_info_tab_contents.

22. Reported in Booth et al., *What We Know about Army Families*, 43–44.

23. Ibid.

24. See the chapters in David R. Segal and Mady Wechsler Segal, eds., *Peacekeepers
and Their Wives: American Participation in the Multinational Force and Observers*
(Westport, CT: Greenwood Press, 1993); Bell and Schumm, "Providing Fam-
ily Support during Military Deployments," 143–44; D. Bruce Bell and Walter R.
Schumm, "Family Adaptation to Deployments," in *Pathways to the Future: A Re-
view of Military Family Research* (Scranton, PA: Marywood University, Military
Family Institute, 1999), 109–18; and Suzanne Wood, Jacquelyn Scarville, and
Katherine K. Gravino, "Waiting Wives: Separation and Reunion among Army
Wives," *Armed Forces and Society* 21, no. 2 (1995): 217–36, https://doi.org/10.1177
/0095327X9502100204.

25. Meadows et al., *Deployment Life Study*, 139; and Christina Collins and Shelley
MacDermid Wadsworth, "Understanding Military Families: Their Characteris-
tics, Strengths, and Challenges," in *Care of Military Service Members, Veterans, and
Their Families* (Washington, DC: American Psychiatric Publishing, 2014), 23–40.

26. Anthony J. Faber, Elaine Willerton, Shelley R. Clymer, Shelley M. MacDermid,
and Howard M. Weiss, "Ambiguous Absence, Ambiguous Presence: A Qualitative Study of Military Reserve Families in Wartime," *Journal of Family Psychology* 22, no. 2 (2008): 222–30, https://doi.org/10.1037/0893-3200.22.2.222;
Joyce A. Baptist, Yvonne Amanor-Boadu, Kevin Garrett, Briana S. Nelson Goff,
Jonathan Collum, Paulicia Gamble, Holly Gurss, Erin Sanders-Hahs, Lizette
Strader, and Stephanie Wick, "Military Marriages: The Aftermath of Operation Iraqi Freedom (OIF) and Operation Enduring Freedom (OEF) Deployments," *Contemporary Family Therapy* 33, no. 3 (2011), 199–214, https://doi.org
/10.1007/s10591-011-9162-6.

27. Andres and Coulthard, "Children and Deployment," 177–90.

28. See Elin Gustavsen, "The Privatized Meaning of Wartime Deployments: Examining the Narratives of Norwegian Military Spouses," *Ethos* 45, no. 4 (2017):
514–31, https://doi.org/10.1111/etho.12176. See also Gustavsen, *Constructing
Meaning after War*.

29. Jocelyn Bartone, "Missions Alike and Unlike: Military Family Support in War and Peace," in Moelker et al., *Military Families and War in the 21st Century*, 193–209.

30. See review in Booth et al., *What We Know about Army Families*, 75. See also Dennis K. Orthner and Roderick Rose, *SAF V Survey Report: Deployment and Separation Adjustment among Army Civilian Spouses* (Chapel Hill: University of North Carolina, Army Family Development Report, 2005), 6–7, https://silo.tips/download/saf-v-survey-report-data-source.

31. See Stephanie Brooks Holliday, Amy DeSantis, Anne Germain, Daniel J. Buysse, Karen A. Matthews, and Wendy M. Troxel, "Deployment Length, Inflammatory Markers, and Ambulatory Blood Pressure in Military Couples," *Military Medicine* 182, no. 7 (2017): e1892–e1899, https://doi.org/10.7205/MILMED-D-16-00327.

32. Brighita Negrusa and Sebastian Negrusa, "Home Front: Post-Deployment Mental Health and Divorces," *Demography* 51, no. 3 (2014): 895–916, https://doi.org/10.1007/s13524-014-0294-9; and Sebastian Negrusa, Brighita Negrusa, and James Hosek, "Gone to War: Have Deployments Increased Divorces?" *Journal of Population Economics*, 27, no. 2 (2014), 473–96, https://doi.org/10.1007/s00148-013-0485-5.

33. Bonita M. Smith, Andy R. Brown, Terri Varnado, and Sarah E. Stewart-Spencer, "Deployments and Marital Satisfaction of Civilian Male Spouses," *Journal of Military and Government Counseling* 5, no. 1 (2017): 70–85, https://mgcaonline.org/wp-content/uploads/2013/02/JMGC-Vol-5-Is-1.pdf#page=73.

34. R. Blaine Everson, Carol Darling, Joseph R. Herzog, Charles R. Figley, and Dione King, "Quality of Life among U.S. Army Spouses during the Iraq War," *Journal of Family Social Work* 20, no. 2 (2016): 124–43, https://doi.org/10.1080/10522158.2017.1279578.

35. E. Trey Asbury and Danica Martin, "Military Deployment and the Spouse Left Behind," *The Family Journal: Counseling and Therapy for Couples and Families* 20, no. 1 (2012): 45–50, https://doi.org/10.1177/1066480711429433; and Kathryn E. Faulk, Christian T. Gloria, Jessica Duncan Cance, and Mary A. Steinhardt, "Depressive Symptoms among US Military Spouses during Deployment: The Protective Effect of Positive Emotions," *Armed Forces and Society* 38, no. 3 (2012): 373–90 https://doi.org/10.1177/0095327X114287.

36. Benjamin R. Karney and John S. Crown, *Families under Stress: An Assessment of Data, Theory, and Research on Marriage and Divorce in the Military* (Santa Monica, CA: RAND Corp., 2007), 165.

37. Dennis K. Orthner, Roderick Rose, and Richard Fafara, *Supporting Families during Military Separations: The Value of Formal and Informal Support* (Chapel Hill, NC: Jordan Institute for Families, 2004).

38. Diane L. Padden, Rebecca A. Connors, and Janice G. Agazio, "Stress, Coping, and Well-Being in Military Spouses during Deployment Separation," *Western Journal of Nursing Research* 33, no. 2 (2011): 247–67, https://doi.org/10.1177/0193945910371319.

39. Sandra Dursun and Kerry Sudom, "The Well-Being of Military Families: Coping with the Stress of Military Life among Spouses of Canadian Armed Forces Members," in Moelker et al., *Military Families and War in the 21st Century,* 128–44.

40. Mary Keeling, Simon Wessely, Christopher Dandeker, Norman Jones, and Nicola T. Fear, "Relationship Difficulties among U.K. Military Personnel: Impact of Sociodemographic, Military, and Deployment-Related Factors," *Marriage and Family Review* 51, no. 3 (2015): 275–303, https://doi.org/10.1080/01494929.2015.1031425.

41. Manon Andres, Gary Bowen, Philippe Manigart, and René Molker, "Epilogue," in Moelker et al., *Military Families and War in the 21st Century,* 320–30.

42. Bell and Schumm, "Providing Family Support during Military Deployments," 143–44.

43. Bartone, "Missions Alike and Unlike," 200.

44. See Christopher Dandeker, Claire French, Catherine Birtles, Simon Wessely, "Deployment Experiences of British Army Wives before, during and after Deployment: Satisfaction with Military Life and Use of Support Networks," in *Human Dimensions in Military Operations—Military Leaders' Strategies for Addressing Stress and Psychological Support,* Meeting P-HFM-134, Paper 38 (Neuilly-sur-Seine, France: RTO, 2006), 38-1-38-20, http://www.rto.nato.int/abstracts.asp.

45. Erin Sahlstein Parcell and Katheryn C. Maguire, "Turning Points and Trajectories in Military Deployment," *Journal of Family Communication* 14, no. 2 (2014), 129–48, https://doi.org/10.1080/15267431.2013.864293.

46. Elizabeth M. Collins, "Rest and Recuperation for the Troops" (June 29, 2011), https://www.army.mil/article/60773/rest_and_recuperation_for_the_troops.

47. Dandeker et al., "The British Military Family," 109.

48. Andres and Coulthard, "Children and Deployment," 180.

49. Ibid., 116–17.

50. Bell et al., *USAREUR Family Support during Operation Joint Endeavor,* 42–43; D. Bruce Bell, Jocelyn Bartone, Paul T. Bartone, Walter R. Schumm, Rose E. Rice, and C. Hinson, "Helping U.S. Army Families Cope with the Stresses of Troop Deployment in Bosnia-Herzegovina." Paper presented at the Biennial International Meetings of the Inter-University Seminar on Armed Forces and Society Conference, Baltimore, MD, October 1997.

51. See Margaret C. Harrell, "Army Officers' Spouses: Have the White Gloves Been Mothballed?" *Armed Forces and Society,* 28, no. 1 (2001): 55–75, https://doi.org/10.1177/0095327X010280010.

52. Booth et al., *What We Know about Army Families,* 110.

53. See Thomas E. Trail, Carra S. Simms, and Margaret Tankard, *Today's Army Spouse Survey: How Army Families Address Life's Challenges* (Santa Monica, CA: RAND Corp., 2019), xii.

54. See the literature reviews in Donetta Doris Quinones, "Military Wife Participation in the Family Readiness Group during the Deployment Cycle" (PhD

diss., Walden University, 2019), 24–44; and Catherine Louise Wiberg, "Leadership Techniques for Successful, Sustainable Army Reserve Component Family Readiness Groups" (PhD diss., Colorado Technical University, 2019), 20–38. Both dissertations are available online. See also the chapters in Leandra Hinojosa Hernández and Jennifer Belding, eds., *Military Spouses with Graduate Degrees: Interdisciplinary Approaches to Thriving in Uncertainty* (Lanham, MD: Lexington Books, 2019).

55. Myriam Levesque McCray, "Infidelity, Trust, Commitment, and Marital Satisfaction among Military Wives during Husbands' Deployment" (PhD diss., Walden University, 2015), 47.

56. Hawkins et al., *What We Know about Military Family Readiness*, 78; and Burrell et al., "Impact of Military Lifestyle Demands on Well-Being, Army, and Family Outcomes," 45–47.

57. Elizabeth S. Allen, Galena K. Rhoades, Scott M. Stanley, and Howard J. Markman, "On the Home Front: Stress for Recently Deployed Army Couples," *Family Process* 50, no. 2 (2011): 235–47, https://doi.org/10.1111/j.1545-5300.2011.01357.x.

58. Tomforde, "Emotional Cycle of the Deployment," 87–106.

59. Andres and Coulthard, "Children and Deployment," 188.

60. Data conveyed in Blaisure et al., *Serving Military Families in the 21st Century*, 53.

61. For a review, see Hawkins et al., *What We Know about Military Family Readiness*, 33.

62. See Meadows et al., *Deployment Life Study*, xxi.

63. Booth et al., *What We Know about Army Families*, 42.

64. Abigail M. Yablonsky, Edie Devers Barbero, and Jeanita W. Richardson, "Hard Is Normal: Military Families' Transition within the Process of Deployment," *Research in Nursing and Health* 39, no. 1 (2016): 42–56, https://doi.org/10.1002/nur.21701.

65. Walter R. Schumm, D. Bruce Bell, and Benjamin Knott, "Factors Associated with Spouses Moving Away from Their Military Installation during an Overseas Deployment," *Psychological Reports* 86, no. 3c (2000): 1275–82, https://doi.org/10.2466/pro.2000.86.3c.1275.

66. E. W. Van Vranken, Linda K. Jellen, Kathryn H. M. Knudson, David H. Marlowe, and Mady W. Segal, *The Impact of Deployment Separation on Army Families* (Report NP846) (Washington, DC: Walter Reed Army Institute of Research, 1984), 3–4.

67. See Hawkins, *Army of Hope, Army of Alienation*, 46.

68. See multiple chapters in Moelker et al., *The Politics of Military Families*, and Moelker et al., *Military Families and War in the 21st Century*.

69. Rachael Gribble, Laura Goodwin, Sian Oram, and Nicola Fear, "'Happy Wife, Happy Soldier': How the Relationship between Military Spouses and the Military Institution Influences Spouse Well-Being," in *The Politics of Military*

*Families: State, Work Organizations, and the Rise of the Negotiated Household* (London and New York: Routledge, 2019), 138–51.

70. See Margaret C. Harrell, *Invisible Women: Junior Enlisted Wives* (Santa Monica, CA: RAND, Corp., 2001), 12–13.

71. Blaisure et al., *Serving Military Families in the 21st Century*, 56.

72. See Morten G. Ender, Paul T. Bartone, and Thomas A. Kolditz, "The Fallen Soldier: Death and the U.S. Military," in *Handbook of Death and Dying: The Responses to Death*, vol. 2. (Thousand Oaks, CA: Sage, 2003), 544–55.

73. Soldiers are killed during peacetime but most in accidents—military training or in personal situations such as vehicle accidents. See Ender et al., "Fallen Soldier." The casualty process ramps up during wartime or a mass casualty event, becoming more elaborate and encompassing. See Morten G. Ender, Mady Wechsler Segal, and Sandra Carson Stanley, "Role Conformity and Creativity: Soldiers as Administrators and Caregivers after Loss," *Journal of Personal and Interpersonal Loss* 4, no. 1 (1999): 1–23, https://doi.org/10.1080 /10811449908409714.

74. Van Vranken et al., *Impact of Deployment Separation on Army Families*, 10–11.

75. Harrell, "Army Officers' Spouses," 63.

76. Harrell, *Invisible Women*, 33–34.

77. Christopher M. Tarney, Cristobal Berry-Caban, Ram B. Jain, Molly Kelly, Mark F. Sewell, and Karen L. Wilson, "Association of Spouse Deployment on Pregnancy Outcomes in a US Military Population," *Obstetrics and Gynecology* 126, no. 3 (2015): 569–74, https://doi.org/10.1097/AOG.0000000000001003.

78. David M. Haas and Lisa A. Pazdernik, "A Cross-Sectional Survey of Stressors for Postpartum Women during Wartime in a Military Medical Facility," *Military Medicine* 171, no. 10 (2006): 1020–23, https://doi.org/10.7205/MILMED.171 .10.1020.

79. Susanna Didrickson, "Facing Uncertainty on Two Fronts: The Experience of Being Pregnant While One's Husband Is Deployed" (PhD diss., University of Arizona, 2015), 19–22.

80. For a review, see Hawkins et al., *What We Know about Military Family Readiness*, 113–24.

81. For a review of the literature, see H. Thomas De Burgh, Claire J. White, Nicola T. Fear, and Amy C. Iverson, "The Impact of Deployment to Iraq or Afghanistan on Partners and Wives of Military Personnel," *International Review of Psychiatry* 23, no. 2 (2011): 192–200, https://doi.org/10.3109/09540261.2011.560144.

82. Jennifer Rouse, "Military Dads Can Now Watch Birth of Child," *Corvallis Gazette-Times* (May 24, 2005), https://www.gazettetimes.com/.

83. See Ziff's findings in both "'Honey, I Want to Be a Surrogate'" and "'Mommy Deployment.'"

84. See Abby E. Murray, "Military Spouses, Advanced Degrees and the Myth of Keeping Busy," in *Military Spouses with Graduate Degrees: Interdisciplinary*

*Approaches to Thriving amidst Uncertainty* (Lanham, MD: Lexington Books, 2019), 143–61.

### 3. "The Big Group Hug"

1. See Gerry J. Gilmore, "82nd Airborne Division Becomes 'Waterborne' in New Orleans," *Department of Defense News* (September 21, 2005), https://archive .defense.gov/news/newsarticle.aspx?id=17253#:~:text=NEW%20ORLEANS %2C%20Sept.,20.

2. Blaisure et al., *Serving Military Families in the 21st Century,* 149.

3. Ibid., 51.

4. *The Best Years of Our Lives,* directed by William Wyler (1946; RKO Radio Pictures), 2:52:00, https://www.imdb.com/title/tt0036868/.

5. David R. Segal, *Recruiting for Uncle Sam: Citizenship and Military Manpower Policy* (Lawrence: University of Kansas Press, 1989), 60–61.

6. See Jerry Lembcke, *The Spitting Image: Myth, Memory and the Legacy of Vietnam* (NY: New York University Press, 1998), 169.

7. For a sampling, see Frances M., Doyle, Karen J. Lewis, and Leslie A. Williams, "Named Military Operations: U.S. Military Operations from January 1989 to December 1993," *Armed Forces and Society* 23, no. 2 (1996): 285–98, https:// www.jstor.org/stable/45347066.

8. Charles R. Figley, "Weathering the Storm at Home: War-related Family Stress and Coping," in *The Military Family in Peace and War* (New York: Springer, 1993), 173–90; and Hosek et al., *How Deployments Affect Service Members,* 55–56.

9. Blaisure et al., *Serving Military Families in the 21st Century,* 51.

10. Hosek et al., *How Deployments Affect Service Members,* 23, 33.

11. Figley, "Weathering the Storm at Home," 173–90 and ibid.

12. Ibid.; and ibid.

13. See Charles W. Hoge, Carl A Castro, Stephen C. Messer, Dennis McGurk, Dave I. Cotting, and Robert L. Koffman, "Combat Duty in Iraq and Afghanistan, Mental Health Problems, and Barriers to Care," *New England Journal of Medicine* 351, no. 1 (2004): 13–22, https://doi.org/10.1056/NEJMoa040603; and later Terri Tanielian and Lisa H. Jaycox, eds., *Invisible Wounds of War: Psychological and Cognitive Injuries, Their Consequences, and the Services to Assist Recovery* (Santa Monica, CA: RAND Corp., 2008), xxi.

14. Heidi Cramm, Deborah Norris, Kelly Dean Schwartz, Linna Tam-Seto, Ashley Williams, and Alyson Mahar, "Impact of Canadian Armed Forces Veterans' Mental Health Problems on the Family during the Military to Civilian Transition," *Military Behavioral Health* 8, no. 2 (2019): 148–58, https://doi.org/10 .1080/21635781.2019.1644260.

15. See Matthews, *Head Strong,* 69–88.

16. Meadows et al., *Deployment Life Study*, xxv. See also the review literature in Hawkins et al., *What We Know about Military Family Readiness*, 97; see also Trail et al., *Today's Army Spouse Survey*, 56.

17. See chapters in Segal and Segal, *Peacekeepers and Their Wives*. See Lynne M. Knobloch-Fedders, Leanne K. Knobloch, Samantha Scott, and Hannah Fiore, "Relationship Changes of Military Couples during Reintegration: A Longitudinal Analysis," *Journal of Social and Personal Relationships* 37, no. 7 (2020): 2145–65, https://doi.org/10.1177/0265407520917461.

18. Bell and Schumm, "Providing Family Support during Military Deployments," 139–52; and Figley, "Weathering the Storm at Home," 173–90.

19. Meadows et al., *Deployment Life Study*, xxi.

20. Booth et al., *What We Know about Army Families*, 43–44.

21. Walter R. Schumm, D. Bruce Bell, Morten G. Ender, and Rose E. Rice, "Expectations, Use, and Evaluations of Communications Media among Deployed Peacekeepers," *Armed Forces and Society* 30, no. 4 (2004): 649–62, https://doi.org/10.1177/0095327X0403000407.

22. Bell and Schumm, "Providing Family Support during Military Deployments," 139–52; and Wood et al., "Waiting Wives," 217–36.

23. See Jay A. Mancini, Catherine Walker O'Neal, and Mallory Lucier-Greer, "Toward a Framework for Military Family Life Education: Culture, Context, Content, and Practice," *Family Relations* 69, no. 3 (2000): 644–61, https://doi.org/10.1111/fare.12426.

24. Blaisure et al., *Serving Military Families in the 21st Century*, 281.

25. Bell and Schumm, "Providing Family Support during Military Deployments," 139–52; and Figley, "Weathering the Storm at Home," 173–90.

26. Moelker et al., *Military Families and War in the 21st Century*.

27. Rachel E. Pye and Leanne Simpson, "Family Functioning Differences across the Deployment Cycle in British Army Families: The Perceptions of Wives and Children," *Military Medicine* 182, no. 9 (2017): e1856–e1863, https://doi.org/10.7205/MILMED-D-16-00317.

28. "Stop-loss" is a policy implemented by the U.S. military that established across the board or individual involuntary extension of the active-duty service members to be retained beyond their established end of the term of service date. See Evan M. Wootan, "Banging on the Backdoor Draft: The Constitutional Validity of Stop-Loss in the Military," *William & Mary Law Review* 47 (February 2005): 1063–98, https://heinonline.org/HOL/Page?handle=hein.journals/wmlr47&div =28&g_sent=1&casa_token=&collection=journals.

29. See Terri Tanielian, Lisa H. Jaycox, David M. Adamson, and Karen N. Metcher, "Introduction," in *Invisible Wounds of War: Psychological and Cognitive Injuries, Their Consequences, and Services to Assist Recovery* (Santa Monica, CA: RAND Corp., 2008), 3–17.

30. Reporters Dana Priest and Anne Hull and photographer Michel du Cille received a Pulitzer Prize for their *Washington Post* investigative journalism

NOTES TO PAGES 72–80    197

reporting on conditions at the Walter Reed Army Medical Center and the mistreatments of wounded service members. Information is available at The Pulitzer Prizes, *The Washington Post, for the work of Dana Priest, Anne Hull, and photographer Michel du Cille,* https://www.pulitzer.org/winners/washington-post-2.

31. For background on casualties in Iraq and Afghanistan, see Mathew S. Goldberg, "Casualty Rates of U.S. Military Personnel during the Wars in Iraq and Afghanistan," *Defence and Peace Economics* 29, no. 1 (2018): 44–61, https://doi.org/10.1080/10242694.2015.1129816; and Mary Keeling, Heidi Williamson, Victoria Williams, James Kiff, and Diana Harcourt, "Body Image Concerns and Psychological Well-Being among Injured Combat Veterans with Scars and Limb Loss: A Review of the Literature," *Military Behavioral Health* 9, no. 1 (2020): 1–10, https://doi.org/10.1080/21635781.2020.1792013.

## 4. "I Have No Idea about Services"

1. See Blaisure et al., *Serving Military Families in the 21st Century,* 118–19.
2. See Sofia K. Ledberg and Chiara Ruffa, "Military Families: Topography of a Field," in *Handbook of Military Sciences* (Cham, Switzerland: Springer, 2020), 1–16.
3. Booth et al., *What We Know about Army Families,* 104.
4. See Jennifer Mittlestadt, *The Rise of the Military Welfare State* (Cambridge, MA: Harvard University Press, 2015), 10–11.
5. Booth et al., *What We Know about Army Families,* 103–28; Bernard D. Rostker and K. C. Yeh, *I Want You! The Evolution of the All-Volunteer Force* (Santa Monica, Calif.: RAND Corp. 2006), 582; and Allen Rubin and Helena Harvie, "A Brief History of Social Work with the Military and Veterans," in *Handbook of Military Social Work* (Hoboken, NJ: John Wiley & Sons, 2012), 3–20.
6. See the chapters about Finland and Sweden in Moelker et al., *The Politics of Military Families,* 169–83, 253–66.
7. Booth et al., *What We Know about Army Families,* 104.
8. Ibid.
9. See Kenona H. Southwell and Shelley M. MacDermid Wadsworth, "The Many Faces of Military Families: Unique Features of the Lives of Female Service Members," *Military Medicine* 183, no. 1 (2016): 70–79, https://doi.org/10.7205/MILMED-D-15-00193.
10. D. Bruce Bell, Mary L. Stevens, and Mady W. Segal, *How to Support Families during Overseas Deployments: A Sourcebook for Service Providers* (Arlington, VA: U.S. Army Research Institute for the Behavioral and Social Sciences, 1996), 21; and Richard W. Bloom III, "A Reason to Believe: The Sustenance of Military Families," in *The Military Family in Peace and War* (New York: Springer, 1993), 173–90.
11. Gustavsen, "The Privatized Meaning of Wartime Deployments," 514.

12. A year later, Rear Detachment Commanders were no longer the least deployable. Division commanders learned that exceptional leadership was required on the home front and rotation of RDCs was instituted. See Ender, *American Soldiers in Iraq*, 6–9.

13. See Military Pay Charts at *Military Payrates, 2020*, accessed October 10, 2022, https://www.militaryrates.com/military-pay-charts-01_05_2020. Base pay for an E4 with four years of military service is $2,507.35. Base pay for an LTC with eighteen years of military service is $9,277.66.

14. See Schumm et al., "Factors Associated with Spouses Moving Away from Their Military Installation during an Overseas Deployment," 1275–82.

15. See Daniel Burland and Jennifer Hickes Lundquist, "The Best Years of Our Lives: Military Service and Family Relationships—A Life Course Perspective," in *Life-Course Perspectives on Military Service* (New York: Routledge, 2013), 171.

16. James A. Martin and Dennis K. Orthner, "The 'Company Town' in Transition: Rebuilding Military Communities," in Bowen and Orthner, *Organization Family*, 163–77.

17. Booth et al., *What We Know about Army Families*, 103–27; Rostker and Yeh, *I Want You!*, 582; and Rubin and Harvie, *A Brief History of Social Work with the Military and Veterans*, 3–20.

18. See the chapters in Moelker et al., *Military Families and War in the 21st Century*.

19. Gail L. Zellman, Susan M. Gates, Joy S. Moini, and Marika Suttorp, "Meeting Family and Military Needs through Military Child Care," *Armed Forces and Society* 35, no. 3 (2009): 437–59, https://doi.org/10.1177/0095327X083308.

20. Booth et al., *What We Know about Army Families*, 104.

21. Barabara R. Sarason, Irwin G. Sarason, and Regan A. R. Gurung, "Close Personal Relationships and Health Outcomes: A Key to the Role of Social Support," in *Personal Relationships: Implications for Clinical and Community Psychology* (New York: John Wiley & Sons, 2001), 15–42.

22. Van Vranken et al., *The Impact of Deployment Separation on Army Families*, 7.

23. Jay A. Mancini and Gary L. Bowen, "Families and Communities: A Social Organization Theory of Action and Change," in *Handbook of Marriage and the Family* (Boston: Springer, 2013), 781–813, https://doi.org/10.1007/978-1-4614-3987-5_32.

24. Mady W. Segal and Jesse J. Harris, *What We Know about Army Families* (Special Report 21; Contract No DAAL03–86-D-0001) (Alexandria, VA: U.S. Army Research Institute for the Behavioral and Social Sciences, 1993), 35.

25. For a brief review of these studies, see Blaisure et al., *Serving Military Families in the 21st Century*, 118–19.

26. Hawkins et al., *What We Know about Military Family Readiness*, 4.

27. Ibid.

28. For example, see Dorothea Halbe, "Language in the Military Workplace—Between Hierarchy and Politeness," *Talk and Text* 31, no. 3 (2011): 315–34, https://doi.org/10.1515/text.2011.014.

## 5. "They Take the Brunt of the Deployments"

1. Military One Source, *Military Community Demographics*.
2. The numbers fluctuated some over the decade of the 2000s. For example, during the 2000s, U.S. active-duty military personnel averaged just 1,250,000 children. In 2009 the U.S. Army had the most significant number at 548,572, followed by 2004 numbers of the Air Force (328,175), Navy (306,844), and the Marines (104,066). Military children can retain the dependency status until age eighteen and through twenty-three if they are full-time college students and older if they or other family members have special needs. "Military children" is a seemingly generic term. "Military" refers to the part of their childhood or adolescence spent in a family where at least one parent or guardian served in the active-duty military—meaning it was their full-time occupation. "Children" connotes people between the ages of birth and twelve years of age. "Adolescence" refers to teenagers and young adults, while "adults" refers to those in their twenties and older.
3. National Guard and Reserve children and adolescents are typically excluded in research studies. However, the current wars in Iraq and Afghanistan are activating Guard and Reserve service members and deploying them. Scholars are becoming increasingly interested in these families, and the research literature will be reviewed for these groups as it becomes available. See Nameeta Sahni, "Perceptions of Those Left Behind: An Exploration of Family Dynamics within Military Reservist Families during the 2003 Iraq Wartime Deployment" (PhD diss., Alliant International University, 2005).
4. See Stephen J. Cozza, Joscelyn E. Fisher, Jing Zhou, Jill Harrington-LaMorie, Lareina La Flair, Carol S. Fullerton, and Robert J. Ursano, "Bereaved Military Dependent Spouses and Children: Those Left Behind in a Decade of War (2001–2011)," *Military Medicine* 182, nos. 3–4 (2017): e1684–e1690, https://doi.org/10.7205/MILMED-D-16-00101.
5. Rachel Lipari, Anna Winters, Kenneth Matos, Jason Smith, and Lindsay Rock, "Military Child Well-being in the Face of Multiple Deployments," in *The Routledge Handbook for War and Society: Iraq and Afghanistan* (New York: Routledge, 2011), 283–93.
6. See Booth et al., *What We Know about Army Families*, 89–102. Chapter 6 of the volume reviews the literature on army children. See also Morten G. Ender, "Voices from the Backseat: Growing Up in Military Families," in *Military Life: The Psychology of Serving in Peace and Combat, Volume 3: The Military Family* (Westport, CT: Praeger Security International, 2006), 138–66; see chapter in Ender, *Military Brats and Other Global Nomads;* and Edna J. Hunter and D. Stephen Nice, eds., *Children of Military Families: A Part yet Apart* (Washington, DC: Superintendent of Documents, U.S. Government Printing Office, 1976). For a recent and excellent review of the British experience, see Walter Busuttil and Angela Busuttil, "Psychological Effects of Families Subjected to Enforced and

Prolonged Separations Generated under Life Threatening Situations," *Sexual and Relationship Therapy* 16, no. 1 (2001): 207–28, https://doi.org/10.1080/14681990123566.

7. Children of military personnel are more likely than any other occupational background to serve in the military but appear equally likely as their peers to make a career of it. For research studies on endo-recruitment, see Gary Lee Bowen, "Intergenerational Occupational Inheritance in the Military: A Reexamination," *Adolescence*, 21, no. 83 (1986): 623–29, https://www.proquest.com/docview/1295935247?pq-origsite=gscholar&fromopenview=true&imgSeq=1; John H. Faris, "The All-Volunteer Force: Recruitment from Military Families," *Armed Forces and Society*, 7, no. 4 (1981): 545–59, chrome-extension://efaidnbmnnnibpcajpcglclefindmkaj/https://journals.sagepub.com/doi/pdf/10.1177/0095327X8100700403; George W. Thomas, "Military Parental Effects and Career Orientation under the A.V.F.: Enlisted Personnel," *Armed Forces and Society*, 10, no. 2 (1984): 293–310, chrome-extension://efaidnbmnnnibpcajpcglclefindmkaj/https://journals.sagepub.com/doi/pdf/10.1177/0095327X8401000209; and Leonard Wong, "Recruiting from Within: Military Brats Entering the Officer Corps" (presentation at the Biennial Conference of the Inter-University Seminar on Armed Forces and Society, Baltimore, MD, October 21–23, 2001).

8. Brian Roller and Lee E. Doerries, "Occupational Inheritance in Service Academy Cadets and Midshipmen," *Journal on Educational Psychology*, 2, no. 2 (2008): 43–46, chrome-extension://efaidnbmnnnibpcajpcglclefindmkaj/https://files.eric.ed.gov/fulltext/EJ1066413.pdf.

9. See Hill, *Families under Stress;* and Elise Boulding, "Family Adjustments to War Separation and Reunion," *Annals of the American Academy of Political and Social Sciences*, 272, no. 1 (1950): 59–67, https://doi.org/10.1177/000271625027200109.

10. Dennis K. Orthner, Martha M. Giddings, and William Quinn, "Growing Up in an Organization Family," in Bowen and Orthner, *Organization Family*, 117–39.

11. For an excellent review of the British experience, see Busuttil and Busuttil, "Psychological Effects of Families," 207–28.

12. See Vernon A. Barnes, Harry Davis, and Frank A. Treiber, "Perceived Stress, Heart Rate, and Blood Pressure among Adolescents with Family Members Deployed in Operation Iraqi Freedom," *Military Medicine*, 172, no. 1 (2007): 40–43, https://doi.org/10.7205/MILMED.172.1.40; Stephen J. Cozza, Ryo S. Chun, and James A. Polo, "Military Families and Children during Operation Iraqi Freedom," *Psychiatric Quarterly*, 76, no. 4 (2005): 371–78, https://doi.org/10.1007/s11126-005-4973-y; Stephen J. Cozza and Alicia F. Lieberman, "The Young Military Child: Our Modern Telemachus," *Zero to Three*, 27, no. 6 (2007): 27–33; Angela J. Huebner, Jay A. Mancini, Ryan M. Wilcox, Saralyn R. Grass, and Gabriel A. Grass, "Parental Deployment and Youth in Military Families: Exploring Uncertainty and Ambiguous Loss," *Family Relations*, 56,

no. 2 (2007): 112–22, https://doi.org/10.1111/j.1741-3729.2007.00445.x; and Kristin Mmari, Kathleen M. Roche, May Sudhinaraset, and Robert Blum, "When a Parent Goes Off to War: Exploring the Issues Faced by Adolescents and their Families," *Youth and Society* 40, no. 4 (2009): 455–75, https://doi.org/10.1177/0044118X08327873.

13. See his interview in the documentary *Brats: Our Journey Home,* 2006. Written and directed by Donna Musil. Brats without Borders, 38:38 minutes.

14. Andy J. Merolla, "Relational Maintenance during Military Deployment: Perspectives of Wives of Deployed U.S. Soldiers," *Journal of Applied Communication* 38, no. 1 (2010): 4–26, https://doi.org/10.1080/00909880903483557.

15. Leonard Wong and Stephen Gerras, *The Effects of Multiple Deployments on Army Adolescents* (Carlisle, PA: Strategic Studies Institute, 2010), vii.

16. Huebner et al., "Parental Deployment and Youth in Military Families," 112–22.

17. A military family off-site is an occasion for military leadership and spouses to retreat from the offices and the military post for team building and preparation for the impending deployment.

18. See Moira A. Fallon and Teresa J. Russon, "Helping Military Families Who Have a Child with a Disability Cope with Stress," *Early Childhood Education Journal* 29, no. 1 (2001): 3–8, https://doi.org/10.1023/A:1011348620920, and "Adaptation to Stress: An Investigation into the Lives of United States Military Families with a Child Who is Disabled," *Early Childhood Education Journal,* 30, no. 3 (2003): 193–98. See also Stephen J. Cozza, *Workgroup on Intervention with Combat Injured Families* (Bethesda, MD: Uniformed Service University of the Health Sciences, Center for the Study of Traumatic Stress, 2009), http://www.usuhs.mil/csts.

19. Booth et al., *What We Know about Army Families,* introduction.

20. See Remi M. Hajjar and Morten G. Ender, "Boredom, Fragmentation, and a U.S. Army Unit in Eastern Europe," *Journal of Political and Military Sociology* 48, no. 2 (2021): 223–54, https://doi.org/10.5744/jpms/2004.

21. Ender, *Military Brats and Other Global Nomads,* 83–99.

22. See Ann E. Aydlett and American School Counselor Association, *Dealing with Deployment: A Small-Group Curriculum for Elementary and Middle School Students,* School Counselor Reference Series (Alexandria, VA: American School Counselor Association, 2008); Andrew Briggs and Pam Atkinson, "Adapting the Model: Therapeutic Work with Children from Army Families," *Journal of Social Work Practice,* 20, no. 1 (2006): 51–67, https://doi.org/10.1080/02650530600565951; Anita Chandra, Laurie T. Martin, Stacy Ann Hawkins, and Amy Richardson, "The Impact of Parental Deployment on Child Social and Emotional Functioning: Perspectives of School Staff," *Journal of Adolescent Health* 46, no. 3 (2010): 218–23, https://doi.org/10.1016/j.jadohealth.2009.10.009; Christina Mitchell Rush and Patrick Akos, "Supporting Children and Adolescents with Deployed Caregivers: A Structured Group Approach for School Counselors," *Journal for Specialists in Group Work,* 32, no. 2 (2010): 113–25, https://doi.org/10.1080

/01933920701227034; and Mona P. Ternus, "Support for Adolescents Who Experience Parental Military Deployment," *The Journal of Adolescent Health* 46 no. 3 (2010): 203–6, https://doi.org/10.1016/j.jadohealth.2009.12.019.

23. Rozlyn C. Engel, Luke B. Gallagher, and David S. Lyle, "Military Deployments and Children's Academic Achievement: Evidence from Department of Defense Education Activity Schools," *Economics of Education Review* 29, no. 1 (2010): 73–82, https://doi.org/10.1016/j.econedurev.2008.12.003.

24. Barnes et al., "Perceived Stress, Heart Rate, and Blood Pressure," 40–43.

25. Examples of deviance include carrying a knife or gun to school, using alcohol, or thoughts of suicide.

26. Examples include higher rates of anxiety, stress, depression, and psychotropic drug prescriptions.

27. Courtney L. Gosnell, Dennis R. Kelly, Morten G. Ender, and Michael D. Matthews, "Character Strengths and Performance Outcomes among Military Brat and Non-brat Cadets," *Military Psychology* 32, no. 2 (2020): 1–12, https://doi.org /10.1080/08995605.2019.1703434.

28. Harrell, "Army Officers' Spouses," 55–75.

29. Booth et al., *What We Know about Army Families*, 81.

30. Wong and Gerras, *Effects of Multiple Deployments on Army Adolescents*, vii.

31. The U.S. Army does have a policy allowing service members to remain at post and not moving so a child can complete their senior year in the same locale. It is known as the High School Senior Stabilization Program, established on December 14, 2000, by the U.S. Army Chief of Staff. It allows for an "initiated assignment procedure to schedule Permanent Change of Station (PCS) moves to occur at times that avoid disruption of the school schedule for Soldiers who have Family members who are high school seniors. The policy was expanded to include Soldiers with Family members in their junior year." U.S. Army Human Resources Command, *High School Senior Stabilization Program* (August 9, 2021), https://www.hrc.army.mil/content/High%20School%20Senior %20Stabilization%20Program.

32. I have not published these results independently. They are part of a larger study. See Ender, *Military Brats and Other Global Nomads*, 83–99.

33. See Carlton-Ford et al., "Iraqi Adolescents," 53–75.

34. See Ian Shapira, "He Was a Baby When His Dad Died in Afghanistan. He's 18 Now, and the War Still Isn't Over," *Washington Post* (November 26, 2019), https://www.washingtonpost.com/dc-md-va/2019/11/26/he-was-baby-when-his -dad-died-afghanistan-hes-war-still-isnt-over/?arc404=true.

35. National Academy of Sciences, *Returning Home from Iraq and Afghanistan Preliminary Assessment of Readjustment Needs of Veterans, Service Members, and Their Families* (Washington, DC: The National Academies Press, 2010), 79–80.

36. See Abigail H. Gewirtz and Tori S. Simenec, "Strengthening Parenting in Deployed Military Families," in *Parent-Child Separation: Cause, Consequences, and Pathways* (Cham, Switzerland: Springer, 2022), 209–28.

37. Deborah Harrison and Patrizia Albanese, *Growing Up in Armyville: Canada's Military Families during the Afghanistan Mission* (Waterloo, Ontario: Wilfrid Laurier University Press, 2016).

38. Ibid., 108–44.

## 6. "He Has a Laptop"

1. See Claude S. Fischer, *America Calling: A Social History of the Telephone to 1940* (Berkeley: University of California Press, 1992).

2. See Thomas E. Miller, "New Markets for Information," *American Demographics* (April 1995): 46–54.

3. Saqib Shah, "The History of Social Networking," *Digital Trends* (May 14, 2016), https://www.digitaltrends.com/features/the-history-of-social-networking/.

4. See Lynne M. Borden, Octavia Cheatum, Kyle R. Hawkey, Michelle W. Kuhl, Amy Majerle, Jessie H. Rudi, Michelle D. Sherman, Burgess Smith, David Steinman, and Lara Westerhof, *Social Media Communication with Military Spouses* (Minneapolis: University of Minnesota, 2015), https://reachmilitaryfamilies .umn.edu/sites/default/files/rdoc/Social%20Media%20Communication %20with%20Military%20Spouses.pdf.

5. See Kimberly Williams, *2016 Status of Forces Survey of Active Duty Members (SOFS-A) Selected Results on Active Duty Members and Families: Technology, Relationships, Child Care, Counseling, Impact of Deployments, and Military OneSource* (Department of Defense, Office of People Analytics, 2018), http://download .militaryonesource.mil/12038/MOS/Surveys/2016-SOFS-Briefing-MCFP.pdf; and Defense Manpower Data Center, *2013 and 2014 Status of Forces Surveys of Active Duty Members (SOFS-A) Briefing on Leading Indicators, Military OneSource, Financial Health, Family Life, Access to Technology, Impact of Deployments, and Permanent Change of Station (PCS) Moves* (Defense Manpower Data Center Research, Surveys, and Statistics Center, 2014), https://www.militaryonesource .mil/leaders-service-providers/sp-l-deployment/findings-from-the-status-of -forces-surveys-of-active-duty-members.

6. An example is Patrick H. O'Keefe, "Using Facebook to Communicate with Husbands While Deployed: A Qualitative Study of Army Wives' Experiences," *Journal of Military and Government Counseling* 6, no. 2 (2018): 119–38, https:// mgcaonline.org/wp-content/uploads/2018/07/JMGC-Vol-6-Is-2.pdf.

7. See the chapter titled "Baghdad Calling: Soldier Communications with Other Fronts," in Ender, *American Soldiers in Iraq*, 103–13.

8. Ariane Ollier-Malaterre, Jerry A. Jacobs, and Nancy P. Rothbard, "Technology, Work, and Family: Digital Cultural Capital and Boundary Management," *Annual Review of Sociology* 45 (2019): 425–47, https://doi.org/101146/annurev-soc -073018-022433.

9. See Morten G. Ender, "E-mail to Somalia: New Communication Media between Home and War Fronts," in *Mapping Cyberspace: Social Research on the Electronic*

*Frontier* (Oakdale, NY: Dowling College Press, 1997), 27–52; Morten G. Ender and David R. Segal, "Cyber-Soldiering: Race, Class, Gender and New Media Use in the Military," in *Cyberghetto or Cybertopia?: Race, Class, and Gender on the Internet* (Westport, CT: Greenwood, 1998), 65–82; and Ender, *American Soldiers in Iraq*, 103–13.

10. See Morten G. Ender and David R. Segal, "V(E)-mail to the Foxhole: Soldier Isolation, (Tele)communication, and Force-Projection Operations," *Journal of Political and Military Sociology* 24, no. 1 (1996): 83–104, https://www.jstor.org /stable/45294092.

11. D. Bruce Bell, Walter R. Schumm, Benjamin Knott, and Morten G. Ender, "The Desert Fax: A Research Note on Calling Home from Somalia," *Armed Forces and Society* 25, no. 3 (1999): 509–20, https://doi.org/10.1177/0095327X990250030; and Hosek et al., *How Deployments Affect Service Members*, 43–44.

12. See Booth et al., *What We Know about Army Families*, 39–40.

13. Ender, "E-mail to Somalia," 27–52.

14. See Douglas Kellner, *The Persian Gulf TV War* (Boulder, CO: Westview Press, 1992), 86–89.

15. See Ender and Segal, "V(E)-mail to the Foxhole," 83–104.

16. By 2004, the U.S. military engaged in a new defense posture in Iraq known as Full-Spectrum Operations. FSOs include a combined element of combat operations, training and employing Iraq security forces, and providing essential services in Iraq such as providing electricity, promoting governance, and fostering economic pluralism. See Peter W. Chiarelli and Patrick R. Michaelis, "The Requirement for Full-Spectrum Operations," *Military Review* 84, no. 4 (2005): 4–17, chrome-extension://efaidnbmnnnibpcajpcglclefindmkaj/https:// smallwarsjournal.com/documents/chiarelli.pdf.

17. See Martha Raddatz, *The Long Road Home: A Story of War and Family* (NY: G. P. Putnam's Sons, 2008), 23.

18. See Ender, *American Soldiers in Iraq*, 103–13.

19. See "Honor the Fallen," *Military Times.com*, https://thefallen.militarytimes.com /army-spc-frances-m-vega/256873. SPC Vega, married and a military brat, is the first woman soldier of Puerto Rican descent to die in combat in Iraq.

20. See Ender, "E-mail to Somalia," 27–52.

21. For an excellent description of a forward operating base, see Leonard Wong and Stephen Gerras, *CU @ The FOB: How the Forward Operating Base Is Changing the Life of Combat Soldiers* (Carlisle Barracks, PA: Strategic Studies Institute, 2006).

22. See *Iraq Coalition Casualty Count*, http://icasualties.org/. The site is not an official Department of Defense website. It remains a reliable and ongoing source of casualties in Iraq and Afghanistan—meaning injuries and fatalities—by location, nationality, time, and status. Retrieved November 11, 2017.

23. The objective was to honor the DD Form 93. This official document is for all deployed military personnel including DOD civilians and contractors on which

to indicate who should be personally notified in case of emergency or death as well as their beneficiaries.

24. Gustavsen, "The Privatized Meaning of Wartime Deployments," 514.

25. Pew Research Center, *Mobile Fact Sheet: Social Media,* accessed October 15, 2022, https://www.pewresearch.org/internet/fact-sheet/mobile/.

26. Hajjar and Ender, "Boredom, Fragmentation, and a U.S. Army," 225–26.

27. Ibid., 237.

28. See Sarah P. Carter and Keith D. Renshaw, "Spousal Communication during Military Deployments: A Review," *Journal of Family Issues* 37, no. 16 (2016): 2309–32, https://doi.org/10.1177/0192513X14567956.

29. Ibid.

30. Hawkins et al. *What We Know about Military Family Readiness,* 96–97.

31. Ibid., 97–98.

32. See Steven L. Sayers and Galena K. Rhoades, "Recent Advances in the Understanding of Relationship Communication during Military Deployment," *Journal of Family Psychology* 32, no. 1 (2018): 1–2, https://doi.org/10.1037/fam0000417.

33. Leanne K. Knobloch, Lynne M. Knobloch-Fedders, and Jeremy B. Yorgason, "Communication of Military Couples during Deployment Predicting Generalized Anxiety upon Reunion," *Journal of Family Psychology* 32, no. 1 (2018): 12–21, https://doi.org/10.1037/fam0000344.

34. For the UK, see Emma Long, "The Spirit of Community, the Army Family, and the Impact of Formal and Informal Support Mechanisms," in *The Politics of Military Families: State, Work Organizations, and the Rise of the Negotiated Household* (London: Routledge, 2019), 184–97.

35. Uroš Svete and Jelena Juvan, "Soldiers' Private Digital Communications as a Factor Disturbing Military Operations Abroad," *Res Militaris* 6, no. 2 (2016), http://resmilitaris.net/.

36. See Manon Andres and René Moelker, "What Happens On-Board Stays On-Board?: The Political Game of Communication between Deployed Military Personnel and their Loved Ones," in *The Politics of Military Families: State, Work Organizations, and the Rise of the Negotiated Household* (London: Routledge, 2019), 267–82.

37. Military sociologists offer some tips in a book chapter. See René Moelker and Manon Andres, "Epilogue: Dating from a Distance: Love and Separation in a Networked Society," in *The Politics of Military Families: State, Work Organizations, and the Rise of the Negotiated Household* (London and NY: Routledge, 2019), 324–32.

38. See Edward A. Benoit III, "Digital V-Mail and the 21st Century Soldier: Preliminary Findings from the Virtual Footlocker Project," *Preservation, Digital Technology and Culture* 46, no. 1 (2017): 17–31, https://doi.org/10.1515/pdtc-2017-0023.

39. Meadows et al., *Deployment Life Study,* xxiv–xxv.

## 7. "Wolf Blitzer Doesn't Talk to Me Anymore"

1. See the debate surrounding what is known as the casualty hypothesis, which holds that the more casualties suffered by the U.S. military during a military intervention during deployment, the greater the increase in the public negative reactions and calls for a withdrawal of those troops. It is sometimes known as "casualty aversion" or "casualty aversion hypothesis" in the literature. One side confirms this finding. See Andrew F. Hayes and Teresa A. Myers, "Testing the Proximate Casualty 'Hypothesis': Local Troop Loss, Attention to News, and Support for Military Interventions," *Mass Communication and Society*, 12, no. 4 (2009), 379–402, https://doi.org/10.1080/15205430802484956; and Andrew F. Hayes and Teresa A. Myers, "Reframing the Casualty Hypothesis: (Mis)perceptions of Troop Loss and Public Opinion about War," *International Journal of Public Opinion Research* 22, no. 2 (2010): 256–75, https://doi.org/10.1093/ijpor/edp044. Other research holds that casualties may increase public support for the intervention. See James Burk, "Public Support for Peacekeeping in Lebanon and Somalia: Assessing the Casualties Hypothesis," *Political Science Quarterly* 114, no. 1 (1999): 53–78, https://doi.org/10.2307/2657991.
2. For reporters, see Roshan Noorzai and Claudia Hale, "Balanced Coverage in Practice: News Reporting of Conflict in Afghanistan," *Journal of War and Cultural Studies* 14, no. 3 (2020): 345–64, https://doi.org/10.1080/17526272.2020.1719608; for veterans, see Hans Schmidt, "'Hero Worship' or 'Manipulative and Oversimplifying': How America's Current and Former Military Service Members Perceive Military Related News Reporting," *Journal of Veterans Studies* 16, no. 1 (2020): 13–24, https://doi.org/10.21061/jvs.v6i1.156; and for the public, see Sean Aday, "The U.S. Media, Foreign Policy, and Public Support for War," in *The Oxford Handbook for Political Communication* (UK: Oxford University Press, 2017), 315–32.
3. Portions of this chapter are reprinted from Morten G. Ender, Kathleen M. Campbell, Toya J. Davis, and Patrick R. Michaelis, "Greedy Media: Army Families, Embedded Reporting, and the War in Iraq," *Sociological Focus* 40, no. 1 (2007): 48–71, https://doi.org/10.1080/00380237.2007.10571298, © 2007 by the North Central Sociological Association, reprinted by permission of Taylor & Francis Ltd., http://www.tandfonline.com, on behalf of the 2007 North Central Sociological Association.
4. Ender, *American Soldiers in Iraq*, 103–13.
5. Bartone, "Missions Alike and Unlike," 193–209.
6. Hitoshi Kawano and Atsuko Fukuura, "Family Support and the Japan Self-Defense Forces: Challenges and Developing New Programs," in Moelker et al., *Military Families and War in the 21st Century*, 302–18.
7. Andres and Coulthard, "Children and Deployment," 177–90.
8. See David R. Segal, "Communication about the Military: People and Media in the Flow of Information," *Communication Research* 2, no. 1 (1975): 68–78, https://doi.org/10.1177/009365027500200104.

9. Individuals wrote both letters and blogs. The significant differences between letters and blogs are time lag and privacy. Letters involve lag time and are private as the intended audience is an individual rather than a group. Blogs are in real time and intended for a broader, public audience of readers. See Brad Knickerbocker, "Soldier Blogs Bring the Front Line to the Folks at Home," *Christian Science Monitor* (April 18, 2005), http://www.csmonitor.com/2005/0419/p01s05-ussc.html.

10. Steven Livingston, *Clarifying the CNN Effect: An Examination of Media Effects According to Type of Military Intervention* (Cambridge, MA: Harvard University Kennedy School of Government, 1997), 1–5, http://www.ksg.harvard.edu/presspol/Research_Publications/Papers/Research_Papers/R18.pdf.

11. Stephen D. Cooper, "Press Controls in Wartime: The Legal, Historical, and Institutional Context," *American Communication Journal* 6, no. 4 (2003): 16, http://www.ac-journal.org/?page_id=693.

12. By 2004, 71 reporters had died covering the war in Iraq. Christopher Paul and James J. Kim, *Reporters on the Battlefield: The Embedded Press System in Historical Context* (Santa Monica, CA: RAND Corp., 2004), 1–2. The Committee to Protect Journalists reports that 204 journalists and media support personnel had been killed between March 2003 and December 2011, making it the deadliest wartime death number ever recorded. See Katherine Fung, "Record Number of Journalists Killed during Iraq War: Committee to Protect Journalists," *Huffpost* (March 13, 2013), https://www.huffpost.com/entry/iraq-war-killed-journalists_n_2907550.

13. Aday, "U.S. Media, Foreign Policy, and Public Support for War," 315–32.

14. Oren Livio and Shani Cohen-Yechezkely, "COPY, EDIT, PASTE: Comparing News Coverage of War with Official Military Accounts," *Journalism Studies* 20, no. 5 (2019): 696–713, https://doi.org/10.1080/1461670X.2017.1417054.

15. Cooper, "Press Controls in Wartime," 6; Paul and Kim, *Reporters on the Battlefield*, 109–14.

16. See Cooper, "Press Controls in Wartime," 5–6.

17. Evan O'Neil and Joel Rosenthal, *Media and the Military: Lessons Learned from the Iraq War, Conference Summary* (NY: Carnegie Council on Ethics and International Affairs, June 2, 2003).

18. Paul and Kim, *Reporters on the Battlefield*, 96–98.

19. Again, the Committee to Protect Journalists, a nonprofit group, reports that 204 journalists and media support workers were killed in Iraq between March 2003 and December 2011. Another 21 were killed in Afghanistan between 2001 and 2013. See Frank Smyth, "Iraq War and News Media: A Look Inside the Death Toll," *Committee to Protect Journalists* (March 18, 2013), https://cpj.org/2013/03/iraq-war-and-news-media-a-look-inside-the-death-to/.

20. Schmidt, "Hero Worship," 13–24.

21. Mark Johnson, "Internet, 'Embedding' Keep Families Close to Soldiers," *Milwaukee Journal Sentinel* (March 26, 2003), http://www.jsonline.com.

22. We suspect the close-ended question forced a listing of a time amount. We should have included a no viewing option. In practice, we estimate the spouses probably viewed coverage once or twice and then constrained themselves after that.

23. Defense Manpower Data Center, *Profile of Service Members Ever Deployed* (June 29, 2009), https://dwp.dmdc.osd.mil/dwp/app/main.

24. See Belasco, *Troop Levels in the Afghan and Iraq Wars, FY2001–FY2012*, 9–13.

25. Ross A. Miller and Karen Albert, "If It Leads, It Bleeds (and If It Bleeds, It Leads): Media Coverage and Fatalities in Militarized Interstate Disputes," *Political Communication* 32, no. 1 (2015): 61–82, https://doi.org/10.1080/10584609.2014.880976.

26. PBS News Hour, "Remembering the U.S. Service Members Who Lost Their Lives during the Afghanistan Exit," *PBS News Hour* (August 30, 2021), https://www.pbs.org/newshour/show/remembering-the-u-s-service-members-who-lost-their-lives-during-the-afghanistan-exit.

27. See Raddatz, *The Long Road Home*, 231–32. Raddatz describes the experiences of soldiers and families of the First Cavalry Division out of Fort Hood, Texas, in April 2004—a deadly month for U.S. forces in Baghdad, Iraq. In addition to the book, the National Geographic television network featured an eight-part series based on the book. See Mikko Alanne, creator, *The Long Road Home*, 8 episodes, November 7—December 19, 2017, National Geographic, DVD, http://channel.nationalgeographic.com/the-long-road-home/.

28. Richard J. Pinder, Dominic Murphy, Stephani L. Hatch, Amy Iversen, Christopher Dandeker, and Simon Wessely, "A Mixed-Methods Analysis of the Perceptions of the Media by Members of the British Forces during the Iraq War," *Armed Forces and Society* 36, no. 1 (2009): 131–52, https://doi.org/10.1177/0095327X0833081.

29. See Cynthia Enloe, *Nimo's War, Emma's War: Making Feminist Sense of the Iraq War* (Berkeley: University of California Press, 2010), 15.

30. See Karen G. Jowers and Patricia N. Kime, "Rules of Engagement: Media Coverage of Military Families During War," in *A Battle Plan for Supporting Military Families* (Springer, Cham, 2018), 333–49.

### Conclusion

1. *The Time Traveler's Wife*, directed by Robert Schwentke (Warner Bros. Pictures, 2009), 1:47:00, https://www.imdb.com/title/tt0452694/.

2. Audrey Niffenegger, *The Time Traveler's Wife* (NY: Scribner, 2003), 3.

3. Ibid., xviii.

4. Brian Baker, "The Pathologies of Mobility: Time Travel as Syndrome in The Time Traveler's Wife, La Jetée and Twelve Monkeys," in *Diseases and Disorders. Routledge Studies in Contemporary Literature* (London: Routledge, 2013), 83–97.

5. Harlene Hayne, Julien Gross, Stephanie McNamee, Olivia Fitzgibbon, Karen Tustin, "Episodic Memory and Episodic Foresight in 3- and 5-year-old Children," *Cognitive Development* 26, no. 4 (2011): 343–55, https://doi.org/10.1016/j.cogdev .2011.09.006; Fatemeh Ahmadi Azar and Farid Parvaneh, "Chaos Theory and Nonlinearity in The Time Traveler's Wife: Reading in Light of Hayles's Theory," *Journal of Educational and Social Research* 8, no. 3 (2018): 19–25, https://www .mcser.org/journal/index.php/jesr/article/viewFile/10313/9943; Kevin Nance, "Anything Can Happen: A Profile of Audrey Niffenegger," *Poets and Writers* (October 9, 2009), https://www.pw.org/content/anything_can_happen_profile _audrey_niffenegger.

6. Anne Demers, "When Veterans Return: The Role of Community in Reintegration," *Journal of Loss and Trauma* 16, no. 2 (2011): 160–79, https://doi.org/10 .1080/15325024.2010.519281.

7. Niffenegger, *The Time Traveler's Wife*, xix.

8. Dana Stevens, "The Time Traveler's Wife," *Slate* (August 14, 2009), https://slate .com/culture/2009/08/eric-bana-and-rachel-mcadams-in-the-time-traveler-s -wife.html.

9. HBO television developed a series *The Time Traveler's Wife*, created by Steven Moffat, six-part series (HBO, 2022), https://www.hbo.com/the-time-travelers-wife.

10. Burton, "Army Wives," 71–89.

11. Tanya Biank, *Under the Sabers: The Unwritten Code of Army Wives* (NY: St. Martin's Press, 2006), xi–xii.

12. Other examples of popular cultural representations of military families include *Married to the Army: Alaska,* executive producer Stephanie Drachovitch, eight-part series, November 18–December 29, 2012 (OWN, 2012)—a reality television show and the British produced *Military Wives*, directed by Peter Cattaneo, 112 minutes (Ingenious Media, 2019). See also Alice Cree, "People Want to See Tears: Military Heroes and the 'Constant Penelope' of the UK's Military Wives Choir," *Gender, Place, and Culture,* 27, no. 2 (2020): 218–23, https://doi.org/10 .1080/0966369X.2019.1615414. There is no shortage of widespread interest in military families as military-themed films such as the 2015 film *American Sniper* increasingly feature the home as much as the war front. See Julien Pomarède, "Normalizing Violence through Front-Line Stories: The Case of *American Sniper*," *Critical Military Studies* 4, no. 1 (2018): 52–71, https://doi.org/10 .1080/23337486.2016.1246995.

13. Burton, "Army Wives," 84–85.

14. Katherine Fugate, creator, *Army Wives,* Season 1, episode 1, "A Tribe Is Born." June 3, 2007, Lifetime, television series, https://www.imdb.com/title /tt0859592/.

15. See Marco Briziarelli, undated, "Social Work or Unpaid: The Ideological Reproduction of Facebooking," *Los uaderno Q,* 21–24.

16. A special thanks to my colleague and psychologist Elizabeth Wetzler for this term, in discussion with the author, March 17, 2020.

17. See the ethnographies of various spouses affiliated with various occupations in Hilary Callan and Shirley Ardener, eds., *The Incorporated Wife* (NY: Routledge, 1984).

18. See Lisa Silvestri, "Surprise Homecomings and Vicarious Sacrifices," *Media, War, and Conflict* 6, no. 2 (2013): 101–15, https://doi.org/10.1177/1750635211347640.

19. Much has been written about adult children from military families. See chapters in Ender, *Military Brats and Other Global Nomads* and the popular Mary Edwards Wertsch, *Military Brats: Legacies of Childhood Inside the Fortress* (St. Louis, MO: Brightwell Publishing, 1991).

20. Meadows et al., *The Deployment Life Study*, xxiv–xxv.

21. See T. E. Narasimhan, "Fishermen Can Now Access Phone, Email, Whatsapp, Skype at Sea," *Business Standard* (September 26, 2016), https://www.business -standard.com/article/current-affairs/fishermen-can-now-access-phone-email -whatsapp-skype-at-sea-116092600572_1.html.

22. Here they are referencing the film of the same name starring Bill Murray. See Morten G. Ender, "Boredom: Groundhog Day as Metaphor for Iraq," in *The Oxford Handbook of Military Psychology* (London and NY: Oxford University Press, 2012), 311–24.

23. See Amy Reinkober Drummet, Marilyn Coleman, and Susan Cable, "Military Families under Stress: Implications for Family Life Education," *Family Relations* 52, no. 3 (2003): 279–87, https://doi.org/10.1111/j.1741-3729.2003.00279.x.

24. Donna Pickering and Tara Holton, *Informal Buddy Support System for Military Reservists* (Washington, DC: DTIC: ADA578905, 2001), https://apps.dtic.mil/sti /pdfs/ADA582929.pdf.

25. See Betty Warner, "The Villages at Belvoir—U.S. Army Garrison Fort Belvoir," *Silo.Tips* (December 10, 2017), https://silo.tips/download/the-villages-at- belvoir-us-army-garrison-fort-belvoir.

26. See any recent college-level marriage and family textbook for this information. See Nijole Benokraitis and Cheryl Buehler, *Marriages and Families: Changes, Choices, and Constraints* (New York: Pearson, 2019), 389.

27. David Crary, "Army's Divorce Rate Soars," *NBC News online* (July 1, 2005), https://www.nbcnews.com/id/wbna8406365.

28. See U.S. Department of Defense, *Service Academies* (Washington, DC: Office of the Secretary of Defense, Document Number: 2015–32926, December 31, 2015), 81761.

29. Harold D. Lasswell, "The Garrison State," *American Journal of Sociology* 46, no. 4 (1941): 455–68, https://www.jstor.org/stable/pdf/2769918.pdf.

30. See Andrew Bacevich, *Breach of Trust: How Americans Failed Their Soldiers and Their Country* (NY: Metropolitan Books, 2013), 32–35.

31. First Lady Dr. Jill Biden continues the efforts at this writing. See Joining Forces. *The White House* (2022), https://www.whitehouse.gov/joiningforces/.

32. Morten G. Ender, "OP-ED: What You Can Do For (Y)our Country," *New York Daily News* (October 12, 2021), https://www.nydailynews.com/opinion/ny-oped

-we-need-national-service-now-20211012-u5y3qvxdm5ebzoackevyll6agq-story
.html.

33. It is not lost on me that the COVID pandemic has somewhat altered traditional work. New pressures for autonomy on when, where, and how people work are emerging. Work and time self-sufficiency certainly will increase at-home work-ing, which has implications for mobile military spouses. Likewise, though, sep-arations will likely continue in sundry different forms of work.

34. Samuel A. Stouffer, Edward A. Suchman, Leland C. DeVinney, Shirley A. Star, and Robin M. Williams Jr., *The American Soldier.* Vol. 1, *Adjustment during Army Life* (Princeton, NJ: Princeton University Press, 1949) and Samuel A. Stouffer, Ed-ward A. Lumsdaine, Marion Harper Lumsdaine et al., *The American Soldier.* Vol. 2, *Combat and Its Aftermath* (Princeton, NJ: Princeton University Press, 1949).

35. See Joseph Soeters, *Sociology and Military Studies: Classical and Current Founda-tions* (New York: Routledge, 2018), 169–80. See also Enloe, *Nimo's War, Emma's War.*

36. Spanner, "Resilient and Entrepreneurial Military Spouses," 233–53.

37. Harriet Gray, "The Power of Love: How Love Obscures Domestic Labour and Shuts Down Space for Critique of Militarism in the Autobiographical Accounts of British Military Wives," *Critical Military Studies* (2022), 1, https://doi.org/10.1080/23337486.2022.2033915.

38. Richard Yarwood, Naomi Tyrrell, and Claire Kelly, "Children, Military Fami-lies and Soldier Citizenship," *Geoforum* 126 (2021): 253–62, https://doi.org/10.1016/j.geoforum.2021.07.009.

39. Hajjar and Ender, "Boredom, Fragmentation, and a U.S. Army Unit in Eastern Europe," 242.

40. Rachel Premack, "Being Away from Home for Weeks on End Can Put Truck-ers' Mental Health at Risk, and There's No Solution in Sight," *Insider* (June 18, 2018), https://www.businessinsider.com/truck-driver-trucking-family-2018-6.

41. Jillian Selzer, "7 Travel Secrets I Learned as the Daughter of a Pilot," *Insider* (Au-gust 12, 2018), https://www.insider.com/travel-secrets-according-to-daughter-of-a-pilot-2018-8.

42. See Rose George, *Ninety-Percent of Everything: Inside Shipping, the Invisible In-dustry That Puts Clothes on Your Back, Gas in Your Car, and Food on Your Plate* (NY: Picador, 2014).

## Appendix

1. Chad Foster, "Readiness and Interoperability in Operation Atlantic Resolve," *Military Review* (January–February, 2018): 92–1001, https://www.armyupress.army.mil/Portals/7/military-review/Archives/English/Foster-readiness-and-interoperability.pdf; and Jesse Granger, "Operation Atlantic Resolve: A Case Study in Effective Communication Strategy," *Military Review* 95, no. 1 (2015): 116–23.

2. See Lionel Beehner and Liam Collins, "Can Volunteer Forces Deter Great Power War? Evidence from the Baltics," *Journal of Strategic Security* 12, no. 4 (2019): 50–68, https://www.jstor.org/stable/26851260#metadata_info_tab_contents.

3. See Ender, *American Soldiers in Iraq,* 10–11.

4. The initial U.S. search in Afghanistan for Osama bin Laden and other perpetrators of 9/11 involved mostly small groups of specialized and varied U.S. forces. While we were interested in some research, these special force units would be highly difficult to access for interviewing of spouses at any time, more so during a war. Although some scholars have.

5. For an excellent discussion of subjectivity and writing the researcher into studies of the military, see Paul Higate and Ailsa Cameron, "Reflexivity and Researching the Military," *Armed Forces and Society* 32, no. 2 (2006): 219–33, https://doi.org/10.1177/0095327X05278171.

6. See Walter R. Schumm, Duane W. Crawford, Janet Crow, Tonya Ricklefs, Kennedy P. Clark, Lorenza Lockett, Roudi Nazarinia Roy, and Yolanda T. Mitchell, "Military Family Research: Methodological Lessons Learned, Often the Hard Way," *Archives of Psychology* 3, no. 2 (2019): 1–22, https://archivesofpsychology.org/index.php/aop/article/view/88.

7. For references, see Charles Kirke, "Insider Anthropology: Theoretical and Empirical Issues for the Researcher," in *Qualitative Methods in Military Studies: Research Experiences and Challenges* (London and NY: Routledge, 2015), 7–30; Eyal Ben-Ari and Yagil Levy, "Getting Access to the Field: Insider/Outsider Perspectives," in Soeters et al., *Routledge Handbook of Research Methods in Military Studies,* 9–18; Greg Scott and Roberta Garner, *Doing Qualitative Research: Design, Methods, and Techniques* (Boston: Pearson, 2013); and Andrea Fontana and James H. Frey, "The Interview: From Structured Questions to Negotiated Text," in *Handbook of Qualitative Research* (Thousand Oaks, CA: Sage, 2000), 645–72.

8. See Helena Carreiras and Ana Alexandre, "Research Relations in Military Settings: How Does Gender Matter?" in *Qualitative Methods in Military Studies: Research Experiences and Challenges* (London and NY: Routledge, 2013), 97–115, Gurney, 99. However, this chapter deals mostly with women researchers and male subjects and less the opposite.

9. Ibid., 103.

10. For a discussion of methods and perspectives in the study of the military, see Donna Winslow, "Military Organization and Culture from Three Perspectives: The Case of Army," in *Social Sciences and the Military* (London and NY: Routledge, 2007), 67–88.

11. Military husbands are also less likely to complete questionnaires. See Leora N. Rosen, Doris B. Durand, and James A. Martin, "Wartime Stress and Family Adaptation," in *The Military Family: A Practice Guide for Human Service Providers* (Westport, CT: Praeger, 2000), 123–38. They received a response rate for military husbands at less than 1 percent of those available.

12. See the two methods books Anselm L. Strauss and Juliet Corbin, *Basics of Qualitative Research: Techniques and Procedures for Developing Grounded Theory* (Thousand Oaks, CA: Sage, 1998); and John W. Creswell, *Qualitative Inquiry and Research Design* (Thousand Oaks, CA: Sage, 1997). More recently, military sociologists have adapted these techniques to the study of military populations. See the eleven chapters in Helena Carreiras and Celso Castro, eds., *Qualitative Methods in Military Studies: Research Experiences and Challenges* (London and NY: Routledge, 2015).

13. Brenda L. Moore, "In-Depth Interviewing," in Soeters et al., *Routledge Handbook of Research Methods in Military Studies*, 116–28.

# Index

Printed in the USA
CPSIA information can be obtained
at www.ICGtesting.com
LVHW040318030224
770776LV00003B/287

9 780813 950051